Multinational Corporations and Governments

edited by
Patrick M. Boarman
Hans Schollhammer

The Praeger Special Studies program—utilizing the most modern and efficient book production techniques and a selective worldwide distribution network—makes available to the academic, government, and business communities significant, timely research in U.S. and international economic, social, and political development.

Multinational Corporations and Governments

Business-Government Relations in an International Context

PRAEGER SPECIAL STUDIES IN INTERNATIONAL BUSINESS, FINANCE, AND TRADE

Praeger Publishers   New York   Washington   London

Library of Congress Cataloging in Publication Data
Main entry under title:

Multinational corporations and governments.

(Praeger special studies in international business,
finance, and trade)
Based on the proceedings of a conference held in late
1973 under the joint auspices of the Center for International
Business and the UCLA Graduate School of Management.
Includes index.
1. International business enterprises—Congresses.
2. Industry and state—Congresses. I. Boarman, Patrick M.
2. Schollhammer, Hans. III. Center for International Business.
IV. California. University. University at Los Angeles. Graduate
School of Management.
HD2755.M83   338.8'8   75-8402
ISBN 0-275-00900-9

PRAEGER PUBLISHERS
111 Fourth Avenue, New York, N.Y. 10003, U.S.A.

Published in the United States of America in 1975
by Praeger Publishers, Inc.

Printed in the United States of America

Effective collaboration between government and business is a central requirement for dealing with most of the major problems facing American society today. Many of today's unresolved issues are a consequence of the failure of business and government, the two primary institutions in this society, to function effectively, individually and in relation to each other. Disappointment at the inability of these two central institutions to function effectively together has led to increasing disenchantment and alienation of the American people with both.

The desire to stimulate action oriented research toward improving this condition led the Norton Simon, Inc. Foundation for Education, with the encouragement of its board of directors, to establish the Norton Simon, Inc. Foundation Commission on the Business/Government Relationship with initial funding of one million dollars. The importance of this issue prompted Dr. Roger Heyns, President, American Council on Education, William W. Scranton, Chairman of the Northeastern National Bank and former Governor of Pennsylvania, and Sol M. Linowitz, Partner of Coudert Brothers, former Chairman of Xerox Corporation, and former Ambassador to the Organization of American States to join with me as the members of the Commission.

Nowhere is the study and understanding of the business/government relationship more important than it is in relation to multinational corporations. These corporations exist because they fill a need that requires worldwide coordination in an era of international interdependence and mutual cooperation.

Under the circumstances, the Commission felt it most appropriate that it support the purpose of the conference on "Multinational Corporations and Governments" that was held in the Fall of 1973 under the joint auspices of the Center for International Business of Pepperdine University and the Graduate School of Management, UCLA.

I congratulate the organizers of the conference, Dr. Patrick M. Boarman and Dr. Hans Schollhammer on their accomplishment and thank them for the painstaking efforts that have gone into the preparation of the conference papers for publication.

——————

Harold Williams is the dean of the Graduate School of Management of the University of California at Los Angeles.

A prime issue for the remainder of the twentieth century is the unfolding confrontation between the "big business" activities of enterprises that have become increasingly multinational and the "small politics" outlook of national states. The political and social structures inherited from the past and appropriate to a world composed of sovereign nation-states are colliding at many points and with growing frequency with immensely powerful technological and economic processes that, unhindered, will produce a true world economy. In this event, national boundaries may become so many "Maginot lines," functionally obsolete and of interest mainly to historians of culture.

The outcome of the confrontation between these two sets of forces—the one arrayed on the side of the perpetuation of national autonomy—the other on the side of the "global village—is by no means predetermined. But probably decisive to that outcome will be the fate of the multinational corporation (MNC), standing as it does as both the arch symbol and prime catalyst of the internationalization of business. Under the circumstances, it is hardly to be wondered at that the MNC should have become the object not only of scientific scrutiny but of demagogy in its various guises. Around it has sprouted a luxuriant growth of myths, half-truths, surmises, and fantasies, many of which cancel each other out.

Thus, for many, it appears self-evident that MNCs jeopardize the sovereignty and independence of nation-states. Yet there are numerous recent instances in which national governments have expropriated—without a moment's hesitation—the assets of foreign companies whose annual revenues exceed the total outputs of the nations in question. The authors of the proposed Burke-Hartke legislation argue that MNCs cause the export of jobs and production from the United States; but politicians in the developing countries claim that MNCs exploit their riches for the benefit of the imperialist "home country" and reserve the choicest jobs for "home country" nationals. Clearly, not all these propositions can be simultaneously true. MNCs cannot at the same time be exporting major economic benefits from the home country, whether in the form of jobs, income, production, or tax payments, and, from the host country. The benefits in question have to end in one geographical area or the other.

The truth is, as always, found somewhere in the interstices of the myths and the easy generalizations. As far as the "home" country effects in the United States are concerned, studies by various agencies, public and private, suggest that far from destroying jobs, MNCs have, on balance, created substantial numbers of new jobs. These jobs are the result of the "pull effect" of the MNCs' investments abroad on U. S. exports, which take the form of intermediate or accessory products required to maintain a foreign plant or complement its product lines. On the other hand, MNCs' foreign investments have a "push effect" on the economies of host countries, including the diffusion of capital and knowhow into areas deficient in them, the establishment of training programs, and the associated expansion of the employment base for local nationals. These developments are bound to have positive effects on host countries.

At bottom, MNCs are business enterprises like any others, with the virtues and defects inherent in such enterprises. Their peculiarity lies in the fact that they serve needs which require worldwide cooperation and the yielding-up of some national sovereignty. MNCs have been extraordinarily successful, in spite of the national and international regulatory mazes that surround them, in responding to the needs of consumers. If they have exhibited weakness, it is in two areas: (a) failure to make clear their contributions to nation-state economies; and (b) failure to approach constructively and imaginatively the problem of how to cope with the myriad overlapping and intersecting legal and regulatory frameworks of both home and host country.

Recent developments involving increased activities by a variety of national governmental agencies and international organizations are indicative of the urgency and the significance of this latter task. No multinational enterprise can escape from interacting with governmental agencies of both the host and the home country on a broad range of issues. For this reason, a multinational firm's failure to develop a systematic and comprehensive approach to its governmental relations will invariably reduce its operational effectiveness. The repercussions from this neglect can be long-lasting and quite impossible to offset by merely focusing on internal operating efficiency.

Although international executives are increasingly concerned with devising plans for a systematic approach to governmental relations, the existing information on this subject is still very limited. To ameliorate this situation, the Managerial Study Center of the Graduate School of Management, University of California, Los Angeles and the Center for International Business, Pepperdine University organized with the support of the Norton Simon Foundation on the Business-Government Relationship, a three-day conference on "Multinational Corporations and Governments: Business-Government Relations in an International Context." This conference brought together government officials from the United States and other countries, members of international organizations, international business executives, academicians and administrators to share their expertise, experience and opinions on the interactions between multinational enterprises and governments. This book documents the results of this endeavor and reflects the breadth and complexity of the issues involved.

The contributions are grouped into six parts. Part I treats of the fundamental issue of national sovereignty vs. the global orientation of multinational enterprises. Professor Neil H. Jacoby's study points to the rising hostility toward multinational business operations as reflected in a variety of restrictive governmental regulations and he proposes a number of institutional and behavioral measures for reducing the frictions between multinational firms and governmental agencies. He emphasizes particularly the need for an international agency that would develop and endorse the implementation of a "code of conduct" for multinational firms in the pursuit of their global business activities. Prof. Robock, in contrast, argues that it is essentially the role of the home governments to control and restrain the foreign operations of their enterprises. He begins with the premise that there is an inherent conflict between the activities of multinational enterprises seeking to maximize their economic objectives on a supranational level and the nation-states (under whose jurisdiction they operate) seeking to maximize their own national goals. In Professor Robock's opinion, this inherent conflict cannot be entirely eliminated; but it is the responsibility of the home governments of multinational firms to control these enterprises in such a way that this conflict situation is not unnecessarily aggravated.

Professor Behrman's study is a comprehensive analysis of the reasons for controlling multinational business operations, the agencies that should be involved, and how the controls should be implemented. The concluding paper in Part I by Patrick M. Boarman addresses the thesis that MNCs contribute to international monetary turmoil by virtue of their power to move large sums of money from one center to another. He concludes that it would be a serious error for governments to penalize MNCs (e.g., by imposing restraints on the international flow of capital) for sins in the monetary field actually committed by governments themselves.

In Part II, the contrasting policies of two major nations—the United States and Canada—toward MNCs are examined. Stanley Katz outlines the rapid increase in U. S. investments abroad in the last decade and a half and the reasons therefor and discusses the special problems that are faced by a country whose MNCs are the world's most powerful and pervasive. The excitement and alarm provoked by the "American challenge" of a few years ago is viewed as obsolete in the wake of the cheapening of the dollar and the growing attractiveness of the United States itself as a locus for foreign investment.

In his paper, on the functions and purposes of the Overseas Private Investment Corporation (OPIC), Marshall Mays considers the special commercial and political risks facing American investors in developing countries—risks for which private insurance is generally unavailable. He shows how OPIC has influenced the form and behavior of U. S. investments in the developing countries so as to minimize the risk of political friction and maximize the developmental impact of the investments. The paper by A. E. Safarian and Joel Bell focusses on the unique problems faced by a country—Canada—which belongs to the developed group of nations, but which is characterized by a very high degree of foreign ownership as well as by a federal structure which complicates the making and implementation of a unified policy with respect to foreign-based MNCs.

Part III consists of a comprehensive review by Robert Cornell of the impact of MNCs on the direction and composition of international trade (in contrast to their impact on the balance of trade and payments). Cornell finds that the trade of the MNCs does not erode U. S. competitiveness in international trade (as often charged) but in fact supports and amplifies it.

Part IV is concerned with the international ramifications of national antitrust laws. Most MNCs, at least the better known ones, were large in their home countries before they ever moved abroad. And MNC critics profess to see a connection between domestic monopolistic or oligopolistic behavior and the expansion of MNCs' power internationally through such devices as transfer pricing in intercorporate transactions. The dilemma for national policy is how to deal with the allegedly "anti-competitive" behavior of firms, a significant part of whose activities may take place in other national jurisdictions. Messrs. Aibel and Baker examine—from the private and government point of view respectively—the most popular current theses respecting the international antitrust issue and assess their validity, or lack of it.

The potential conflict between national interest and the global orientation of the operations of multinational firms has been frequently documented in cases involving developing countries. Part V of the book focuses specifically on multinational business activities in developing countries, their economic contributions, and their implications for governmental relations. Walter Chudson's paper analyzes the evolution of a foreign investment policy in the developing countries and presents a range of significant issues concerning the transfer of technology to the developing countries— a process in which the multinational firms are key agents. Anant Negandhi's paper presents the results of a comparative survey dealing with behavioral and operating characteristics of U. S.-based multinational firms as compared to local enterprises in six different countries. Finally, G. Reuber's paper presents evidence of the positive contributions of different types of foreign investments in the context of developing economies.

The final section of the book, Part VI, contains three papers whose aim is to present empirical evidence on the current state of multinational business–government relations and to suggest ways for making these interactions more effective. J. Boddewyn's study stresses six essential principles for structuring governmental relations. From the point of view of multinational firms, governmental relations must be viewed as being important, and unavoidable; they must be organized and managed; they are a top-management function that is legitimate. In addition, Boddewyn emphasizes the necessity for creating a mutuality of benefits.

Whereas most of the papers in this volume are concerned with the relationships between MNCs and nation-states, David Blake's paper brings into relief the ways in which MNCs by their very existence and conscious policies influence international politics, or the relations among states. Lastly, Hans Schollhammer's study reflects the results of an investigation into the current state of governmental relations of a small group of U. S. and European-based multinational firms and how some of their executives perceive the need for and implementation of a positive program of governmental relations in an international business context.

The conference from which this book resulted was a joint venture of the Center for International Business, Pepperdine University, and the Graduate School of Management of the University of California at Los Angeles. The editors wish to express their thanks to all who contributed to the success of the enterprise and especially to the support provided by the Norton A. Simon Foundation for the Business-Government Relationship. It is their hope that, however the conflict between nation-states and the multinationals is resolved, it will be so on the basis of the production of factual, nonhysterical and patient research such as is represented in the papers included in this volume.

CONTENTS

LIST OF TABLES

xvii

LIST OF FIGURES

FIRMS AND GOVERNMENTS IN CONFLICT

MULTINATIONAL
CORPORATIONS AND
NATIONAL
SOVEREIGNTY
Neil H. Jacoby

After 25 years of spectacular expansion in a liberalizing world
economic order, the multinational business corporation (MNC) has,
of late, entered an environment of increasing hostility. Both in
their home and in host nations, MNCs confront a rising tide of
criticism and suspicion that, unless allayed, could lead to punitive
restraints. The evidence of this ominous trend is plain to see.

THE RISING HOSTILITY TOWARD
MULTINATIONAL BUSINESS

Fear of "loss of control" of their national destinies because of
massive foreign private investment has caused Canada and Australia
to enact laws for screening such investments in the future. Nationalization and expropriation of the property of foreign-owned companies
appear to be increasing, especially in Latin America and the Middle
East. At the instigation of the former Allende government of Chile,
the United Nations launched a comprehensive inquiry into the role
of MNCs and their impacts upon the process of economic development,
and the staff of the Department of Economic and Social Affairs
recently published a critical report.[1] Alleged interference by
International Telephone and Telegraph Company in the internal
politics of Chile led to the creation of a special Subcommittee of
the U. S. Senate under the chairmanship of Senator Frank Church,
whose report criticized the behavior of ITT.[2] (The Subcommittee
might also have criticized the Allende government of Chile for
expropriating the property of foreign investors without paying the

---

Neil H. Jacoby is professor, Graduate School of Management,
University of California, Los Angeles.

prompt and adequate compensation required by international law.)
Many observers believe that MNCs created the money crises of
1971 and 1973.[3] Labor unions in the industrialized nations are
becoming increasingly concerned about the ability of the MNC to
move production operations from one country to another in order to
avoid high wages or other onerous demands by national unions.
They propose to create multinational labor organizations to bargain
with multinational enterprises on the international allocation of
corporate investments, in addition to the traditional matters of
wages, hours, and working conditions.[4]

The most powerful blow against multinational business would,
however, be struck by the passage of the proposed Foreign Trade
and Investment Act (popularly known as the Burke-Hartke Bill),
first introduced in the U. S. Senate in September 1971 with the
strong support of the AFL-CIO.[5] Its main purposes are to discourage
American business investment abroad and to limit imports into the
United States. American labor leaders castigate U. S.-based MNCs
as "runaway investors" who have "exported jobs" to foreign plants.
They believe that the industrial base of the United States is being
undermined and narrowed by corporate investment abroad. The
Burke-Hartke Bill would greatly increase the taxation of profits
from foreign investment by U. S. corporations. It would impose
import quotas that would freeze foreign trade at the average levels
of 1965-69 and empower the president to prohibit any transfer of
U. S. capital or technology abroad that would, in the judgment of
the president, create unemployment in the United States.

The effects of MNC investment upon world trade, the U. S.
balance of payments, domestic employment, and international
transfers of technology were studied recently by the U. S. Tariff
Commission at the request of the Subcommittee on International
Trade of the Senate Committee on Finance.[6] That study found that
nearly all of the consequences of MNC investment abroad were
favorable to the United States and to the world. Such investment
made a large positive contribution to the U. S. balance of trade
and payments. On the most reasonable assumptions it produced
a gain of about half a million U. S. manufacturing jobs. MNC
foreign investment helped, rather than hindered, the expansion of
U. S. trade in high-technology goods such as aircraft and computers.
MNCs accounted for nearly all of the inflow of $2.3 billion during
1971 on account of royalties and fees paid for U. S. technology.

Academic analysts have concluded that the premises of the
Burke-Hartke Bill are invalid, and that its passage would be
disastrous to American interests and to the cause of world economic
integration.[7] Nevertheless, the threat remains that this bill—which
Walter Wriston has aptly called "the most retrogressive piece of
legislation since the Smoot-Hawley Tariff"—will become the law
of the land.[8]

And so we must ask: What are the causes of this spreading
hostility toward multinational business? Are there valid reasons
for a confrontation between the MNC and the nation-state? What
practical steps can be taken to avoid and to resolve conflicts
between these two powerful institutions of the contemporary world?

I suggest that the major sources of friction fall into three groups.
First, there are frictions based upon ignorance or misunderstanding
of the general public interest; these can be reduced by education
and by subsidizing special interest groups that can show they have
been harmed by MNC investments. Second, there are frictions
arising from disparities between the laws and practices of nations;
these can be dispelled by harmonizing actions. Third, there are
frictions arising from the interpretation of investment agreements.
These can be allayed by the use of international machinery for
settling disputes. Let us examine these several sets of factors in
turn.

FRICTIONS BASED ON IGNORANCE
OR MISUNDERSTANDING

If we are to reduce conflicts between MNCs and national governments, we must first distinguish rhetoric from substance. Governments,
especially in developing regions of the world, commonly complain
that the MNC exerts "external control" in its affairs, "exploits"
its labor and natural resources, realizes "excessive" profits,
which it "drains off" into the hands of foreign investors and fails
to reinvest in local development. However, these allegations
usually shield the real reasons why host governments dislike MNCs.

I suggest that there are three fundamental causes of friction
based on ignorance or misunderstanding: first, a mistaken identification of the American MNC with the imperialistic enterprises of
former colonial powers; second, a widespread belief in the mercantilist
fallacies of international trade; third, the resistance of entrenched
elements of society in host countries to the MNC as an agent of
social and economic change.

The initial experience with foreign corporations of most host
countries in the developing regions of the world was with the
imperial monopolies of Britain, France, Holland, and Spain. These
early companies were the "chosen instruments" of their governments.
They followed the flags of the mother countries into their colonies
to mine and harvest natural resources and to sell manufactured
goods at high profit margins. It was natural that these early MNCs
were regarded as instruments of imperialism by the colonial peoples.
Understandably, these attitudes have carried over to the more
recent American MNC, which is viewed as an instrument of
"neocolonialism" and probably as an agent of the CIA! Yet the
United States does not treat its enterprises as "chosen instruments"

of national policy. Indeed, our country is alone among the great powers in treating them as adversaries. Foreign suspicion of American MNCs would be sharply reduced abroad if American companies and the U. S. government took pains to publicize abroad the real business-government relationships that prevail in the United States.

The leaders of many foreign governments in the Third World are also under the spell of mercantilist thinking about international trade and investment. Subconsciously, if not overtly, they regard it as a zero-sum game in which one nation must lose what the other gains. And, since the foreign-based MNC is considered to have superior experience and bargaining power, it is thought to reap profit "at the expense" of the host nation. In their perspective, international trade is exploitative. The national interest, they believe, is to build up domestic industries whose products will substitute for imports. The ultimate goal is economic autarchy, the assumed way to political and economic independence. Here, again, economic education can help to dispel such illusions. Today, no nation—even such large and powerful political entities as the United States, the Soviet Union, or the People's Republic of China—can go it alone without enormous material sacrifices. For a small nation, autarchy is suicidal.

A third source of hostility to the foreign-based MNC is deeply rooted in the nature of man. This is the resistance to change by the entrenched classes of traditional societies that have a stake in the status quo. They see the MNC as a carrier of new values and ideas that threaten the old ways that have served them well. The MNC introduces the idea of meritocracy instead of aristocracy; of rewarding talent instead of status; of distinguishing people by ability instead of by color or sex; of reducing poverty because affluent people make more profitable markets; of opposing nationalistic barriers because they shrink the size of markets and reduce efficiency.

It is no accident that most complaints about foreign-based MNCs in developing countries emanate from the elites, the intellectuals, the government bureaucrats, and other beneficiaries of the traditional order, rather than from the masses of farmers and workers. Social and economic change is a challenge to the privileged status of the elite, but it is an opportunity for upward social and economic mobility. Conflicts between the MNC and elite groups in the developing nations are difficult to resolve, because the elites control the governments of such countries and purport to speak for their peoples. Much criticism of foreign-based MNCs from such elites should be understood, however, as expressions of self-interest in the status quo rather than concern for the public interest.

Of course, special interest groups within <u>home</u> as well as within host countries oppose MNC investment. The classic example is the opposition of American labor leaders, expressed in their support of the Burke-Hartke Bill, that would deal a lethal blow to U. S. foreign trade and investment. How can a government disarm the opposition of special interest groups that feel threatened by MNC foreign investment? How can it prevent such groups from frustrating that expansion of world trade and investment that is in the general public interest? A promising approach would be a commitment by the federal government <u>to pay compensatory subsidies</u> to industries and workers that can show that they are harmed by such investment. This principle is already incorporated into American foreign trade laws; and it was a powerful instrument in creating the European Economic Community (EEC). The usual formula is to pay compensatory damages on a descending annual scale, and to phase it out after sufficient time has elapsed for the reallocation of resources.

FRICTIONS ARISING FROM DIFFERENCES IN NATIONAL LAWS AND CUSTOMS

Apart from criticisms of MNCs that are grounded upon ignorance or the selfish interests of particular groups in home or host countries, there also are real and substantial complaints by nations about the operation of multinational enterprises that arise from differences between the laws, policies, or customs of the MNC's home government and that of the host government. They can be resolved by the harmonization of national policies. A recent illustration is national policy on trade with the People's Republic of China (PRC). Such trade has been encouraged by Canada, but up to recent times forbidden by the United States. A Canadian subsidiary of an American-based MNC that abided by American policy conflicted with Canadian policy. Fortunately, the new U. S. policy of detente with the PRC removed this source of friction.

A review of the extensive literature on this subject indicates that five substantial causes of friction between MNCs and national governments deserve a high priority upon our attention. They are international disparities in financial accounting practices, in corporate income taxation, in the rules of competition, in international flows of funds, and in the conventions of investment behavior. Hostility would be much reduced if nations could agree upon uniform financial accounting standards, uniform methods of taxing corporate income, and a common code of competition and investment behavior; and if they could find ways of preventing massive international flows of funds owned by MNCs from operating

as a destabilizing influence upon the world monetary order. Let
us consider each of these points.

International Accounting Standards

National governments feel frustrated by the ability of MNC
managers to price goods and services transferred internally from
one affiliate to another so as to minimize the aggregate taxes paid
by the company. Thus, if the income tax rate in an oil-consuming
country is high and in an oil-producing country is low, a multinational oil company may transfer crude oil at a high price from
its producing affiliate to its refining and marketing affiliate, thus
realizing most of the income in the low-tax country. However,
disparities among national accounting practices go far beyond
the special case of flexible "transfer pricing" by MNC managers.
Accounting practices differ sharply among countries in regard to
depreciation, reserves, consolidation of subsidiaries, adjustments
for price inflation, and disclosure of financial results. The result
is that comparisons of the earnings of enterprises in different
countries are of limited value; and that capital is allocated
inefficiently among different uses and nations. As custodians
of the business information system, the accounting profession
bears a responsibility for leadership in harmonizing national
accounting standards and practices. An International Accounting
Standards Committee was formed in London during 1973 for this
purpose.[9] Its work should be supported and accelerated by both
MNCs and national governments, in the interests of reducing an
important cause of friction between these institutions.

Corporate Income Taxation

Taxation of corporate income is another bone of contention
between MNCs and national governments. Governments define
taxable income in a multiplicity of ways, impose taxes at a wide
range of rates, make various allowances for foreign tax payments,
and sometimes doubly tax the same income, first in the country
in which it is earned and then in the nation in which the parent
company is domiciled. Also, some countries wholly or partly
integrate the taxation of corporate income with the taxation of
personal income, whereas others—notably the United States—
do not integrate at all. All of these divergent practices create
inequities as well as opportunities for evasion and avoidance of
tax burdens. Although it is fanciful to expect all nations to adopt
a uniform system of income taxation throughout the world, much
disputation between MNCs and national governments could be

avoided by reducing national incongruities in income taxation.
Fortunately, there has been a movement in this direction, which
merits encouragement and acceleration.

Competition

A third prolific source of alienation between MNCs and
national governments has been differences in concepts and in
legal codes of competition. In general, the U. S. government
imposes the most rigorous definition of competition upon its
enterprises and has been most active in investigating and prosecuting violations of its antimonopoly laws at home and abroad. Its
insistence upon prosecuting violations of the Sherman Act by a
foreign affiliate of an American-based MNC has caused foreign
governments to complain of "extraterritoriality" in the application
of U. S. laws. Although such criticism may be valid, it should
be coupled with criticisms of foreign governments for encouraging
cartelization of their private industries for foreign trade. Also,
the oil-exporting countries have created, in OPEC, the world's
most powerful and successful export monopoly. There is a real
danger that the nations exporting copper, bauxite, coffee, tea,
and other commodities may emulate OPEC. If the world is to
avoid the debilitating path of cartelization and autarchy, international
agreement upon the conditions of effective competition, upon
permissible market behavior by private and public enterprises and
governments, and upon methods of enforcement has become a
central need of our times.

International Transfers of Funds

MNCs played a significant role in the world monetary disorders
that preceded the devaluations of the U. S. dollar in 1971 and 1973.
This was true simply because so large a part of all international
monetary exchange is conducted by multinational corporations.
Although the studies of both the United Nations and the U. S.
Tariff Commission concluded that MNCs played a passive and
reactive role in recent currency disorders, the vast magnitude of
their operations did magnify disorder. World business has outgrown
the institutional arrangements made at Bretton Woods 30 years ago.
Methods for assuring that short-term international transfers of funds
are not destabilizing must be an essential part of the new world
monetary order now being worked out by the leading trading nations.
This will probably mean, among other things, a sharp elevation
in the role of SDRs as an international monetary reserve, and a

corresponding reduction in the role of gold, the U. S. dollar, and
other national currency units.*

An International Code of Investment

The fifth key cause of friction between MNCs and national
governments is lack of congruence in ideas about appropriate
international investment behavior. MNCs and their home governments complain that many host governments fail to live up to the
provisions of investment contracts they have signed, unilaterally
modify such agreements, and frequently expropriate the property
of foreign investors without paying prompt and adequate compensation. Host countries, on the other hand, denounce the interference
by MNCs in their domestic political affairs and the flouting by
MNCs of local customs, such as those regarding the job security
of employees. The United Nations report pointed out that "a
negotiating machinery and set of rules concerning the investment
and other activities of MNCs are yet lacking."[10] The world
needs, as Michael Blumenthal, chairman of the Bendix Corporation
has said, "A GATT for Investment."[11] The broad objective would
be to lay down a set of ground rules for international private
investment, voluntarily agreed upon by both MNCs and national
governments. This would reduce the range for arbitrary action
and thus for disputes and hostility.[12] Hopefully, it would serve
to liberalize the world investment environment, as GATT has
liberalized the world trading regime. As a practical matter, such
an international investment code would first have to be negotiated
among the larger developed nations and later extended to developing
countries. Gradually, it would be expected that nations would
modify their laws and practices to conform with those of the international investment code.

FRICTIONS ARISING FROM INTERPRETATION
OF INVESTMENT AGREEMENTS

Another prolific source of conflict between the MNC and the
host country is differences in the interpretations of investment
agreements. This can be resolved by provision of machinery for
international arbitration to which both parties agree in advance.
Many investment agreements between MNCs and foreign
governments bind both parties to submit any disputes over the

---

*For further discussion of these matters, see Chapters 14 and 15.

interpretation of the agreement to international arbitration. In
the event of a dispute, each of the two parties normally name an
arbitrator of his choice, the two nominees then select a third,
and the three-man panel hears the dispute and renders a judgment
binding upon both parties. The main reason for international
arbitration is that multinational companies are reluctant to submit
disputed issues to the courts of host countries. Arbitration by
an international panel provides, in effect, a trial by judges not
biased toward the laws and customs of one nation. A number of
unofficial international bodies, including the International Chamber
of Commerce, offer their good offices for such arbitration and
maintain panels of persons qualified to judge investment disputes.

There is, however, a crucial drawback to international arbitration by an unofficial agency. If a host government believes that
a foreign MNC has violated its investment agreement, it may not
hesitate to bypass the compulsory arbitration provisions of that
agreement and to act unilaterally.

The world needs an official agency for the international
arbitration of investment disputes, with power to impose penalties
if either party refuses to abide by its awards. For this reason, the
International Centre for the Settlement of Investment Disputes
(ICSID), established in 1965 as an autonomous agency of the
World Bank Group, is a potentially important institution.
ICSID provides conflicting parties with an assured neutral forum
for the settlement of future disputes. It provides conciliation and
arbitration procedures to settle disputes that have already arisen.
ICSID has developed slowly, because governments were required
to obtain the necessary authority to ratify the convention establish-
ing it. As of mid-1973 some 65 states had ratified it—mainly
European, North American, and African. Unfortunately, few Latin
American or Middle Eastern nations have done so.[13]

The arbitration process of ICSID is standard. Each party
selects an arbitrator from panels of prominent economists, jurists,
and bankers of many countries maintained by ICSID. The two
selectees agree upon a third, who acts as president of a tribunal
that hears arguments from both parties and renders a decision
binding upon both. Because of their treaty commitment, and because
the World Bank Group could impose costly penalties, member states
would hesitate before violating a judgment by a tribunal of ICSID.

The first case submitted to ICSID, in December 1971, was a
complaint by Holiday Inns-Occidental Petroleum Corporation against
the government of Morocco. Because this case provided a trial
run for ICSID procedures, a brief account is of interest.

In 1966 Holiday Inns and Occidental Petroleum entered into
joint ventures for the construction and operation of hotels in
Europe and Africa, including inns in the Moroccan cities of Tangier,
Casablanca, Marrakesh, and Fez. The government of Morocco

supplied sites and agreed to lend 60 percent of the estimated completion costs of the hotels. The hotels were to be built and operated by the Holiday Inns-Occidental venture. The original expectation was that the Holiday Inns-Occidental venture would invest an equity of 40 percent. Construction costs proved to be very much less than estimated, however, and after two of the hotels were completed, it became evident that the mortgage loans would cover 100 percent of costs. The government of Morocco then demanded that the Holiday Inns-Occidental venture put up equity money. When this was refused, as unnecessary and not required by the contract, Morocco stopped progress payments on the uncompleted hotels, seized the completed hotels, and operated them under the Holiday Inn name. Holiday Inns-Occidental then complained to ICSID, arguing that their estimates had been made in good faith, that they had taken a business risk, and that Morocco had breached its contract and was damaging the Holiday Inn name by operating the hotels according to inferior standards. Morocco replied that the Holiday Inns-Occidental construction cost estimates were fraudulent and that the agreement should be renegotiated. Holiday Inns-Occidental filed its complaint in December 1971. Two members of the tribunal were appointed by March 1972, but the president did not accept appointment until March 1973. So far, the tribunal has held a number of sessions and issued a number of orders. Whatever the outcome, the proceedings in this case will have cost the parties about one-half million dollars. Yet, the prospect is that both parties will abide by whatever award is made. This case will be a model of conflict resolution by the rule of law.

We may contrast this orderly arbitration of an investment dispute by an official international agency with the arbitrary, unilateral action taken by the government of Libya with respect to its agreements with foreign oil companies. Although all Libyan concession agreements contain provisions committing the parties to arbitration of disputes, the Libyan government has ignored such provisions. It has chosen, instead, to propose and to make radical changes in its agreements after offering the oil companies only a limited time in which to comment upon them. Similarly, the oil nations of the Persian Gulf have unilaterally announced changes in contracts with foreign oil companies.

These cases show that contracts and agreements mean nothing if the signatory parties do not intend to live up to them. A commitment to the rule of law and to the sanctity of contracts is essential to good long-term relations between multinational corporations and national governments. By reducing the risks of international investment, such commitments benefit all parties.

MULTINATIONAL BUSINESS AND INTERNATIONAL
RELATIONS IN THE FUTURE

During the final quarter of this century, economic issues seemed destined to replace questions of security as the primary factor in international relations. Detente among the great powers is underway. There is a new awareness of global economic interdependence. Threatened shortages of food, energy, and basic materials command attention everywhere, along with the dangers of transnational pollution of the land, the air, and the oceans. The world monetary and trading systems are being overhauled. Suddenly the old ideological division, the cold war, the nuclear arms race, and superpower confrontations seem outdated and irrelevant. Improving the quality of human existence and stabilizing the relations between human societies and their physical environments have come to the center of the stage in all nations.

In this emerging era it is vitally important that the causes of friction between multinational business enterprises and national governments be minimized. Multinational enterprise is man's most powerful instrument for world development.[14] If it functions in harmony with national governments it can make an enormous contribution to the well-being of all peoples. If, on the other hand, present conflicts continue, they could become exacerbated. They could lead to economic autarchy, protectionism, and cartelism. This would surely destroy the unifying forces of multinational business, dampen the economic progress of people, and raise the probability of war. Therefore, there is no time to lose in beginning to resolve the conflicts between MNCs and national governments.

NOTES

1. United Nations, Department of Economic and Social Affairs, Multinational Corporations in World Development (New York, 1973).

2. "The International Telephone and Telegraph Company and Chile, 1970-71," Report to the Committee on Foreign Relations, U. S. Senate by the Subcommittee on Multinational Corporations, June 21, 1973.

3. See Wall Street Journal, April 19, 1973.

4. See Wall Street Journal, April 23, 1973. Charles Levinson, secretary-general of the International Federation of Chemical General Workers' Union, stated: "Traditional wage bargaining is just arguing about sharing the pie. We want a voice in baking the pie."

5. See American Enterprise Institute, The Burke-Hartke Bill, Legislative Analysis No. 4. (Washington, D. C., February 22, 1973).

6. See Implications of Multinational Firms for World Trade and Investment and for U. S. Trade and Labor, Report to the Committee on Finance of the U. S. Senate, (Washington, D. C.: Committee on Finance, U. S. Senate, February 1973).

7. See, for example, Eugene D. Jaffe, "In Defense of MNCs: Implications of Burke-Hartke," MSU Business Topics, Summer 1973, pp. 5-14.

8. Walter B. Wriston, "The World Corporation—New Weight in an Old Balance," address to the International Industrial Conference of the Conference Board and Stanford Research Institute, San Francisco, Calif., September 17, 1973.

9. See Wall Street Journal, July 2, 1973.

10. United Nations, op. cit., p. 65.

11. See Business Week, August 18, 1973, p. 12.

12. While serving as the U. S. representative in the Economic and Social Council of the United Nations during 1957, the author sought unsuccessfully to obtain State Department backing for a U. S.-sponsored economic program of the United Nations, including technical assistance, a U. N. Development Loan Fund to finance infrastructure, and an international code to govern investment in agriculture and industry.

13. See Seventh Annual Report, 1972-73 of the International Centre for the Settlement of Investment Disputes, pp. 6-7.

14. This thesis is further elucidated in Chapter 5 of the author's Corporate Power and Social Responsibility (New York: Macmillan, 1973).

2

**THE CASE FOR
HOME-COUNTRY
CONTROLS OVER
MULTINATIONAL
FIRMS**
Stefan H. Robock

The case for home-country controls is not necessarily related to the good or bad intentions of multinational enterprises. Nor does it have to rest on charges of "abuses" or "exploitation" by multinational companies. The case for home country controls over multinational business enterprises is based on the reality that the goals of the multinational firm and the goals of its home country are not identical. To be more concrete, what is "good" for the U. S.-based multinational company is not necessarily what is "good" for the national interests of the United States.

GLOBAL GOALS

By its nature, the multinational enterprise attempts to direct a corporate family of diverse nationalities under its control toward supranational or global goals. The parent and each member of the family have a nationality, having been granted their corporate existence by the authority of a specific sovereign nation. But through bonds of common ownership and common strategy that cut across national boundaries, the family group operates as a transnational system that rationalizes its business operations and maximizes its business goals on a global basis. Such goals may be in harmony or in conflict with the goals of one or more nation-states. Each multinational enterprise tries to maximize its goals on a supranational level. Each nation-state tries to maximize its own national goals. Inevitably, therefore, a potential conflict exists between the multinational enterprise and the nation-state, whether

Stefan H. Robock is Professor of International Business, Graduate School of Business, Columbia University.

it be the home country of the parent or the host country within which
the affiliates are located.

A potential conflict between the public interests of a government
and the private interests of a business firm and its stockholders
is not unique to the field of multinational business. In all business
operations, whether domestic or international, the business enterprise and governments have common interests that overlap and are
in harmony as well as potential areas of conflict where the interests
of the two parties diverge. As a sovereign power, the nation-state
has the ability and—I would add—the responsibility for setting rules
to govern business transactions within and across its national
boundaries that will increase national benefits, protect the public
interest, and resolve conflicts between business and government.

In domestic business operations the general principle that
governments should exercise certain controls is widely recognized.
In the field of international trade and international transfers of
funds, the legitimacy of government controls is a generally accepted
fact of life. And in host countries the justification for government
controls over inbound foreign investment is almost universally
acknowledged. Why should there be any dispute about the general
principle that home countries should establish controls over the
multinational operations of enterprises whose headquarters are
located in that country?

ARGUMENTS AGAINST HOME-COUNTRY CONTROLS

One argument against home-country controls is that the
business interests of the multinational enterprises and the national
interests of the home country are not always identical or harmonious.
Neil Jacoby seems to be making this argument when he states in
his recent book on Corporate Power and Social Responsibility,
"There is no basic conflict between the multinational company's
goal of maximizing profits in each country and overall profit
maximization."[1] But neither the general position that conflict
potentials do not exist nor the specific argument by Jacoby are
tenable. As a partial answer to Jacoby, I would note that in maximizing global profits, a multinational enterprise will use transfer
pricing and other strategies to position profits in those countries
with the lowest tax rates. And this conflicts with maximizing
profits in each country of operation.

A second argument against home-country controls is that the
positive benefits of multinational business operations to the
home country exceed the negative effects. To be sure, the
phenomenal recent expansion of multinational business is impressive
evidence that the mutuality of interests between nation-states and
the multinational enterprise heavily outweighs the divergent interests.

Yet for specific home countries, and for the United States in particular, the attempts so far to demonstrate in an empirical and comprehensive way that benefits exceed costs have not been acceptable by objective standards because of conceptual problems, inadequate data, and bias. In any event, the case for controls does not rest on the issue of whether net benefits are positive. Assuming that they are, home countries can still justify controls as a means of increasing net benefits.

A third argument against home controls is similar to the argument for free trade. The traditional argument for free trade and against controls is that world output from a given set of resources will be increased by international specialization and unfettered free trade among nations. Likewise, the argument is made that the free operation of multinational enterprises across national boundaries can stimulate the movement of productive resources from areas of lesser relative opportunity to areas of greater relative opportunity and improve overall economic efficiency on a world basis.

Most nations agree in principle with the arguments that free trade and the free movement of multinational enterprises will maximize global output. Yet most nations have adopted controls over both trade and multinational enterprises. The reason is simple. Neither of these concepts deals with the distribution among countries of the global benefits, and national control programs are considered necessary to assure a specific nation that it will receive what it considers to be its fair share of the global benefits.

Furthermore, there is not unanimous agreement on the inevitability of greater global benefits arising from multinational business operations. As Stephen Hymer has noted, direct investment "is also an instrument for restraining competition between firms of different nations."[2] And the potential for monopolistic patterns in multinational business is still another reason for rejecting the "free trade" argument.

MNCs AND THE "CRITICAL MASS"

A review of the case for home-country controls leads me to wonder why the issue has been so long in coming to the forefront. The answer seems to be that only recently have multinational enterprises become "a critical mass" in relative size for most investor countries.

The principal multinational enterprises have their home bases in industrialized countries with large domestic economies. And until recently the foreign operations radiating from a specific home country, although large in absolute size, were small enough relative to the total economy to be inconspicuous or not troublesome. Consequently, home countries tended to consider their international business firms as domestic companies with important, but not dominant, foreign operations.

But after two decades during which foreign production has expanded at a much more rapid rate than the economy of the home countries, the relative importance of foreign operations has become of sufficient size to have a critical impact on events in the home country. Just to cite one statistic, Raymond Vernon estimated for 1966 that the total sales of the 187 enterprises on the Fortune 500 list that he has classified as multinationals accounted for between 32 and 39 percent of total sales for all U. S. manufacturing enterprises.[3]

Another significant recent change is that an ever-increasing share of international trade consists of movements within and among multinational enterprises rather than transactions between independent domestic firms located in different nations. As a result of this trend, government officials and legislators concerned with trade policy have found the traditional approaches for controlling international trade less relevant and have had to broaden their horizons to include multinational business activities.

Even more important in focusing attention on home-country controls has been the evolution of international business activities from domestic firms with foreign operations to multinational enterprises with global horizons, operating goals and strategies. I am not anxious to enter into a debate on definitions of the label multinational or international corporation. But Charles Kindleberger in addressing this question of definitions has suggested that an "international corporation is willing to speculate against the currency of the head office because it regards holdings of cash anywhere as subject to exchange risks which should be hedged."[4] By this test, events of the last few years have demonstrated that many U. S. companies have recently become multinational or global in their orientation. And the change toward global strategies and the implications of this change to the balance of payments situation of the United States has not gone unnoticed.

In presenting the case for home-country controls over multinational enterprises, I don't want to leave the impression that home countries have allowed multinational firms to operate with complete freedom. As several of the following chapters will remind us, the United States has had controls over direct investment outflows, over international pricing practices as they affect tax revenues, and is applying to some extent the U. S. antitrust law to the foreign operations of some U. S. multinational companies. In addition, the United States has applied certain programs adopted for national security reasons, such as controls on trade with the Sino-Soviet bloc countries, to the operations of U. S. multinational firms. And the United States has attempted to influence multinational business activities, through tax incentive programs such as the

Domestic International Sales Corporation (DISC), through foreign
risk insurance programs, and through political support for U. S.
foreign investment.

But virtually all of the home-country controls that the United
States currently applies to multinational business operations were
not specifically adopted to control multinational enterprises.
Invariably, the programs had a different or broader objective and
they happened to cast their net over the multinational enterprises.
Control programs that respond directly and comprehensively to the
multinational enterprise phenomenon are still mainly in a discussion
stage in the United States. In contrast, Japan is probably the
most advanced in this direction.

My assignment has been to present the general case for home-
country controls. But the more interesting and more controversial
issues relate to the specific kinds of controls that are likely to
be adopted. And here the debate revolves around the effects of
multinational business operations on the home country's balance
of payments situation, employment, tax revenues, international
political relations, national security goals (such as assuring the
United States of a continuing and dependable supply of foreign
raw materials), and domestic antitrust policies.

Unfortunately, in virtually all of these areas, U. S. policy
making will suffer for some time to come from the inadequacy of
conceptual tools and a critical shortage of factual information
and analysis needed for determining the real impact of multinational
enterprises on the national interests. The United States along with
most other national governments has continued in a traditional path
of collecting statistics as if we were still living in a world of
international trade rather than multinational business. Only
recently, mainly in response to the pressure of the labor unions
for the Burke-Hartke Bill, has the U. S. government even made
a start toward collecting facts and sponsoring research on the
impact of multinational business on the United States. Unfortunately,
most of the research sponsored by the U. S. government has been
of an advocacy nature rather than objective inquiries.

The international business community also deserves its share
of lashes at the stake. U. S. multinational firms have continued
for too long to consider home-country controls as unlikely, unreasonable, and contrary to divine law. They have relied principally on
public relations campaigns that attest to their virtue. They have
neglected to support, to undertake, or to press the U. S. government to undertake the difficult technical studies that would permit
the multinational business community to help shape reasonable and
valid control measures.

MOVING TOWARD SPECIFICS

Let me conclude by trying to provoke some discussion on specific components of home-country programs. In the area of political conflicts the question arises as to whether an investor country that assumes responsibility for representing the interests of its multinational business firms in foreign areas through laws like the Hickenlooper amendment or through political risk insurance programs should also assume the responsibility for screening the expansion plans of multinational firms in order to minimize the potential damage that controversies over international business interests can have on the foreign policy interests of the investor country. One option currently being considered is to untie the United States and the private investor interest by discontinuing political risk insurance. Such an approach would permit the United States to become involved at its option and encourage multinational enterprises to improve their own practices in assessing political risk and in considering alternative strategies for minimizing risk.

In the area of balance of payments effects, the weakness of current research is evidenced by the fact that the business community has argued to both home and host countries that multinational business operations provide net balance of payments benefits. But the balance of payments issue is what we would call a zero-sum game, that is, if one country gains another must lose. Thus one side of the argument must be wrong.

In the area of employment effects of the multinational enterprises on the home country, the principal studies available from government and business are likewise not acceptable. The Harvard study sponsored by the U. S. Department of Commerce reaches conclusions on the positive employment effects of multinational business by examining only nine actual foreign investment decisions. Other studies allege to demonstrate positive employment effects on the home country by comparing the domestic employment trends of multinational companies, which are generally in technologically dynamic growth industries, with domestic employment trends for all industry, including bakeries and brick plants, and by demonstrating that dynamic industries have had above average increases in jobs in the United States.

I happen to believe that the internationalization of business operations has been a logical, inevitable, and desirable trend. I also believe that multinational business enterprises are basically legitimate institutions and that the national and international governmental framework that has been designed for a world of international trade must be reshaped for a world of multinational business. The basic problem is that no multinational government organization exists that matches effectively the geographical reach of the multinational business enterprise and that represents the combined interests of the countries in which the enterprise operates. Thus each of the nation-states has begun to exercise its sovereign power to influence the multinational enterprise as the inherent differences in goals have become apparent. Eventually, some form of international controls may be worked out as a result of the United Nations' recent entry into the area of multinational business controls. But for some time to come the principal controls are likely to be those exercised by individual nation-states or regional groupings such as the European Economic Community. And it is important for both government and business that the controls be well conceived.

NOTES

1. Neil Jacoby, Corporate Power and Social Responsibility (New York: Macmillan, 1973), p. 113.
2. Stephen Hymer, American Economic Review, May 1970, p. 443.
3. Raymond Vernon, Sovereignty at Bay (New York: Basic Books, 1971), 1. 13.
4. Charles P. Kindleberger, American Business Abroad (New Haven, Conn.: Yale University Press, 1969), p. 182.

3

**CONTROL OF THE
MULTINATIONAL
ENTERPRISE:
WHY? WHAT? WHO?
AND HOW?**
Jack N. Behrman

The answers to the questions in the title of this chapter cannot
be provided unless one first sets forth the assumptions as to the
kind of international economic order within which international
companies are to be controlled. There are several proposals
floating around to control the international companies, but few of
them make explicit the underlying assumptions as to the nature of
the world economy that exists or is desired.

There are at least five patterns of world economic order that
can be distinguished and that would give rise to different types
of control mechanisms over international business. They include
(1) a pattern of strong national autonomy and concern for national
self-sufficiency; (2) a move toward regional blocs; (3) the perpetuation of a neoclassical system, leaning toward market efficiency
as the criterion for determining international economic activity;
(4) the development of a techno-industrial structure over the world
based on criteria of company efficiency; and (5) a new pattern of
international industrial integration based on repartition of sectoral
activities over the world under multiple criteria, including efficiency.
Each of these will be discussed in turn in this chapter showing
their impacts on the questions of why, what, who, and how to
control the international companies. Finally, we will examine
whether or not different types of market orientation and different
sectors of business activity would require one or another of these
types of economic order or whether there is a progression from the
first of these "orders" to the fifth.

Jack N. Behrman is Professor of International Business, Graduate
School of Business Administration, University of North Carolina.

NATIONAL AUTONOMY

The objective of national autonomy is still retained as the basic orientation of government policy in a large number of countries in the world, with the developing countries still to go through a stage of primary concern for national self-sufficiency. The extent to which they remain in this stage or move rapidly through it toward a more outgoing orientation will depend on a variety of factors, including political orientations, national will, economic capabilities, natural resources, historical orientations (such as colonialism), etc.

Besides the developing countries, however, there is among the advanced countries a "new nationalism" that encourages them to cut off international or external impacts. This new nationalism reflects the increasing demands by the public and business for government responsibility and interference in the national economy. The responsibilities start with the level of economic activity and employment and the rate of growth of each; they follow with social welfare programs, housing, education, monetary stability, exchange rate stability, resource development, science and technology, and so on. Governments are held politically responsible for success in each of these fields; and the more the total economy is affected by these decisions, the more governments wish to isolate themselves from international disturbances. The international companies are institutions embodying many of the impacts that appear at times to be adverse to national objectives—at the same time that they bring desirable contributions to each of these goals.

Why Control?

The reasons why countries with a nationalistic orientation would want to control the multinational enterprise or other forms of direct foreign investment include the desire for independence from outside influence—both actual and symptomatic; for independence from economic disturbances abroad; for an expanded national industrial base to improve bargaining positions with other countries; and for autonomy over their own national industrial development. Enough has been written already to demonstrate that these are concerns of nearly all host governments, and almost all governments have reacted by imposing some kind of controls over foreign investment—however minor the volume or the impact. Even the United States recently has shown a concern for the increasing influence of foreign investments to the extent of having a bill presented by Congressman Dent proposing to restrict the inflow of foreign investment and to subject it to regulation or negotiation to make certain that it is favorable to the United States.

The first two reasons for control—independence and reduction
of disturbances—mean that there is a concern to separate the host
country economy from decisions made abroad. These concerns may
be deep-seated or merely symptomatic, that is, the government and
the people may be more concerned with the image of foreign dominance
than with the actual independence. The other two reasons—development
of a bargaining base and determination of industrial development—
mean that the host government does not feel that the criteria employed
by others as to the location and growth of industry are appropriate
to the pursuit of its own objectives. It, therefore, needs control
over the selection of industrial sectors and their rate of development.

Control What?

In order to achieve the separation of the national economy from
the economies of other nations, the host government has a variety
of specific regulations or restrictions from which to choose. Not
every country will adopt all, for each of them achieves a different
degree of independence and separation—some of them being only
cosmetic, as with the forcing of local ownership, which "obviously"
removes foreign control. The list includes regulations over entry,
acquisitions, take-overs, ownership, product lines, employment,
research and development, exports, closing a plant, flow of funds,
the selection of directors, the development of local managers and
technicians, the location of the plant, and the extent of local
financing.

The use of any one of these restrictions depends upon the
intensity of the concern for foreign penetration and the type of
impact the investment has. For example, the antipathy toward
acquisitions is based on a fear that all local enterprise in key
sectors may be absorbed by the foreigner. To force establishment
of a new plant permits at least the existing ones to remain in
existence for a time, to demonstrate whether or not they can be
competitive. The cost of such a regulation is considerable to
the host economy, but it is borne, to demonstrate independence.
Efforts to gain control through local ownership of a majority of
shares is a costly and unnecessary move; such control as is
desired can be exercised much better directly by the government
than through local ownership.

National controls over research and development activities
also frequently miss the mark in that they are aimed at achieving
a greater independence on the part of the host country from foreign
technological developments; in fact, most of the regulations reduce
such independence. The reason is that they do not pay enough
attention to the development of local capabilities but instead

emphasize the creation of foreign-owned R&D laboratories; the results are owned by the parent, who decides where to innovate.

The difficulty of achieving the objectives of the controls does not mean that they will not be used. On the contrary, such use is to be intensified with the frustration of each in turn.

Who Controls?

Unless there is a clear intention on the part of the host government to inject the government itself into industrial development and economic decisions, national controls are likely to transfer the decision making from foreign private centers to local private centers. The requirement of local ownership, the development of local managers, and the selection of directors from among national citizens and the development of local technicians all lead toward increasing the control over economic development by private individuals rather than the government. Although this is the result of some of the national control systems, many of them also go further to inject the government into basic investment decisions and therefore to extend its control over the local private sector as well. Given the increasing responsibilities assumed by governments all over the world, it seems highly unlikely that national governments will accept any control mechanism related to foreign investments that does not give them a substantial continuing ability to alter local private decisions also.

Though the control structures are varied, the list of countries that apply national regulations over foreign investments is quite long. In fact there is no country that does not apply some type of discrimination against the foreign investor in some sector of the economy. Even the United States—despite its open policies—restricts foreign investment in banking, coastal shipping, and national-security industries. In addition, it has applied its antitrust regulations in ways that some foreign investors feel discourage investment.

The most effective postwar restrictions were undertaken by Japan; it consciously selected foreign licensing rather than direct foreign investment inflows as the means of stimulating its industrial development. This is a model that many other countries are now attempting to follow, a few successfully. Mexico is the country that has a greater chance of following the Japanese model in some respects—though it has chosen more direct investment than licensing because of its need for capital. The Indian government has injected itself into most agreements on direct investment and foreign licensing; and though Brazil used to be rather open, its regulations are currently significant and are likely to become more restrictive in the future. South Africa is now clamping down on foreign ownership of banks,

forcing the sale of up to 80 percent of the shares to locals. Canada
has been debating the issue of control for some time but has finally
agreed on the initial step of screening new investments and restricting
acquisitions.

Japan coupled its restrictions on foreign investment with a
positive policy on industrial development. This meant that it
selected the key sectors into which foreign investment or foreign
licensing would be permitted to move and supported these decisions
with national economic policies aimed at channeling funds into
the sectors that it wished to promote. Many developing countries
are trying to do the same thing, but this approach is accelerated
by a desire on the part of many of them to prepare for future negotiations at the regional or international levels through the development
of key industrial sectors. No country wishes to go to the bargaining
table with only a few chips. This desire intensifies the drive to
national self-sufficiency—at least in key industrial sectors.

How to Control

The mechanism for national control has been the issuance of
regulations by an appropriate ministry—finance, treasury, economy,
labor, commerce and trade, commerce and industry, or whatever—
and the requirement that negotiations be undertaken with this
ministry prior to approval of a foreign investment. Alternatively,
some incentive may be given to investors within the country, but
these may be withheld from the foreigner until certain approvals
are received from various ministries.

The mechanism, therefore, involves a series of negotiations
with appropriate government officials concerning a pending approval
or the private agreements with local partners.

There are a few countries in which the regulations are set
out quite clearly and no negotiations are required if the arrangement
stays within the constraints indicated. For example, in the Ivory
Coast, companies coming in with less than 50 percent ownership
of a new venture can do so fairly freely, meaning that they do not
have to get approvals from the Ivorian government. However,
foreign companies wishing to have more than 50 percent ownership
have to go through the series of approvals requiring extensive
negotiations with the government.

DIFFERENCES AS TO SECTOR
AND MARKET ORIENTATION

The why, what, who, and how of control over foreign investment
differ markedly according to the sector in which the investment

occurs and to the market orientation of the company. Thus, national
control over activites in the natural resource sector tend to become
more intensive than in some of the industrial sectors. Similarily,
some service sectors are becoming quite sensitive—banking, insurance,
consultants such as in accounting, marketing, and law. These are
being increasingly reserved for local citizens, through regulations
that prohibit any new investment in the area and also force the sale
of existing firms to locals.

The market orientation of the companies has also led to
differences in national controls. For example, in the Andean
Community, * if a foreign-owned affiliate is exporting 80 percent
or more of its total production, the restrictions on local ownership
are removed and 100 percent foreign ownership is permitted. At
the other extreme, where the company is selling only to the national
market, it may similarly be owned 100 percent by foreigners. It
is only where the company is going to be selling in the regional
market, taking advantage of the integration of the Andean countries,
that it is forced to sell out to local citizens. Other countries also
feel that market segmentation makes a difference as to the ability
of locals to take over the activities that foreigners have been
conducting—such as in retail operations in clothing and food. In
these areas the foreigners are being squeezed out through government
regulations—for example, the Philippine retail nationalization law,
and the Africanization of shops owned by Asians and Europeans
in many countries of Africa.

REGIONAL BLOCS

Regional blocs may be based on national autonomy or they may
be moved away from self-sufficiency through regionalism toward
wider international cooperation. Attitudes toward foreign investment
within a regional grouping differ according to the intensity of the
national orientation, according to the past experiences of the
members of the various blocs, and according to whether they include
some advanced countries as members.

Two distinct types of blocs need to be examined from the viewpoint of controls over investment—existing or future blocs, created
by countries in a similar situation for the purpose of regional
economic integration, and those that result from the extension of
a sphere of influence over a region by a dominant advanced country
(or countries). The former include members that are more or less
homogeneous—the European Economic Community, the Andean
Community, etc.; and the latter cut across the developing and the

---

*Bolivia, Chile, Colombia, Ecuador, Peru, and Venezuela.

developed countries, such as the inclusion of the Francophile
countries of Africa in the European Community. The spheres
of influence may be even looser, as was the case with the United
States in Latin America in the not-so-distant past and currently
with Britain in some of its former colonies.

Why Control?

The division of the world into regional blocs is likely to produce
two different types of control mechanisms for foreign investment:
one that would be aimed at facilitating the flow of investment within
the bloc and the other at constricting it between blocs. The latter
has as its objective securing the independence of the bloc from
outsiders. The motive is similar to that of national economies for
autonomy but is simply expanded to all members of the group.

The objective of industrial development within the bloc, again
similar to that under national autonomy, is made more complex by the
desire to balance industrial growth among the members, and this
will require control to make certain that industry is located where
it is desired and grows at the rate desired by all the members.
To enforce this balancing of industrialization, the members must
agree to a harmonization of policies toward foreign investment in
order to prevent competition among them for foreign capital and
technology.

Control of investment within a sphere of influence is likely
to lead to preference for projects undertaken by the dominant,
advanced countries—as in the former French colonies of West
Africa. The preference is likely to be more covert than overt,
through the interpretation of regulations or the process of negotiation. The purpose, of course, is to maintain the predominant
ties to the advanced country, which may be providing substantial
assistance to the less advanced members.

Control What?

As with policies under national autonomy, the regional blocs
would likely control all of the activities indicated above, but they
will add some new ones. In view of their need to balance industrial
development, it will be necessary not only to direct the location
of plants but also to make certain that their volume of production,
product lines, and the technologies used are equitable among
members. In addition, the flow of sales among the members—exports
and imports—must be "equitably" balanced so that no one country
is left in a substantial deficit position. This was one of the problems
that broke the Central American Common Market in the past few years.

Finally, controls will have to be extended over pricing, so that
the agreed-upon dependence on a single source of supply within
the region is not used in a monopolistic way to divert the benefits
from one member to another.

These comments apply to foreign investment within the region—
that is, among the members themselves—as well as to the investor
from outside the region, who might be given a monopoly in a particular
sector. It would simply not be acceptable that he be able to set his
own prices and divert sales or supplies according to his desires
if he unbalanced the benefits among the members.

Who Controls?

The regional groupings that have come close to forming a
concerted policy of foreign investment include the Central American
Common Market and the Andean Community. Others that have yet
to form concerted policies are the European Economic Community,
the Latin American Free Trade Association (LAFTA), the East African
Community (which has virtually broken up), Comecon, and the
Association of Southeast Asian Nations (ASEAN). Spheres of
influence are not yet sufficiently developed to have formed concerted
policies.

At the regional level the problem of who actually controls
foreign investment activities raises a third dimension in addition
to local private citizens or the host government: the possible
rise of a regional government group. In the Andean Community
all three levels are used to force the divestment of foreign-owned
companies into locally owned companies, but if private individuals,
who are citizens of the Andean countries, cannot purchase the
companies, the host government stands ready to do so. There
does not seem to be a preference of either private or government
ownership, just a dislike of foreign ownership. There is, so far,
no clear delineation of the role of the private sector in economic
development within the area. This lack of clarity is also found
in the ASEAN region and throughout LAFTA. The East African Community
also faced the same problem. And Comecon, despite its preference
for socialist enterprises, is moving toward an accommodation with
foreign private enterprise in order to develop new industrial activities under "coproduction" arrangements. These would undoubtedly
be controlled by the socialist governments, in some cases without
any equity shareholding by the foreign investor.

Those companies that do not become "localized" through sales
of shares to nationals remain under government regulations with
respect to borrowing, flow of funds, location, etc. In addition
the national regulations in the Andean Community must accord with
the provisions of Decision 24 under the Treaty of Cartagena, and

the administrative junta has the responsibility to make certain that the treaty rules are adhered to by members. For the "integration industries"—those under complementation agreements—additional regional machinery will have to be set up to assure compliance.

How to Control

The administrative machinery for controlling the foreign investor is more complex at the regional than at the national level. First, agreements are required among the members for the purpose of harmonizing their national regulations or for unifying them under a single regulation. The Andean countries have chosen a route of harmonization, while the Central American Common Market attempted to integrate regionally without a common approach to the foreign investor. Despite an initiative by France some years ago, the European Community has so far avoided developing a single policy toward the foreign investor; it is, rather, seeking to regulate development of particular sectors; for example, the computer industry, aerospace, and aircraft. The policies toward the foreign investor will be set within the policies toward sectoral industrial development within the EEC.

Whether the controls are exercised through an agreement or through industrial policies that cover more than foreign investment relations, there will be a need for administrative bodies to carry out the regulations. These bodies will have to be at the regional level—as with the Andean junta and the secretariat of the Central American Common Market (SIECA). Unless there is a complete unification of regulations, negotiations of the international companies with governments will still be at the national level, under harmonized national legislation and regulations. With unification the negotiations themselves are likely to be centralized at the regional administrative level.

Both the national control mechanisms and the regional control system can be steps toward an international control system. It is highly unlikely that either will be replaced by an international system. Rather, each nation will seek to gain strength at the bargaining table through its own national growth—as is the case with Mexico, India, and Canada et al.—or through an association with others that are seeking to combine for strength. The movement toward blocs means that nations are interested in power relationships and the sharing of benefits as well as in market efficiency. This should not be surprising, given the fact that nation-states have always been concerned with both power and wealth. Neoclassical economics shifted the emphasis, asserting that the absolute level of wealth and prosperity was more important than its relative distribution among nation-states and that wealth and efficiency were

the sources of power and equity; the latter would flow automatically
from the former.

NEOCLASSICAL ORDER

The reestablishment of an international economic order along
neoclassical lines would require substantial controls over foreign
investment and multinational enterprises, but of a different type
than that indicated above. The result would be an international
order based on the free market and operating under criteria of
market efficiency.

Why Control?

The main reason for these controls would be to restructure
the criteria of industrial development and to reestablish competition
as the main driving force in corporate decision making and in
industrial policies of countries. The objective would be the
most efficient use of the world's resources, as dictated by market
forces. To accompany such a reordering of the world economy
there would have to be a new international monetary system—to link
national "free markets" effectively—and a strengthening of the
General Agreement on Tariffs and Trade (GATT) to remove government
barriers to trade. (Neoclassical economics does not require the
removal of barriers to the movement of capital or people.)

Under this approach the basic purpose of controls would be
to remove two types of interference in the market: those of governments and those of oligopolistic enterprises. Those proposing
this approach view the resurrection of competitive private enterprise
under the neoclassical system as the primary means of achieving
the economic goals of nations and the world economy: "Private
enterprise is seen as the most important single developmental
factor; if left to itself, private enterprise would bring rapid
economic development, would increase social welfare, and would
lay the groundwork for sound and stable political democracy."[1]

To be consistent with the classical criteria, an international
control mechanism would have to turn back the clock on the
development of the international corporation—not leaving that
corporation "to itself" but forcing its dissolution into competitive
units and restructuring a competitive world economy.

Control What?

The activity of the international control body would be directed
at expanding the concepts of antitrust legislation as they exist in the

United States, the deconcentration of key industries, the reduction
of the size of dominant companies, the break-up of combinations
within and across national boundaries, the elimination of oligopolistic
industries, the dispersion of financial centers, and the reintroduction
of a self-regulating market. In other words, all anticompetitive
activities would have to be regulated out of existence.

Given the difficulty of achieving these goals on a national
scale, it would appear almost impossible to do so at the international
level—particularly since there is no evidence that any country in
the world, including the United States, really would adhere to the
neoclassical concept of a world economic order. One strong reason
is that this approach makes no distinction among different types
of international activities and their quite different impacts on
government responsibilities. No government will, for example,
give up control over its financial and money markets to the spread
of multinational banking, though it _might_ permit a multinationaliza-
tion of cosmetics or shoes.

Who Controls?

The proposals for the creation of a GATT for international
investment fits with the approach of reintroducing a neoclassical
world economy. The present GATT is based on the concepts of a
world order embodying the principles of free trade under a "nondis-
criminatory, multilateral system of trade and payments." The rules
of the GATT are those aimed at providing maximum leeway for private
decisions in trade around the world. Similarly, the International
Monetary Fund (IMF) was directed at removing interferences of
governments in the international money market and therefore permitting
and encouraging the stabilization of exchanges and maximizing
the freedom of private citizens to make decisions in international
trade and finance. Coupled with the IMF, GATT was to give
day-to-day control over international economic activities to the
private sector—under generalized rules that were directed at
restricting interferences of governments.

The atrophy of both of these institutions indicates that this
particular approach to world economic order is no longer acceptable
to nations.

How to Control

In order to implement a GATT for international investment there
would have to be basic agreement as to the specific rules to be
applied against governments and against the international corporations. The present GATT was not formed as an information-gathering

unit, but as a rules-applying organization. In order to apply the
neoclassical criteria, the regulations would have to be directed
against both—that is, against any activity that interfered with a
competitive world market. The rules would have to be precise,
and they would have to provide the opportunity of appealing infractions of the rules to a court of arbitration for judicial settlement.

The proposals to form a GATT for international investment that
is merely directed at obtaining information out of which a set of
rules will eventually be determined are not predicated on any
assumptions about the structure of the international economic
order that is desirable. To set up an organization that is to gather
facts without any reference to the particular problems that are to
be solved appears to be a prescription for frustration and cacophonic
dialogue. The first meetings would be taken up with discussions
as to which problems are most important and therefore which types
of data would be gathered. This discussion would be predicated
on the underlying assumptions as to the type of world economic
order that would be desired. Eventually, a direct posing of this
question would be required.

Without some agreement as to the next steps toward a new
international economic order, the international companies will
be handled within the first two alternatives already discussed.
However, the multinational enterprise offers at least the possibility
of moving toward an international cooperative order, by using it
to achieve either its own ends or those of governments.

TECHNO-INDUSTRIAL ORDER

One alternative international approach, inveighed against by
the leftist economists and by socialists, is to let the multinational
corporation establish the nature of a new international economic
order. It would be one oriented around the more technically advanced
industries. The basic structure of the new order would be determined
by the criteria of company success. These in turn are likely to
include the growth of the corporation, increasing efficiency (as
determined by a continuous effort to reduce costs, not necessarily
to maximize profits) by increasing productivity, and innovation
in the advanced-technology fields.

In the view of George W. Ball, former undersecretary of state,
the multinational enterprise is the means of achieving the objective
of a new order, including the demise of the nation-state in favor
of a supranational government guided by the MNC: "The multinational
corporation not only promises the most efficient use of world resources,
but as an institution, it poses the greatest challenge to the power of
a nation-state since the temporal position of the Roman Church began
its decline in the 15th century." Ball further urges the advantages

of increasing size of economic units, guided under the multinational corporation: "I know of few things more hopeful for the future than the growing determination of American business to regard national boundaries as no longer fixing the horizons of their corporate activity. . . . If Europe and Latin America get on with the establishment of larger trading units, then the multinational corporation has a bright future. Indeed, it could be the harbinger of a true world economy."[2] What is meant by a "true world economy" is not clear; but in the context of Ball's other statements, it implies either operation through a supranational government or domination of the economic activities of the world by large corporations operating in the market economy. In some of his statements he has implied that the multinational corporations should be permitted to form a type of world government apart from the regularly constituted governments themselves. This would imply the spread of the techno-industrial structure from the advanced countries to the developing countries. The result would be domination by the advanced industries and the centers of decision making such as New York, Chicago, Los Angeles, Paris, Frankfurt, London, and Milan.

Why Control?

The why of control under this approach to world order is to pave the way for the growth of the multinational enterprise under criteria of its own efficiency, in an effort to achieve an integrated world economy, not under the "dead hand" of bureaucratic governments. That system would be clearly a "growth-oriented" system.

Control What?

What would be controlled would be government interference in activities of the MNC. Government regulations in different countries would be harmonized in order not to make decisions by companies difficult and not to interfere with the most efficient use of resources as seen by the companies themselves. Examples of what would be harmonized include patent law, tax law, production standards, quality control regulations, licensing arrangements, rights of establishment, remittances of funds, local borrowing regulations, etc. Rather than these regulations constraining the corporation, they would restrain governments and facilitate the growth and dominance of the MNCs.

Who Controls?

In order to force governments to abide by this approach, an international institution would have to be set up that would be, in fact, supranational. This would be necessary because governments would tend to intervene whenever the activities of corporations did not accord with national interests as governments saw them.

Again, the problem of setting up such an international institution begins with an agreement on the type of international order to be established; or, as Ball says, if the nations agree to integrate economically (a new order) the MNC can do it for them best. Undoubtedly, if governments do not act to control the multinational enterprise, it will gradually and inexorably produce a world that is organized by the leading enterprises. However, this result is unlikely, given the initiatives being taken to create national autonomy and regional blocs. It seems unlikely that governments will step aside to permit the multinational corporations to assume the role of governments internationally.

There is, of course, the possibility that a few countries would permit greater leeway to the MNC among themselves, but even these are likely to make distinctions among the sectors in which freedom is accorded—for example, high technology but not banking or retailing.

How to Control?

To support a movement toward a techno-industrial world order, a variety of "codes of behavior" have been proposed on the part of companies as well as international organizations. These codes have been directed largely at governments, encouraging them to behave in ways that will provide "a favorable climate for investment" and therefore to permit the spread of international corporate activities.

Recognizing that a one-way code would be unacceptable, proposals have also been made for "codes of good behavior" on the part of corporations. These codes are based on the assumption that if companies act as "good corporate citizens" they should then be left alone to determine what is in their interest, and, therefore, also in the interests of host countries. Given the research that is now being done and the hearings that are taking place on the many aspects of MNC activities, it seems unlikely that governments will stand aside even if companies can demonstrate that they are operating in a "socially responsible" manner. Social responsibility does not meet all of the concerns of governments, not even the most important of them.

Although the Organization for Economic Cooperation and Development (OECD) has been discussing the desirability of

international codes for investment, it has not been able to push
the matter very far, principally because the developing countries
have shown that they are uninterested in this approach. The
developing countries are more concerned with maintaining national
control over the foreign companies.

INTERNATIONAL SECTORAL INTEGRATION

It is my own view that no international economic order will be
acceptable to governments presently or in the near future unless it
includes a means of determining the location of industrial activities
worldwide—among the advanced countries and between them and the
developing countries. The beauty of the neoclassical system was
that it left these kinds of decisions to the free play of the market.
But as evidenced in the observations of many critics of this system,
the result was not seen as equitable in the sense of locating industry
where it would be most effective in using (and conserving) the
world's resources or in accelerating growth around the world.
Consequently, governments have felt it necessary to interfere in the
market not only domestically but internationally. They have sought
to relocate or to alter the location of industry according to what
they consider to be their national interests. No new international
economic order can, in my view, become viable unless it focuses
directly on this problem—that is, the location of industrial activity
around the world. Specialization among large sectors of activity,
with trade among them, is no longer acceptable (and is not necessary
for growth); specialization within sectors may be acceptable. New
criteria of economic decision making will be required, and new
means of control by governments or by international institutions.

Why Control?

The objective of controlling the multinational enterprise under
this approach to a new international economic order would not be
that of constraining the company simply to reduce its decision-making
power. Rather, it would be to guide this power toward fulfillment
of the industrial policies agreed upon among nations. These
industrial policies would likely be quite specific in the sense
of giving priority to specific industrial sectors and also in the
sense of dividing industrial activity within sectors among a variety
of countries. The precise objective would be to make certain that
each country shared equitably in the development of industry, the
diversification of employment, the development of research and
technology, and the opportunity to participate in selling to expanding
world markets. The overall objective of governments would be to

direct the growth and structure of international industrialization,
and to ensure the making of adjustments between the advanced and
developing countries—especially through what might be called
"mobile" industries. The mobile industries include those in which
it is feasible to split production activities and locate them in
diverse places, more or less close to the final market. This
capability means that it is possible to locate specific production
activities almost anywhere in the world, especially where there
are low labor and low transport costs.

To support these industrial policies, a complementary policy
on the attraction and control of foreign investment would be desirable.
The objective would be quite different from that of the preceeding two
approaches in that the multinational enterprise would be induced
to mutate in various ways suitable to the objectives of industrial
growth around the world rather than being seen as a distinct and
long-lived institution that needs to be guided or controlled apart
from the other economic policies pursued by governments.

Control What?

The types of control exercised over the multinational corporation
would be set by the particular industrial policies to be implemented.
For example, controls over the service sectors would probably not
be encompassed within the particular type of control—they would
be handled under the orientation of national autonomy or the regional
blocs, as discussed earlier. However, the extractive sector and
the various manufacturing sectors would likely be included. Among
these, some key sectors would be selected for priority treatment—
petroleum development, petrochemicals, automobiles, metalworking,
textiles, pharmaceuticals, electronics, etc. These sectors would
be seen as amenable to guidance from an international organization
as to where they might be located, what kinds of products and
technology would be appropriately developed in new economies,
what research and development activities might be undertaken, and
what assistance might be given to the host countries by advanced
countries or by the host countries to make certain that the repartition
of each industrial sector was viable both from the standpoint of
the international companies and from that of the world markets.

In addition, the MNC would be directed so as to make a
maximum contribution to multinational projects such as pollution
control, minimum nutrition, aerospace, resource development in
the seabed, etc. These will require multiple governments and
multiple companies as participants, under new agreements and
institutional arrangements. The MNC is an efficient mechanism
for implementing these projects.[3]

Who Controls?

In order to undertake this kind of guidance of the foreign investors, a new international organization would be required. None of the existing organizations fits; nor would they be capable of stretching their umbrellas wide enough to encompass these activities. This includes OECD, UNIDO, GATT, or other UN-related agencies. The new institution would have responsibility for overseeing both the industrial policies that affect foreign investment and the foreign investment regulations. It would also set priorities over the first efforts at repartition of specific sectors and over the countries that would be first served. For example, the absence of substantial investment in Africa is the result of a series of obstacles that are considered overpowering in a market-type economy. In the absence of the regional organization, international companies question whether or not their activities will be viable there. Only if a concerted effort was made by international organizations to create the requisite conditions for international investment will the volume of such investment expand as it should in order to accelerate indus- trialization in that region. This suggestion is not the same as that requiring "favorable conditions" for investment under past rules of the game.

The institution does not need to have large funds; rather, it needs to have substantial and appropriate information and the power of persuasion, which will bring both governments and private enter- prise together. The way in which it would be able to do so would be to have more information than anyone else, some incentive programs, and a reputation for giving good advice.

How to Control?

The major authority of the new institution would be to gather information appropriate to developing sectoral priorities and to guiding the repartition of industrial activity in each sector. The gathering of this information would be for the purpose of making studies on the basis of which competent advice could be given to corporations and governments about the international structure of each industrial sector. In addition, the institution would be able to initiate programs for cooperative industrial development among countries in such things as the development of the resources of the seabed, petroleum development in the seas, aerospace, pollution control, and environmental protection. Finally, the institution should be permitted to review the industrial plans of various nations to make certain that, even if they were directed toward significant self-sufficiency, there would be room for international investment to open the country to international competition and to provide it access to opportunities in the international markets.

The controls under such a system would be highly selective—focusing on those companies that could help implement cooperative projects and those sectors in which repartition programs seemed viable. Not all international business would be encompassed and not all companies in any sector, nor all countries. Agreements would be tailored to the specific purposes sought. But the overall organization would continuously seek new ways to guide international companies to the objectives sought by governments.

SIMULTANEOUS CONTROL SYSTEMS OR PROGRESSION?

It remains to question whether or not these different approaches to world economic order could exist simultaneously or whether they constitute a stepped progression from national self-sufficiency to international industrial cooperation. If the answer is that they constitute a stepped progression, then the question arises as to how to facilitate the movement from the first to the succeeding ones.

At present a considerable part of the discussion of international codes or controls assumes that all international business is quite similar and that all international investors are multinational enterprises. Distinctions among the different types would soon lead us to a recognition that a variety of controls are likely to be used, each based on a different assumption as to the nature of the world order that is desirable in that particular industrial sector or that economic activity. For example, banking and services are increasingly likely to be controlled by national regulations, while petroleum will undoubtedly be placed more and more under international agreements. These distinctions would indicate that the precise control mechanisms will likely vary at the same time in the same country according to the industrial sectors or the market orientations of the companies being controlled.

Whatever the choice among these five avenues of control, new organizations will be required. They will need to have the capability of encouraging the stepped progression or of completing several control systems that lead to international economic cooperation. What remains to be developed is an understanding of the fact that different orientations to a new international economic order can exist simultaneously—sector by sector and country by country—and will lead to different kinds of control mechanisms over foreign investment.

In order to determine the kinds of control and who will exercise them requires first a dialogue on the nature of the international economic order and the differences that are implied by the different impacts of various industrial sectors and types of international business. What will then be needed is a conference that seeks to disaggregate the types of business, the industrial sectors, the market orientations, and the precise impacts that are of concern to governments. Out of this should come an appreciation of the different types of control that are feasible and desirable.

To move along this path, a new institution will be needed to gather information directly relevant to decisions as to the nature of the new international economic order and the role of industry and industrial cooperation within it. To facilitate this, emphasis should be placed on key sectors, particularly the mobile industries— chemicals and petrochemicals, textiles, autos, electronics, food processing, pharmaceuticals and cosmetics, etc. With this initiative would come a much better understanding of the way in which industrial development is taking place around the world and the extent to which the advanced and developed countries need to cooperate in order to achieve the most effective use of the world's resources by nonmarket as well as market criteria.

NOTES

1. "Business and Developing Countries," The Liebold Institute, 1973, p. 3.

2. Quoted in ibid., pp. 31 and 69.

3. I have detailed these views in "Sharing International Production through the Multinational Enterprise and Sectoral Integration," Law and Policy in International Business 4, no. 1 (1972):1-36.

4

MULTINATIONAL FIRMS AND THE INTERNATIONAL MONETARY SYSTEM

Patrick M. Boarman

Those who direct the destinies of great multinational firms must often feel the urge to voice Hamlet's bitter complaint: "The time is out of joint: o cursed spite, that ever I was born to set it right." The paradox of the multinational enterprise in our time is that, on the one hand, it is the symbol and cutting edge of a still-accelerating technological and economic process that has shrunk the planet to the global village; on the other hand, it is also perceived to be the most egregious misfit in a world that, in political and in ideological terms, appears to be moving in the opposite direction, toward an ever more intense preoccupation with exclusively nationalistic concerns. The technological revolutions of the last several decades—in communications, transportation, information processing, production and distribution—must have as their logical terminus and as a precondition for the reaping of their full fruits an ever more open, an ever more integrated world economy. But this conflicts head on with the reigning political Weltanschauung in which national economic autonomy is the categorical imperative to which every other consideration is subordinated. The logical terminus of a continuous movement along this path is the closed economy and international economic disintegration.

NATIONAL AUTONOMY VS. MULTINATIONAL BUSINESS

The preceding statement puts the matter in stark and doubtless oversimplified terms, but it makes clear the essential choice that

At the time this chapter was written, Patrick M. Boarman was Director of Research, Center for International Business, Pepperdine University, Los Angeles. Currently, he is President, Patrick M. Boarman Associates, Palos Verdes, California.

confronts us: Shall the political structures of the world, now for
the most part obsessively nationalistic, shift (however gradually)
to accommodate and make the most of such phenomena as the
multinational enterprise, or shall the latter, on the contrary, be
swallowed up in the end in the maw of national autonomy?

Some people who are quite knowledgeable on the evolving
role of the multinational firm consider it unlikely that there will
be any significant moving away from national economic autonomy,
so that policies aimed at multinationals will continue to be capricious
to a degree and inimical to the interests not only of multinational
firms but of the nations applying the policies. These experts
expressly preclude any return to the received classical conception
of international economic order as naive, nationalistic (that is,
involving the imposition of our American point of view on the rest
of the world), and normative. What is wrong with being normative,
which means to say having a conception of what should be, I
cannot quite fathom. In any event, the assumption that the ad-
herents of a classical type of international economic order are the
prisoners of an American point of view is simply wrong. The
adherence by responsible scholars to the classical conception, or
to any conception, must be presumed to be based on its inherent
logic and its accord with the facts. To abandon a position that is
correct in all respects except that it is unpopular or inconvenient
is to be merely opportunistic.

Sadly, opportunism, rather than principle, is characteristic
of much of what currently passes for policy in the international
economics arena. Like it or not, we are told, the rest of the
world will simply not be budged from the course on which it is
now embarked, a course of proliferating controls, of rising
economic nationalism, and of obsessive subordination of external
economic concerns to internal ones. One way out of the dilemma
has been suggested by Jack N. Behrman, a noted authority on
multinational business at the University of North Carolina and a
contributor to this volume.* It is that we create a "new institution,"
aimed not at constraining multinational enterprises but of using
them to develop the appropriate responses to the innumerable
hazards of the nationalistic universe in which they are forever
compelled to operate.

One can be hopeful about the prospects for bringing such an
institution into being. But this hope must be set alongside the
fact that such an institution will require far greater cooperation
by the MNCs with each other than they have thus far given any
indication they can muster. Paradoxically, it is probably only
the government (or governments) that dispose of the authority and

---

*See Chapter 3.

the power needed to establish the institution intended to avert increased government control! Furthermore, serious obstacles to any concerted action by MNCs inhere in the antitrust laws of a number of major countries. The clear record, anyhow, is that the MNCs to date have shown no ability and not much interest in speaking with one voice on any subject. Their record in this respect is dismal when compared with what the labor unions have been able to accomplish in their anti-MNC campaign. Never have so few— the MNCs—been under attack by so many.

I submit that the proposed exit from the dilemma is in reality not available and that we have here a case of wanting somehow to secure the benefits of international trade and investment without paying the price in the form of yielding up the amount of national sovereignty and the amount of national autonomy that these benefits require. I am not referring here so much to international or trans-national arrangements—rules of the game—that might be adopted to regulate MNCs, though this would clearly require a significant movement away from national autonomy. I have in mind rather the urgent need for national economies to permit the consequences of their international activity, both in trade and investment, to be fully felt at home. And the yielding up of sovereignty in this sense, as the price of the increased benefits obtainable from the inter-nationalization of business, takes us back, in fact, to the elements of the selfsame classical conception of international economic order that is being rejected by many as utopian.

ORDER VS. DISORDER IN INTERNATIONAL MONETARY AFFAIRS

It is above all international monetary order that was and remains a vital component of international economic order. And nowhere, perhaps, is the conflict between national autonomy and economic welfare more evident than in the relationships of contemporary multinational enterprises to the international monetary system—which brings me to my theme proper.

There are three basic points I would like to develop, and so that they will be clearly in view, I shall state them briefly now and supply the argumentation later. First, multinational firms are widely thought to be responsible in greater or less degree for recent international monetary crises. This is not true. It is not corporate treasurers or even international banks who are to blame for the recurrent upheavals in the world's money. It is rather governments who have created the mess and governments who must clean it up, whereby some have a bigger job to do than others.

Second, multinational enterprises, and international business generally, function best under a regime of fairly stable rates of

exchange (as opposed to flexible rates). Third, an effective system
of stable exchange rates, that is, one not subject to frequent
devaluations and revaluations, is feasible only in the context of
a continuous international adjustment process, which process will
involve continuous concessions of some national economic autonomy
to the requirements of the international economy on the part of
the major nations.

On the first point: It is true that there is a vast basin of
international liquidity—the figure most often cited is $268 billion—
that is under the control of private institutions on the financial
scene and that can be tilted in any direction indicated by the
"nervous Nellies" of the foreign exchange markets. Some $65 to
$75 billion of these liquid assets are estimated to be under the
control of U. S. multinationals, and it is clear that the movement
of only a small portion of such funds, which would greatly over-
shadow the central reserves of any single nation, could easily
produce monetary upheavals. The $268 billion seem less horrendous,
however, in the light of the fact that the amount of liquid funds in
other private hands that theoretically could be mobilized to exploit
disequilibrium among currencies is still larger, namely, the entire
panoply of domestic liquid assets, so that the flights of funds from
one center to another that have characterized the most recent
monetary crises could have occurred even without the intervention
of the multinational firms.

It is also true that multinational companies do not always have
the information or even the wish to exploit through speculation
differences among national currencies. They are, in a variety of
ways that could be adduced, neither as monolithic or as rapacious
as their image would have one believe. "Most do not invest their
cash effectively. They prefer to place temporarily idle funds in the
U. S. regardless of the opportunities available in foreign money
markets."[1]

Holding minimum amounts of cash and current assets in a
subsidiary may be a good way to reduce exposure to the risk of
devaluation; it is not usually the most profitable way to run a
multinational enterprise, since the effort entailed in remitting
cash to the parent causes other protective measures to be overlooked.
In their simulation model of such behavior by MNCs, Robbins and
Stobaugh show losses in the tens of millions of dollars resulting
therefrom.

But even if multinationals were more monolithic, more sophisticated, and more single-minded in the exploitation of disorderly
conditions in foreign exchange markets than they actually are, it
would be inappropriate to fix the blame for currency chaos on them.
To blame is the government or governments that have created the
conditions of monetary uncertainty that induce the MNCs to take
defensive and/or speculative actions.

MNCs AND MONETARY STABILITY

The relationship between MNCs and the international monetary system is a symbiotic one and leads to my second contention, namely, that MNCs function best in a system where currency relationships are fairly stable and predictably stable over the long term. An international monetary system in which exchange rates of the major economies are stable over the long run will offer little incentive for MNCs to get involved in a foreign exchange transaction for its own sake, and this will be good for the system. Likewise, a system of stable rates is good for MNCs because it eliminates the money cost, time, and effort of hedging against currency risks and leaves more time for the real business of the firm in the context of the nonmonetary risks it would customarily encounter.

The immense support that flexible rates, gliding bands, crawling pegs, etc., have been able to garner is, in any event, mystifying. If monetary stability is a desideratum of policy internally, and few presumably question this, why should it be any less desirable internationally? International money is, after all, the existing pattern of exchange rates. Where these parities are constantly in motion, that is, where international money is inherently unstable and unpredictable, the results for trade and investment must inevitably be as noxious as would be a dollar at home that continuously fluctuated in value geographically and temporally. It is true that in the recent period of floating, international business has apparently not registered significant declines. But the period has been too short and the presence of distorting influences (including the world business momentum fed by world inflation coupled with government interventions to limit floating) too significant to permit of any unambiguous judgments on this point. Nor is it clear that we have yet averted the major danger implicit in floating, namely competitive devaluation, whose end effect, given reprisals, would be to constrict trade, as in the 1930s.

The problem is compounded when the world is offered as its ultimate value anchor in lieu of gold (which is supposed to fade away, though it is doing a rather slow fade in increasing in value in a few years from $40 to $190 per ounce) an SDR (a special drawing right) that is to be defined as the average value of a unit of a basketful of currencies, each one of which is subject to floating in greater or lesser degree. A system of floating rates anchored to an SDR that itself is floating is not a mechanism to inspire confidence, to say the least.

Even under a system of exchange-rate stability, an element of exchange-rate risk is present, which conditions in a very direct way every major financial decision taken by multinational firms. The exchange rate is absolutely crucial, but we must distinguish two variants of a stable rate system: one, a system embodying long-term stability of rates; two, a system of stable rates subject, however, to frequent major revaluations or devaluations to overcome fundamental disequilibrium. Behavior under the first system will attend only to the possibility of gain or loss within the limited band of rate movement permitted. The putative gains or losses may, in this case, be so small as to be interesting only to foreign exchange specialists. In a system of wider, though still stable bands, defensive and speculative behavior by MNCs may occur. And here it is appropriate to break a lance for speculation. I emphasize this because of the invidious comparison that is often made between the defensive actions that the MNCs take in foreign currency markets (supposedly legitimate) and their purely speculative actions (supposedly illegitimate).

A POSITIVE VIEW OF SPECULATION

Speculation has a bad name but it is, of course, one of the most constructive activities that occurs in a market-oriented system, chiefly because it eliminates large random swings in prices and production over time. But the conditions under which the speculative activity occurs must not frustrate these smoothing effects. Speculation in foreign currency markets, where the chances of a currency going up or down are fairly even, will actively smooth the rate and make for a more stable system. But speculation in a system in which very large changes—revaluations or devaluations—are expected to occur, and especially where these changes are of the one-way sort, are destructive; more precisely, they are disequilibrating rather than equilibrating. The destructive or negative consequences of such speculation are not to be blamed on the speculator, but on the conditions that render his acts destructive and negative in the macro sense.

One-way or riskless speculation in foreign currency markets occurs because the different national economies in question are moving on divergent tracks. Chronic weakness and chronic strength of currencies are characteristics of such a system and speculators, including MNCs, will quite rightly bet that if internal policies or structures of the countries do not change, devaluation or revaluation or both will occur, and in directions and in amounts that can be roughly anticipated. It follows that their behavior, conditioned by these assumptions, will tend to make the expectations self-fulfilling.

Now the nub of the argument here is that the structural divergences in question will not be overcome, short of a major change in currency parities, unless and until some degree of national autonomy in economic matters and some purely national priorities and preferences are renounced or are cut back.

The argumentation applies equally to a system of flexible rates, since the need for such a system in the first place arises only in situations in which national autonomy in matters economic will take precedence over international economic adjustment. If the rate of exchange, rather than the national economy, takes the burden of the adjustment, the less productive economy, or the more inflated economy, will have the declining currency, and the stronger economy will have the appreciating currency. Unless national structures are compelled to move by policy measures to close the structural gap (or the weak economy is induced to do so by a change in currency parities), the pressure will remain on the weak currency and speculation will again be one-way and destructive.

Of course, in "clean floating" it is also true that the rate may fall low enough or rise high enough, even in the presence of significant inelasticities of demand, to bring economic forces into play that will prevent further declines (or rises) in rates. The trouble is that governments have a direct stake in the behavior of the rate and will normally not let it move to the limits required for the overcoming of the existing disequilibrium. It was, for instance, quite obvious that the strengthening of the dollar in late 1973, which tended to reduce the competitiveness of U. S. exports gained in the successive devaluations of the dollar, was a cause of concern to U. S. government officials, and that the decision to remove restrictions on U. S. capital exports was not unrelated to that concern.

Floating in the real world is always dirty floating. A surplus country will not passively look on while the depreciating currency of a deficit country progressively undermines its own export business. Indeed, as noted above, the danger of a recurrence of competitive depreciation of the beggar-my-neighbor type is even more likely under a system of flexible rates, where no formal declaration is needed to effect it, than under a system of stable rates.

Lastly, even where a currency sinks internationally to a level at which it is seriously undervalued in real terms (by an amount more than sufficient to overcome the fundamental disequilibrium) the threat is posed of a "bargain basement sale" of the country's currently produced goods and capital assets to foreigners, while simultaneously the cost of imports is raised. Both forces in conjunction may, under certain often realized assumptions, exacerbate inflation in the country with the declining currency and, under the mantle of defensive tactics, lead to major disruptions, including controls on imports and exports and capital movements, of the customary patterns of trade and investment.

A government that depends on public support will not long be able to persist in such a course. It is evident that at some point it will find it necessary to modify domestic policies to prevent undue movements in the rate of exchange, much as under a system of stable rates with reserves it is compelled at some point to take steps to prevent continuous loss or continuous accumulation of reserves. What this means, in sum, is that the vaunted autonomy of the national economy, which rate flexibility allegedly makes possible, is an illusion.

But a system of flexible rates has the further negative effect that, since government interventions under dirty floating are not predictable on any easily analyzable criterion, dealers in the currency, be they MNCs or others, are confronted by major new uncertainties that tend to cause wide swings in rates over short periods. This latter effect of dirty floating was dramatically in evidence in the summer of 1973 with the U. S. dollar swinging in value by literally enormous margins in percentage terms.

REDUCING NATIONAL SOVEREIGNTY

There are other alleged exits from the nasty dilemma that inheres in the attempt to enjoy the benefits of international trade and investment and yet remain fully autonomous nationally. They include such gimmicks as increasing international liquidity, including a significant expansion of the use of SDRs, currency swaps, and the like. There is not time here for a detailed examination of these devices. Suffice it to say that as solutions to the problem of international disequilibrium they are equally as illusory as flexible rates. They merely distract attention and effort from the real need, which is for each nation in the system to permit the structure of its economy—structure being taken in the broadest sense—to stay in balance with the other important national economic structures. And that means inevitably giving up a measure of domestic economic sovereignty. This does not require such sovereignty to be abandoned; nor does it mean that MNCs, for instance, cannot be required to conform to certain national require-ments and international requirements—codes of behavior, rules of the game, or whatever. It does mean that there must be a concession of some national sovereignty to the requirements of the international economy—enough to preclude significant and chronic international disequilibrium. In this respect, what I am suggesting is that, indeed, we go back to the essentials of the classical model of international economic order.

If you tell me that won't work, that in the age of Keynes and full employment and any number of other domestic goals that nations will persist in achieving, my prescription is utopian, then there is no future for the multinational enterprise. For it is precisely in such a context—of economic nationalism, of economic particu-larism, and the resulting chronic international disequilibria that it produces—that the MNC will trouble the exchanges and trigger

monetary upheavals, will be condemned and punished for same,
will be found guilty of numerous other contraventions of the national
economic good, will be regulated, will be controlled, and in the
end will be dissolved.

If Keynes were alive, all of this would have the flavor for him,
I am sure, of deja vu. In one of the most unabashed expressions
of national economic chauvinism, he wrote, in the early 1930s:

> National self-sufficiency, though it cost something,
> may be becoming a luxury which we can afford if we
> happen to want it. We do not wish to be at the mercy
> of world forces working out, or trying to work out some
> uniform equilibrium according to ideal principles, if they
> can be called such, of laissez-faire capitalism. We
> wish to be our own masters, and to be as free as we can
> make ourselves from the interferences of the outside
> world.[2]

Whereas Keynes was candid enough to concede that national
autonomy comes at a cost, namely, the benefits to be derived
from the international division of labor, contemporary economic
nationalists nurture the illusion that they can have it both ways.
It cannot be done and the sooner this is recognized and admitted,
the better, and not just for multinational firms.

NOTES

1. S. Robbins and R. Stobaugh, Money in the Multinational
Enterprise (New York: Basic Books, 1973).

2. John Maynard Keynes, Yale Review 22 (Summer 1933):757-60.

BUSINESS-GOVERNMENT INTERACTIONS IN MULTINATIONAL OPERATIONS

5

U.S. GOVERNMENT POLICIES IN THE FIELD OF INTERNATIONAL INVESTMENT

S. Stanley Katz

Let me begin, as most prudent government officials do these days, by stating that I am writing not as an official U. S. government spokesman but rather as an individual with some day-to-day involvement in the formulation of U. S. policies in the international investment area.

Aside from the purely bureaucratic reasons for this sort of opening disclaimer, I have an even more legitimate one: it's simply that there is still an element of policy uncertainty in this area and we do not have clearly defined procedures concerning some types of international investment.

Unlike international trade, where theory, practice, and policies go back 150 years, investment of the type we are witnessing today is a relatively new development in international commerce, and its theoretical framework, its practices, and, consequently, government policies to address some aspects of it are still in the formative stages.

What I would like to do, therefore, is to sketch very briefly what is emerging as the central thrust of U. S. policy in five key areas of international investment.

The areas I will cover are (1) foreign direct investment in the United States, (2) foreign portfolio investment in the United States, (3) U. S. investment in industrialized countries, (4) U. S. investment in developing countries, and (5) the investment activities of the multinational corporations.

S. Stanley Katz is Deputy Director, International Economic Policy and Research, U. S. Department of Commerce.

FOREIGN DIRECT INVESTMENT
IN THE UNITED STATES

By foreign direct investment we usually mean investment in
"bricks and mortar" rather than in security issues, and generally
such investment is for the purpose of building or acquiring substantial ownership (that is, 10 percent or more) in manufacturing or
distribution facilities. Foreign direct investment in the United
States is referred to as "reverse investment," which probably
reflects something of our historical attitude about the direction
in which investment is supposed to flow; but it is nonetheless a
convenient shorthand term to describe such investment.

As with all types of international investment, foreign direct
investment in the United States has been increasing dramatically.
In 1962 the book value of foreign investment in the United States
amounted to under $8 billion; by year-end 1973 the total had more
than doubled to over $17 billion.

Foreign currency revaluations vis-a-vis the dollar in the past
several years have made the United States a highly attractive
place to invest for non-Americans in terms of both asset values
and production costs and, consequently, we expect that in the
next few years we will see an increase of several billion dollars
in the book value of foreign investment in the United States.

In effect, we are now seeing a reversal of the situation that
prevailed in the 1950s and 1960s when the dollar was overvalued
and U. S. investment capital flowed in large volume to countries
of Europe with relatively lower dollar-denominated asset costs
and growing national regional markets.

According to most analysts, the United States derives some
net benefit from this type of foreign investment. Such investment
is generally made by the more technologically advanced industries
and is frequently a vehicle for the introduction of new products,
processes, or technology originating abroad for which the scale
of the U. S. market is an important consideration. Foreign investment of this type can therefore be expected to make a positive
contribution to overall U. S. productivity, income and employment,
and to economic welfare. From a trade and payments viewpoint it
brings in some capital and can serve to displace future imports.

In addition to the recent changes in currency parities, a
number of other factors underlie the current and expected growth
in foreign investment.

One background factor is a dimly perceived undercurrent
of U. S. economic nationalism and the fear that tariffs or other
barriers may some day limit or otherwise restrict exports to the
United States. Another is the growing experience, confidence, and
scale of operations of the foreign-based multinational companies.

Other factors include the size and growth of the U. S. market; the ease of establishing a U. S. investment base that can be used to serve all 50 states; the efficient U. S. marketing and distribution system; relatively less costly raw materials and other inputs; and the greater availability and mobility of labor. On this point, while U. S. labor costs are high, so is our productivity, and foreign labor costs have been rising more rapidly than our own. When the indirect costs of foreign social benefits are included, the differences between U. S. and foreign labor costs have virtually disappeared.

U. S. government policy has been favorably disposed toward foreign investment in the United States since the earliest days of the Republic. There is, in fact, a little-known quote from Alexander Hamilton dated 1791 to the effect that the United States should welcome foreign investment; and this continues to be the official policy today at both the federal and state government levels.

Both levels, in fact, have programs designed to facilitate reverse investment. Against the charge that in doing so they are inviting competition by foreign firms, the point is made that such competition is generally already in the U. S. market in the form of imports. What is being encouraged is a shift in the location of the production unit to the United States, which, not incidentally, serves to neutralize special exporter incentives or favorable cost differentials enjoyed by the foreign firms in their home countries.

PORTFOLIO INVESTMENT

There is a long-standing preference on the part of foreign investors for portfolio investment in the United States, both because of the range of instruments available here and because of traditionally more cautious attitudes about long-term, illiquid commitments in other countries.

Without attempting to discuss foreign portfolio investment in any detail, it is interesting to note how rapidly this kind of investment has been growing. Foreign holdings of U. S. securities increased from $10 billion in 1960 to almost $37 billion in 1973. In 1972, for example, foreign portfolio investment in the United States increased by $8.5 billion, one-half of which represented new purchases and one-half increases in the value of outstanding holdings.

The tempo of foreign portfolio investment seems clearly to have been accelerated by two factors: dollar devaluation and depressed prices of U. S. stocks in relation to earnings. The likelihood that the dollar is now somewhat undervalued plus share prices that are highly attractive to foreign investors with plenty

of liquidity seem to have created a considerable stimulant to
foreign portfolio investment.

On the other hand, U. S. holdings of foreign securities have
increased from less than $10 billion in 1960 to almost $25 billion
at year end 1973. In 1973, U. S. investment in foreign securities
rose more than $3 billion.

As a general policy proposition, foreign portfolio investment
in the United States is considered to be largely a function of the
market, and U. S. government intervention does not seem necessary
or desirable at this point in time. We see some favorable effect
accruing to our balance of payments from these financial capital
inflows, although repatriation of earnings is an offsetting factor.
One problem, of course, is that foreign investment in U. S.
financial instruments tends to be highly interest-sensitive and is
subject to a number of nonmarket influences. Consequently,
short-term capital movements may have an economically destabilizing
effect.

Saying that we look favorably on foreign portfolio investment
does not imply that at least some parts of the U. S. government
would not become highly exercised by a threatened foreign takeover
of major U. S. firms or industries. In the past, that did not seem
to be much of a likelihood. But with heightened foreign interest in
U. S. equity markets, the rapid build-up of dollars in the oil-
producing countries, and some recent cases of actual or threatened
foreign takeover attempts, we find that U. S. attitudes are not
too different from those of other nations around the world. Certainly
some of the investment-restricting legislation proposed recently by
the Congress has indicated that we like to have domestic companies
American-owned. Such legislative purposes are likely to reflect
increasing public and Congressional concern over possibly large-
scale petro-dollar investments in the United States by oil-exporting
nations during the next few years.

U. S. DIRECT INVESTMENT ABROAD
IN DEVELOPED COUNTRIES

When we speak of U. S. foreign investment, the kind that
comes most immediately to mind is overseas direct investment by
U. S. companies, mainly of the multinational variety and in other
industrialized nations. As with other forms of investment, this
type of U. S. foreign investment has increased rapidly over the
past few decades. In 1960 the total book value of U. S. direct
investment abroad was about $32 billion, some $19 billion of it
in the industrialized countries, including $11 billion in Canada
and $7 billion in Europe.

By year end 1973 the worldwide total was $107 billion, of which about $74 billion was in the developed countries, including $28 billion in Canada and $37 billion in Europe.

The interesting thing here is the changing geographic pattern of these investments. The industrialized countries as a whole had a greater share of our direct investment in 1973—69 percent—than in 1960, when they had about 59 percent. This pattern supports the observation that capital (a) is in short supply and (b) flows to areas where its scarcity is respected in terms of its rate of return and safety.

The surge of U. S. investments to Europe during the 1950s and 1960s was largely a consequence of the confluence of two main factors: first, the development of the Common Market, which American firms found highly attractive from a marketing viewpoint; and second, the overvalued dollar, which permitted U. S. firms to buy foreign assets at bargain prices and presented artificially reduced costs of foreign production in terms of U. S. dollars. Together these two conditions exerted a strong pull on U. S. investment.

Fortunately or unfortunately, recognition lagged behind the fact, and it is only now, with the effect of these two investment-attracting factors having largely dissipated, that governments are pondering how to deal with the rapid growth of U. S. investment abroad. Hence we have such things as the Burke–Hartke Bill and the proposed OECD code of conduct for foreign investors that would appear to be largely responses to conditions that caused problems in the past decades but that seem to present only lesser-magnitude problems today. Now, in fact, it is the dollar that is undervalued, the U. S. market that appears to have the most vigorous growth prospects, and the U. S. economy that is increasingly attractive to foreign investors.

U. S. DIRECT INVESTMENT
IN DEVELOPING COUNTRIES

As the figures cited earlier indicate, the relative interest of U. S. investors in the developing countries has diminished, and today a smaller proportion of our total foreign investment is located in these countries than was the case a few years ago. In 1960 we had about $12 billion of direct investments in these countries—about 38 percent of our total foreign investment. At year end 1973 the figure had risen to $28 billion, but that was only 26 percent of the total. In Latin America our direct investments rose from $8 billion to $18 billion while the percentages dropped from 25 to 17 of the total. The kinds of investments U. S. companies

are undertaking have also been changing too: Worldwide as well
as in Latin America, investment is shifting from agriculture and
natural resources to manufacturing, processing, distribution, and
services.

From a policy viewpoint, the developing countries present a
special challenge. High on the agenda of the world's unfinished
business is the need to do something decisive about accelerating
their development; and of all the bilateral and multilateral agents
of development that have been tried—infrastructure, health services,
education, industrial capital, technical assistance, etc.—private
investment, properly directed and monitored, but properly rewarded
as well, is perhaps one of the real keys to unlocking a sustainable
increase in the developing countries' growth and development.
Multinational corporations obviously have a special role to play
in this process.

INVESTMENT BY MULTINATIONAL CORPORATIONS

The multinational corporations have been of interest to the
Department of Commerce for some time, particularly in terms of
their impact on our trade and payments position, domestic employment, and income generation. The department published two volumes
of studies on the MNC.

As far as the United States is concerned, multinational corporations are not really that new a phenomenon. They go back to at
least the 1850s; and in 1900 about one-half of the then-existing
50 largest U. S. corporations had significant overseas operating
interests.

However, today's multinationals are different in terms of a
new management and operational dimension that emerged during
the 1940s and 1950s. Multinationals had always been characterized
by the concept of a common corporate strategy. The new element
that goes beyond that concept is the capability of having the
management of that strategy emanate from a common "nerve center"
based on a rapid flow of information and, if necessary, people
from the nerve center to the overseas branches.

At about the same time that this change in the MNC was taking
hold, national governments began to understand the significance
of Keynesian economics and grasped the idea that it was possible
to pursue income and full employment objectives within national
boundaries. As nations began to articulate these national economic
goals and priorities, they were confronted by multinational business
entities that could move across national boundaries, institute
policies, and undertake activities that could frustrate these government efforts. While national governments were attempting to
achieve economic goals within the confines of their national frontiers,

they found that important elements of their economic fortunes were
under the control of the multinationals who were attempting to
maximize other objectives without regard to national boundaries.

This difference in viewpoint led to some conflict and the
conflict has not ended, as we all know from the continuing debate
over the Burke-Hartke Bill, from foreign expropriations, from the
Andean Investment Code, and from consideration being given to
codes of MNC conduct by the international organizations.

From a broad policy perspective, perhaps the most significant
impact of multinational enterprise derives from the internationalization of production and the resulting start toward developing a more
integrated world economy based on international comparative
advantage. This internationalization of production is regarded by
some analysts as the most important development since the industrial
revolution, and if the developing countries grasp the significance of
this for their own development, the MNCs can be enlisted to serve
as a major tool for accelerating growth and raising living standards
over that vast area of the world.

Multinationals can contribute to these development objectives
in a variety of ways. Clearly, they are an important channel for
the transmission of much-needed technology to the developing
countries. Beyond technology, the multinationals have proven
ability in marshalling and deploying financial resources, in
identifying and developing managerial expertise, and in applying
modern and effective techniques for maximizing production, exports,
and economic returns.

The articulation of such external investment with local and
national customs and attitudes—and suspicions—has led to frictions
with indigenous economic interests and host governments, and,
in some cases, has produced an antiforeign investment bias
antithetical to the capital needs and goals of developing countries.

The future ability of multinational corporations in assisting
the development of the developing world rests on the possibility
of working out a modus vivendi between the companies and the
national governments that presents a sufficient balance of autonomy
and profitability for both parties. As far as U. S. MNC investment
is concerned, our policy is not based on whim, but is a response
to real economic considerations.

SUMMARY

To sum up, U. S. policy in the investment field continues
to evolve, but has traditionally been predisposed toward a relatively
free, basically market-oriented allocation of scarce capital resources.
We do not favor either deliberate or arbitrary government incentives
to attract, nor discrimination to repel, foreign investment, particu-

larly when such measures distort normal trade and investment patterns. There is, however, growing concern over the possibility of large-scale petro-dollar investments in the United States, and this area will have to be watched closely. Finally, private capital investment has an important but still underrealized role to play in accelerating the development of the developing countries and, hopefully, the MNCs will make a contribution toward this important objective.

6

THE PROTECTION OF
OVERSEAS INVESTMENT
Marshall T. Mays

The Overseas Private Investment Corporation (OPIC) is the U. S. government agency engaged in selectively encouraging and protecting U. S. private investment in developing countries. OPIC affords protection in the sense of seeking to assure a sound basis of establishing an investment through formal approval by the host government, a sound basis of assuring political viability grounded in mutual benefits for both the host economy and the U. S. investor, and, if a loss as a result of political action nevertheless occurs, indemnity through insurance or guarantees for the insured interest.

OPIC'S FUNCTIONS

In this brief review I will deal only with OPIC's insurance functions. However, it should be noted that OPIC also is a financing agency, using both direct loans and guarantees of loan funds supplied by institutional lenders and, occasionally, operating companies.

The best way of examining OPIC's role in investment protection is to put it in the overall context of U. S. policy and the historical evolution of our investment-encouragement programs. The United States affords protection to the international law rights of U. S. private overseas investors through normal diplomatic espousal. In some cases this protection is reinforced by treaties of friendship, commerce, and navigation (FCN) that commit each government to assure reciprocal treatment to the investments of the other country's nationals and to provide fair compensation in the event of nationali-

---

Marshall T. Mays is President, Overseas Private Investment Corporation.

zation or expropriation of investment interests. Few FCN treaties
have been negotiated with developing countries in recent years,
however.

The United States has long sought to promote universal
recognition of the principle of "prompt, adequate, and effective
compensation" for expropriation as a tenet of international law.
U. S. law governing administration of foreign economic assistance
programs and U. S. participation in international development banks
directs the Executive Branch to enforce this international law
principle by imposing sanctions in the form of withholding aid
benefits from a nation that fails to meet this test in the treatment
of U. S. private investment.

This legal stance and the threat of sanctions may have some
deterrent effect upon a government contemplating confiscation of
a U. S. private investment. However, they offer no assurance of
effective protection. An increasing number of governments,
particularly in Latin America, have challenged both the existence
of international law requiring "prompt, adequate, and effective
compensation" and the right of a foreign government to intervene
in any way to assert or enforce this law in their sovereign realms.
Further, the aid-withholding sanction is of no real significance to
a government that needs or receives little or no capital or arms
aid on concessional terms from the United States. Even in the
case of an aid recipient, the threat of such sanctions after a
public position on confiscation has been taken by a nationalist
regime is more likely to harden its defiance than cause it to
yield to the United States. The attempts by U. S. directors of
the international banks to block loans to countries that have
confiscated U. S. private properties has usually been opposed
by both developed and developing countries on grounds that
development finance should not be an instrument of big power
pressure.

Finally, the United States itself is frequently reluctant to
risk jeopardizing its other interests—military, political, commercial,
or larger investments—by engaging in a rough confrontation with a
government that has mistreated a U. S. investor.

THE NEED FOR POLITICAL RISK INSURANCE

Given these realities, other forms of assurance have been
needed by U. S. companies and banks contemplating new investments
in countries where security against expropriation and confiscation
was not reasonably predictable. This uncertainty could stem from
political instability, ambiguous or threatening laws, a servile
judiciary, or simply a track record too limited to permit confidence.

Or the economic capacity of the country to make full indemnity for
an expropriation could be so weak as to create fears of confiscatory
treatment.

In addition, investment in countries with chronic foreign exchange
problems or administratively determined foreign exchange controls
may be vulnerable to another political risk—exchange blockages or
refusal by exchange controllers to carry out previously existing
policies on conversion of the local currency earnings or capital
of a foreign investor. No U. S. policy pronouncement or diplomatic
espousal could protect against this risk.

Finally, the risk of destruction because of war or insurrection
is abnormally high in some countries, particularly developing
nations whose governments are the targets of insurgents or countries
that are adjacent to hostile neighbors or involved in regional tribal
conflicts. Again, U. S. policies and pronouncements or sanctions
are of no use in protecting U. S. investments against this risk.

Private insurance against these three political risks is, for
all practical purposes, not available to either export creditors or
investors. Governments interested in promoting exports have long
provided insurance to their exporters and export financing banks
against these political risks. The public purpose justifying these
public insurance programs was to enable domestic exporters to
offer deferred settlement terms at competitive interest rates. From
this point, the insurance of long-term capital transfers (that is,
investment) was a small step.

The U. S. government was the first to establish political risk
insurance for its foreign investors. The purpose was not primarily
to afford protection to its citizens, as a general benefit of government, but rather to promote a new public policy: the encouragement
of U. S. investment in the recovery of Western Europe after World
War II. The investment insurance program was an element of the
Marshall Plan. Later, as aid programs moved from European
recovery to mutual security with threatened countries of Asia and
southern Europe to a global system of development cooperation,
the investment insurance program was extended as a complement
to official aid transfers, as an investment incentive activity rather
than as an investment protection program. It was limited to new
investments welcomed by the governments of developing countries
that signed a bilateral agreement instituting the program.

One should not exaggerate the distinction between an investment protection program and an investment incentive program.
To be an effective incentive to investment in areas of high political
risk, the program must offer protection that investors believe may
not otherwise be available. Two kinds of protection are afforded:
deterrence of confiscatory or discriminatory treatment on exchange
controls by a host government and indemnity for insured losses.

There are some important distinctions, however. The U. S. investment incentive program is confined to new investments, for which no commitment has been made prior to registering a request for insurance. It is limited to projects responsive to the developmental needs of the host countries. The bilateral program agreement that traditionally has been negotiated by the United States is assumed to have some investor-protection effect, but it is designed more to establish a procedure for settlement of disputes between the insurer and the host government than to commit the host government to respect the rights of the insured. By contrast, the bilateral agreements obtained in the 1960s by the West German government were full-fledged investment-protection agreements, establishing the rights of the German investor as well as providing for operation of the German investment insurance program.

Under the present management of the Overseas Private Investment Corporation the investment insurance program has focused greater attention on another objective: to influence the form and behavior of U. S. investments so as to minimize the risk of political friction and maximize the developmental impact of the investments. This is done through screening of insurance applications, discussion and negotiation with applicants, special terms of insurance contracts, and general terms obligating the insured investor to meet certain requirements in his behavior.

OPIC'S OBJECTIVES

Thus OPIC has four objectives, one primary and three supportive: (1) to serve as an incentive to mutually beneficial investment; (2) to deter mistreatment of the U. S. investor; (3) to provide indemnity for insured losses; and (4) to influence the quality—political and economic—of investments.

How well have these objectives been achieved? No simple, objective answer is possible, because it depends on a judgment of what would have happened if the program had not been available. As to its incentive effect, scores of anecdotes can be cited in which the insurance was an essential requirement of decisions to invest—not the only or necessarily the primary requirement, but an essential condition. A 1971 survey by Business International Research of nearly 400 U. S. companies and banks active in overseas investment found that 46 percent considered political risk insurance essential to their decisions to invest in developing countries; 47 percent said it was "desirable" but not essential. The "essential" vote was 70 percent among companies in the mineral extractive field. We believe at least half of investors would say today that insurance is essential. Most of those who do not consider insurance necessary probably will not buy it, as the fees are not low. (Over a 20-year insurance term, OPIC's basic and standby fees can add up to about half of the total amount of the investor's original capital in a project.) Consequently, a very large majority of those who have bought OPIC insurance in recent years considered it an important requirement of the decision to invest. Since about $5 billion of U.S. investment has been insured over the two-decade life of the program, we might reasonably say that at least half of this amount of investment would not have occurred if it could not have been insured.

These investors—in some 3,000 projects in 92 countries—now represent considerable experience in relying on the insurance sold by OPIC and its predecessor agencies. Even so, OPIC's experience is still too limited to provide an actuarial basis for managing and pricing investment insurance. A relatively small number of foreign investments has been expropriated over the past two decades in the developing countries, and very few of these expropriation cases have been outright confiscations. Only 16 insured U.S. investments have been expropriated, and of these the taking government has paid or committed itself to pay adequate compensation in four cases. War and insurrection losses have occurred in only six insured U.S. investments. Claims on inconvertibility insurance have been surprisingly small.

The incidence of expropriation has been too small and concentrated in too few countries to draw any conclusions about the effect of investment insurance in deterring expropriatory or confiscatory treatment of foreign investments. No investment was insured in Cuba. The bulk of U.S. investment was insured in Chile, and both insured and uninsured were expropriated—along with hundreds of wholly indigenous companies. None of the investments recently expropriated or threatened with expropriation in Peru were insured against expropriation—OPIC's program agreement in Peru has always been limited to inconvertibility insurance. There have been several cases, however, that point in the direction of a deterrent effect of insurance. The Allende government in Chile expropriated Kennecott's uninsured equity without any compensation, but it committed itself to full payment of Kennecott's loan investment in the same project—and in an amount reduced by Allende to almost exactly the amount of OPIC insurance on the loan.

As I pointed out earlier, the OPIC system of bilateral program agreements and related procedures is not primarily an investment-protection system. Many have assumed, however, that it also had some deterrent effect on confiscation-minded governments. No proof of this belief can be offered. The system involves a written approval by the host government of OPIC's insuring each project, with specific reference to the bilateral agreement with that government that gives OPIC subrogation/succession and international arbitration rights. It is debatable whether a revolutionary regime willing to risk international opprobrium by confiscating foreign investments would be deterred by the prospect of facing OPIC in court or in arbitration or would, in fact, recognize the validity of the OPIC agreements with predecessor governments.

MINIMIZING POLITICAL RISK

The real deterrence will always be a politician's judgment—rational in some cases and emotional in others—of where the current government's interests lie. If its interests seem to lie in violating the rights of a foreign investor, it will have little difficulty in finding a legal rationale and a political justification for the act.

It is from this base of realism that OPIC has progressively refined its risk-management and heightened its involvement in counseling investors on politically viable forms of investment and economic practices. Premium rate variations have been established related to judgment of the risk of expropriation in a proposed investment, imposed coinsurance requirements, rejected projects with excessive economic advantages or protections for the U. S. investor, and rejected projects of little developmental benefit to the host country. In some cases OPIC has required a certification by an independent consultant to the host government that the project's economic terms were fair to both parties.

OPIC believes real protection lies in these directions—essentially that investment modes and terms compatible with the political and economic interests of the host country are likely to be the best security against political attack.

Most of the other national investment insurance agencies now attach little importance to formal international agreements protecting the rights of insured or insurer.

Among the dozen other national agencies of OECD countries only the French and Swedish investment insurance programs are required by law to operate under bilateral investment protection agreements. Apart from the franc zone cooperation agreement, France has been able to sign only three such agreements in two years. The Canadian program originally had such a mandatory legal requirement, but it was removed quite early because of the apparent unavailability of other countries willing to participate as cosignatories. Canada has insured investments in Mexico and Guatemala without a program agreement or investment protection treaty.

Agreements have not been sought by Japan, Australia, Denmark, or Norway. The Japanese take the position that an investment guaranty, like an export credit guaranty, should be protected only by diplomatic representation in the event of a host government action requiring an insurance payout.

The United Kingdom policy, as reported by the Development Assistance Committee of the OECD, is that insurance should not require an investment protection agreement. On that basis the U. K. program is available, "in principle," to insure in all developing countries except Rhodesia.

Germany, starting in the early 1960s, was able to negotiate 42 formal investment protection agreements with developing countries, including four in Latin America: Dominican Republic, Chile, Colombia, and Ecuador. The German report to the OECD notes that the German standard agreement is not reconcilable with a strict reading of the Calvo Doctrine, so that the outlook for effective agreements in Latin America is not bright. Nevertheless, the German program has proceeded to insure investments in 14 Latin American countries and some 20 other countries with which there is no effective bilateral agreement. The German decision to proceed without an agreement is based on analysis of the laws and judicial practice of the country concerned, its political trends affecting foreign investor-interests, or the possibility of obtaining an International Centre for the Settlement of Investment Disputes arbitration clause in the German investor's arrangements with the host government. This approach has resulted in excluding only eight developing countries.

Because of the changing situation in many countries of Latin America, OPIC has been considering alternative arrangements where subrogation rights cannot be formally obtained or OPIC-host government arbitration is not obtainable. In these cases special program limitations adapted to individual countries and projects might be substituted for the blanket approach to protection of OPIC's interests.

7

ISSUES RAISED BY
NATIONAL CONTROL
OF THE MULTINATIONAL
ENTERPRISE

A. E. Safarian
Joel Bell

The increased scope of multinational corporations in the past two decades has been accompanied by growing concern about the national consequences and by widespread efforts to regulate such corporations. In this chapter we review briefly the policy responses by Canadian governments to the high degree of foreign (particularly American) direct investment in Canada and the reasons for these responses. These and other likely policies are posing fundamental challenges to multinational corporations as they now exist. In addition, however, important questions have been raised with respect to government-business relations generally and with regard to government-to-government relations both within Canada and externally. Our reflections on these issues arise from recent Canadian experience, but they are by no means relevant only to Canadian experience.

SUMMARY OF CANADIAN POLICIES

Canadian governments have traditionally been highly receptive to foreign direct investment in Canada and generally remain so today in practice (if not always in rhetoric) regardless of their political complexion. Neither the federal government nor any provincial government has yet proposed policies that suggest a major reversal of this comparatively open approach to foreign direct investment. At the same time, three more or less distinct sets of federal government policies have emerged in recent years that suggest a significant, if evolutionary, change in the treatment

A. E. Safarian is Professor of Economics and Dean, School of Graduate Studies, University of Toronto; Joel Bell is an Economic Advisor to the Prime Minister of Canada.

of foreign direct investment and ultimately the degree of reliance on it. We do not wish to suggest that these appeared in a logical and consistent way, much less that the relationship to other policy objectives has been entirely clarified. Nevertheless, these policies do fall into certain patterns and do reflect certain objectives that are worth describing before their governmental and business effects are explored.

One set of policies directly limits the degree of foreign ownership as such. Heavy public investment in some parts of transportation, communications, atomic energy, and hydroelectric industries has historically ensured an important Canadian presence. In addition, certain industries have been designated "key sectors." In these cases the foriegn owners have either been required to divest their interests down to a minority position (broadcasting, banking) or no further controlling mergers with foreign firms are permitted (insurance, sales finance companies). Changes in taxation had the practical effect of preventing the establishment of further foreign-controlled newspapers and periodicals, whether by merger or a new undertaking. Restrictions on foreign control exist in several other specific cases, such as satellite communication, and the government has announced it will restrict foreign control in uranium. Other policies are aimed at the extent of Canadian ownership, or directorship participation rather than voting control as such. One policy intended to affect the degree of foreign ownership is a lower rate of withholding tax on dividends paid abroad when a corporation has a degree of Canadian ownership. The freedom of owners to select directors in all federally incorporated companies is to be limited by proposed legislation requiring that a majority of directors be resident Canadians not otherwise associated with the company; this proposed legislation will obviously have a much greater effect in foreign-controlled than domestically controlled firms. Federal policy also encourages, to a minor extent, Canadian participation in the holding of lease rights in federal territory.

A second policy approach attempts to improve the performance of the subsidiary by reducing certain costs and/or increasing certain benefits believed to be associated in part with the parent-subsidiary relationship, for example, in such matters as manufactured exports, domestic sourcing of supplies, and research capacity. A variety of methods have been used to date to reach such objectives ranging from "moral suasion" and the seeking of information to financial incentives and administrative pressures. For example, the granting of financial support for industrial research on technology is made conditional upon undertakings to develop any results for the benefit of Canada. Another prominent example is the examination of Canadian production wherever the government has an opportunity to do so. Both examples, be it noted, apply to foreign-owned and domestically owned firms.

Some people believe that one consequence of such techniques as requiring some Canadian shareholdings or greater Canadian participation in the directorships of foreign-controlled companies will be to affect various aspects of the performance of such companies. While both economic performance and direct questions of sovereignty are involved, we also might note here the extension of U. S. law and policy to Canada through the parent-subsidiary relationship. The federal government has attempted to mitigate the impact of such extraterritorial measures with respect to U. S. antitrust and trade legislation in particular.

THE FOREIGN INVESTMENT REVIEW AGENCY

By far the most ambitious attempt to increase the net benefit from direct investment, however, is the Foreign Investment Review Agency. This legislation empowers an agency to examine proposed takeovers of Canadian businesses by nonresidents or by nonresident-controlled corporations for the purpose of advising the Cabinet on whether the acquisition would be of "significant benefit" to Canada. If the transaction does not involve such benefit—and the purchaser is unable or unprepared to make such modifications in his plans of operation as would permit a finding of significant benefit—the acquisition would be disallowed by the Cabinet on the advice of the agency and the minister responsible (the minister of industry, trade, and commerce). These provisions apply only to transactions involving the shifting of effective "control" of business carried on in Canada (either by a Canadian or a foreigner) to a foreign-controlled firm or person.

A similar procedure is included in the pending legislation for the establishment of new businesses in Canada—by persons not formerly carrying on any businesses in Canada, or by persons whose former line of business was "unrelated" to that of the new enterprise. This class of transactions will only be brought under the legislation at such later date as the government chooses to proclaim these separate provisions. This would not affect the expansion of existing foreign-controlled operations—nor the undertaking of ventures in related lines of business by foreign-controlled firms in Canada, neither of which is covered by the proposed legislation.

The factors that are to be examined in assessing the existence of "significant benefit" are set out in the legislation as follows:

(a) the effect of the acquisition or establishment on the level and nature of economic activity in Canada, including, without limiting the generality of the foregoing, the effect on employment, on resource

processing, on the utilization of parts, components
and services produced in Canada, and on exports
from Canada;

(b) the degree and significance of participation by
Canadians in the business enterprise or new business
and in any industry or industries in Canada of which
the business enterprise or new business forms or
would form a part;

(c) the effect of the acquisition or establishment on
productivity, industrial efficiency, technological
development, product innovation and product variety
in Canada;

(d) the effect of the acquisition or establishment on
competition within any industry or industries in
Canada; and

(e) the compatibility of the acquisition or establishment with national industrial and economic policies,
taking into consideration industrial and economic
policy objectives enunciated by the government or
legislature of any province likely to be significantly
affected by the acquisition or establishment." [1]

This procedure and these criteria reflect the view that no
categoric judgments are possible on foreign investment generally
or on the effects of multinational enterprises on the host economy.
There is a bias against certain categories of foreign investment in
the sense that those investments that offer no significant benefit
to Canada, even if there is no evidence of detriment, would be
disallowed. The purpose of the review, however, is not the
disallowance of foreign investments, but the separation of the
beneficial investments from those that have little or nothing to
offer Canada, or that are actually frustrating Canadian industrial
objectives.

This process obviously involves the exercise of discretion
within statutory limits and puts the multinational firm in the position
of having to discuss its proposed investments with the Canadian
government. The government would seek to satisfy itself on the
merits of the proposed investment and, in some circumstances,
to secure undertakings from the parent firm that ensure these
benefits. The result might well be changes in the performance or
structure of the firm from what might otherwise have prevailed—
aiming at the achievement of more efficient operations. It is
hoped that any artificial constraints on the opportunities of a
Canadian subsidiary to undertake various activities such as
export activities can be minimized and that any inefficient industrial
structures, not necessarily directly related to the level of activity
within the subsidiary, can be modified. The authorities might well

identify influences external to the firm that account for the performance
and look to other government policies to achieve improved results.

ASSUMPTIONS OF THE REVIEW PROCESS

The beliefs that underly the review process are that there is
frequently a range of possible alternatives open to many international
investors with respect to their Canadian activities, each point on
which range offers a different mix of benefits and costs; and that
some such investments (most likely some takeovers) offer no
significant advantages to Canada. Everything else being equal,
the policy involves a preference for Canadian enterprises.

The government's view of the screening process is based upon
the belief that the international markets through which foreign
direct investment flows into Canada are subject to considerable
interference. Tariffs and other barriers affect trade; exchange
rates are administered to some degree; capital movements are
influenced or directly controlled; taxes and subsidies affect
investment decisions and are intended to do so; international
investors quite logically attempt to minimize the risks they perceive
in foreign direct investments compared to domestic; and some
industries are quite uncompetitive so that resource allocation can
be inefficient. The nature of the foreign direct investment that
results is not that of an efficient market allocation. This is so
even though investors are acting perfectly rationally from their
own perspectives.

Since many of these factors are beyond the control of the
Canadian government, a review process is conceived of by the
government as an instrument for dealing with these forces so as
to achieve that activity in Canada that is economically rational
and internationally competitive. Gains of international rationaliza-
tion and what is deemed an appropriate mix of activities are the
government's objectives for the review process.

Given the very high levels of investment in Canada subject
to the forces noted above, no Canadian government could fail to
give attention to them.

Only time will tell whether the large foreign-controlled sector
of the Canadian economy can be made more compatible with
Canadian industrial objectives by this procedure. Only time will
tell also whether the review agency will be diverted, in part, from
these purposes to ones that are less likely to serve industrial
efficiency. While Canadian participation in the economy is
stimulated by other policies affecting the industrial environment,
the review process might also have some effect in assisting the
achievement of a greater Canadian presence in its business
enterprises.

A third set of policies attempts to remedy certain problems of the Canadian economic environment and/or to supply incentives to Canadian entrepreneurial activity. An increase in the degree of Canadian ownership over time is one of several objectives that these policies are expected to achieve. Under the new tax law the small-business incentive is available only to Canadian-controlled private corporations; for example, federal estate taxes have been eliminated, potentially reducing the sale of private Canadian corporations to nonresidents; and Canadian corporations can now deduct as an expense the interest paid on funds borrowed to finance the purchase of shares in other corporations. One of the more significant examples of this policy approach is the Canada Development Corporation, approved by Parliament in 1971, designed partly to supply more financial and industrial entrepreneurship in Canada and to give a greater Canadian presence in industry. As various policies affecting business operations come up for review, one can probably expect further changes that have as their purpose the stimulating of entrepreneurship in Canada. While these may not discriminate between Canadians and foreigners, Canadians might well make greater use of them than their foreign counterparts.

In recent years some provincial governments have also enacted legislation affecting the degree of foreign ownership and control of Canadian firms. The "key sector" approach has been followed in several provinces, notably with regard to some provincially incorporated financial institutions and some aspects of the publication industry. Two provinces also have legislation giving the government discretionary powers in requiring further processing of natural resources. Several provinces are considering restrictions on the foreign ownership of land. The Province of Ontario now requires that a majority of the directors of Ontario companies be Canadian residents.

REASONS FOR GOVERNMENT POLICIES

In order to appreciate the issues posed for governments and corporations, it is important to consider the reasons for these policies.[2] What follows is necessarily conjectural and controversial in parts, given our still imperfect knowledge of multinational corporations and given the different values with which people approach the phenomenon. There is no denying, however, that significant parts of public opinion and of opinion makers conceive of the issues in this way and that Canadian governments have reacted accordingly and even on occasion given some leadership on the issue.

The perception many Canadians had of this question even a decade ago was that of capital shortage in Canada, which led to a dependence on borrowing abroad that could be modified by policies dealing with the financial industry as such or by policies affecting the use of Canadian savings. The present perception is based on the major issues of industrial organization, specifically the large oligopolistic corporation, but complicated by the political and economic questions raised by its locus in two or more national jurisdictions.

Something as complex as this does not lend itself to simple analytical conclusions, but Canadian policies might be understood in part in terms of a look at the benefits expected from them for national political and economic welfare. These benefits are conceived partly in terms of psychic income. This can be thought of broadly in terms of a sense of well-being resulting from an increase in national independence and pride; from the perception that control over decisions that affect the economic environment rests closer to home (either with Canadians in the private sector or elected representatives); or more specifically in terms of policies that increase cultural identity and/or distinctiveness with respect to the United States in particular. One might note that this need for cultural identity and/or distinctiveness is felt more keenly among English-speaking Canadians than among French-speaking Canadians, is heard more often from the rich industrial base of southern Ontario than elsewhere, and is particularly prevalent among those working in media that are continuously inundated by the communications spillover from the United States. Nevertheless, the spirit of national identification and pride has captured the imaginations of a growing number of Canadians.

A second expected benefit that is related to the first but goes well beyond it is the greater control or effectiveness of national policy that more domestic ownership of industry or national regulation of multinationals is expected to bring. In principle, at least, a national government may incur less difficulty in implementing some types of policy where its jurisdiction reaches all or most of the units it is trying to affect—and that is true also for domestically owned multinationals, as the United States is discovering. Moreover, the existence of regulating instruments presents at least the opportunity to implement some policies in a more coordinated and more effective manner. The multinational firm undoubtedly considers the jurisdiction of the government through such instruments when responding to stated policy objectives of host governments.

A third potential benefit arises from gains in real income, perhaps because real income both internationally and nationally is expected to increase (for example, where the competitive or productivity effects of multinationals with respect to each other and to domestic firms are enhanced); perhaps because more of the international gains possible through the multinational are expected to accrue to Canada, as with the review agency; or perhaps because the policy initiatives selected by government in response to the multinational challenge enhance Canadian entrepreneurial capacities, as with the Canada Development Corporation.

There are certain costs or at least constraints to set against the policies aimed at realizing these benefits, however, some of which are as conjectural as the expected benefits. Some of the policies aimed at inducing ownership or performance results may involve tax concessions or subsidies that Canadians may not wish to undergo beyond certain limits or provable outcomes. There are different views about how much Canada has gained from heavy and prolonged reliance on foreign direct investment and about what might have been achieved by alternative forms of access to foreign techniques or greater reliance on domestic capacities. Still, there is a wide recognition that significant gains did accrue to Canada through new technology, competitive stimulus, product variety, economies of scale and specialization, and tax revenues flowing from higher levels of activity or efficiency. There is a wide desire also not to lose them, whether by our policies or those of foreign governments or by restrictions on firms that are inhibiting in nature. For example, some have strong reservations about the effectiveness of regulatory intervention in achieving significant gains. These reservations are enhanced by their view that the costs of unregulated foreign direct investment may not be such as to justify the intervention, or that the intervention itself may create problems.

AREAS OF UNCERTAINTY

There are evidently many hazy areas here, which is one reason why policy has developed slowly in Canada as well as elsewhere and a reason for the use of the several policies at the same time. Often it is not known what the reaction effects will be, both private and public. Will the intended results of the policies be realized, or will they be frustrated by the acts of the firms affected? Will other governments take steps that offset the anticipated benefits? Will provincial governments oppose the policies strenuously and make use of the instruments available to them to negate the purpose and effect of the federal policy? There is also disagreement on both the meaning and the value attached to national independence. To what extent and in what respects is it to be treated as a "tradeoff" with economic welfare, for example, where that proves necessary? Despite the concern of many Canadians with the issue and the occasional strong reactions on particular questions, our guess is that most Canadians are unwilling to pursue domestic ownership objectives if they themselves have to forego important economic benefits, and that (except for some "key sectors") they are unwilling to accept domestic ownership as such as a sufficient proxy for the objectives of improved performance by the firm.* Moreover, as will be noted shortly, federal policies with respect to foreign firms may have very uneven regional and group effects within Canada, or may clash with differing regional policies or objectives, considerations that would hamper any elected government and particularly that of a federal state.

Put another way, governments in Canada have been concerned to preserve or to assert their power either by locating decision-making power in the private Canadian-owned sector, which they believe may be more responsive to government policies (by means of domestic ownership provisions), or by assuring more certainly that organizations will respond to public policies (by means of public ownership or regulation). We need hardly add that such objectives are mixed with the response to pressures from private domestic interests reflecting a variety of motives. In the case of multinational firms the object has been partly to attempt to secure better performance often arising in a variety of specific contexts as noted earlier. More broadly, however, the object can be described as (1) effective implementation of a set of national industrial policies generally, in the context of an industrial structure that already includes a high degree of foreign ownership, and (2) the expectation that domestic ownership or effective regulation of foreign-controlled firms will achieve these objectives without other and (to some governments) less agreeable options, such as public ownership. We should add, however, that Canadian governments have been prepared to engage in both regulation and public ownership to achieve national or provincial objectives or to deal with crises, even when their general political stance favored private ownership and minimum regulation.

It is also true that the concerns of private Canadian groups are equally varied on these issues and, indeed, that this is one reason why governments have moved cautiously and, at times, more slowly than many would have preferred. The reconciliation of the different views of provincial governments, given the regional economic disparities in Canada, is necessarily of importance in a federal state. In addition, various policy options could have very uneven effects by regions and by income groups. There is a distinct probability, for example, that highly restrictive policies with regard to foreign direct investment would have a proportionately

---

*Among other things, it is notable that public opinion polls tend to show a high and increasing degree of concern with the questions raised by heavy foreign control of Canadian industry but to rank the issue of foreign control quite low when it is placed among a number of issues of national concern.

greater effect, on the average, on lower-income regions and lower-income groups, barring major offsetting policies by taxes and transfers. Private motives obviously vary all the way from concern for national identity and even survival to outright protection for special interests with or without recourse to arguments regarding national interest. All we wish to emphasize for the moment is the evident result, in such circumstances, of emphasis on rather pragmatic policies that reconcile such interests and minimize the conflict with other policy objectives while moving in the directions noted. This heterogeneity of the environment makes for less clarity in the policies and less vigor in the enforcement. There is less agreement on the welfare effects and less agreement on the policy itself. In addition, the dominance of standard of living in the motivations that underlie policy in this area means that nationalism per se is not actively pursued, except in certain "key sectors."

ISSUES POSED FOR BUSINESS AND GOVERNMENT

The interests of multinational firms and of national governments frequently converge—it is not accidental that very few industrial countries block such firms from their national environment. It is equally clear that significant divergences of interest occur. It could hardly be otherwise given the different objectives of firms as against governments and the different "constituencies" over which a multinational firm and a national government attempt to realize their objectives. Both, of course, must settle for something less than they might consider first-best, given constraints both internal and external to them. We hasten to add that the interests of the multinational firm are not monolithic or unchanging: The definition of these by the officers of a subsidiary firm may frequently coincide with those of the host government in conflict with those of the parent management. The subsidiary management may be urging, for example, the expansion of domestic activity through research and international marketing when the parent is less enthusiastic about such expansion in the subsidiary. The outcomes in terms of the distribution of authority and activity can vary widely by firms.

What becomes relevant then are a series of questions the answers to which will ultimately determine the future relations of multinational firms and governments. What will governments do individually and together if they are to regulate multinational firms (their own as well as those headquartered elsewhere) so that their concerns about the negative effects are met? What should governments agree to avoid doing in order to realize or to avoid dissipating the benefits from such firms? What can the firms themselves do in either case? And, where there is no apparent reconciliation or where governments decide to block entry by multinational firms, how can one devise efficient alternatives to foreign direct investment in terms of international transfers of technology and/or the development of domestic firms to efficiently undertake the activities in question?

Policies on the multinational firm are likely to involve a wide variety of techniques. We would expect further attempts at national regulation or restriction of entry and encouragement to alternative forms of international technical transfer or domestic enterprise. We would also expect attempts to reach intergovernmental agreements on those issues that are most likely to prove negotiable, such as tax and subsidy policies. In the next section we will speculate on some consequences of this increasing control of multinationals or of policy harmonization toward them.

Meanwhile, we should emphasize what is at stake. What is involved in large part is a conflict over the international distribution of industrial activity and its proceeds as represented by the technological transfer and technological control embodied in the multinational firm. Governments have not hesitated to influence to their national advantage the terms of trade with regard to goods, services, and portfolio capital, partly because market outcomes are distorted by the power of multinational enterprises in what are frequently oligopolistic industries, by the distortions of the actions of other governments, and by the distortions in international location decisions that come from the fact that a foreign economy is regarded as more risky or is culturally or politically less familiar to the decision makers in the head office of a multinational enterprise. Governments are hardly likely to leave unattended the international distribution of gains through multinational firms, particularly since the large corporation in any case attracts government attention for a variety of other reasons. As governments see the issues, what is at stake is the degree to which they are able to increase everything from the real national income to the national control of economic activity, as well as mixtures of the two. Disaggregating from the national level, it is important to note again that these potential gains may involve potential losses that in both cases fall unevenly on different groups and regions within a country, a fact that considerably complicates judgments on the welfare effects of such policies as well as the policy role of the central government. This is especially the case in a federal state that has regional governments to articulate these views and influence the outcome through policy instruments constitutionally available to them.

CHALLENGES TO MULTINATIONALS

Two points follow from the preceding discussion. One is the challenge to the multinational corporation as a private capitalist institution, to persuade each of two or more governments that their nations gain from its activities. Second, what is much more awkward, they must persuade governments, each of which is trying to increase its share of the net benefits, that it has made the best deal possible with the corporation as regards the corporation's operations and its impact on the economy and community. The corporation has certain advantages here in that governments often lack information on the feasible range of negotiation on terms, or in varying degrees feel bound by contract and/or the reactions of the firms or other governments. Current experience with petroleum is just one of many instances of how quickly such "deals" can evaporate when bargaining power shifts. Of course, the obverse of all this is the challenge to governments to obtain their objectives without losing the investment or damaging other policy objectives, short of situations where they have decided to do without such firms.

The challenge, we suggest, is not only to multinational business. Where foreign ownership of industry is widespread, as in Canada, attempts to regulate the foreign-owned firms are likely to affect the domestically owned firms as well. It is difficult to imagine any other outcome eventually when, in many industries, each set of firms occupies an important role in the industry. If through its policies the government attempts to stimulate exports of foreign-owned firms by a variety of measures, for example, it is unlikely to leave the domestically owned firms out of such an attempt. The point applies a fortiori if an integrated approach to policies affecting an industry is adopted. There is a challenge, in brief, to the nature of government-business relations generally and not just the relations of government to foreign-owned firms or to multinational enterprises.

While the attempt by multinational firms to persuade governments that each is benefiting as much as is feasible in some national sense is complicated enough, it pales by comparison with the role of such firms when the reconciling task of group and regional differences in costs and benefits within a country is added. The political process, after all, has much more to do with such group and regional questions than the somewhat less identifiable "national interest." Business is frequently advised to anticipate and serve the political and economic objectives of a country if it is to live in that country. One would have thought that too much direct involvement of corporations in such reconciliations of the political process would be fraught with dangers, especially for those whose "foreignness" might be expected to make them both hesitant to engage in such actions or vulnerable if they do. In Canada, however, inertia, ideology, and the constitutional division of powers, along with a growing willingness to accept the technocratic role of corporations in presenting their case to

governments and the public, all effectively reduce the political
risks to corporations, regardless of ownership, which take an
active role in public policy issues of this kind. The corporation
on its part recognizes the need to respond to these group, regional,
and government pressures if only to avoid less agreeable measures.

Enough has been said to suggest certain consequences for the
government-to-business relation, for federal-provincial relations
within Canada, and for the relationship of the Canadian to other
governments. Let us take these in turn.

BUSINESS-GOVERNMENT RELATIONS

The relation of government to business, especially but not
only to multinational firms, is already being considerably changed,
with internal changes in the firms themselves as one consequence.
Clearly the first effect is for more government intervention with
regard to large firms in general and multinational firms in particular.
Much will depend on what methods governments decide to use, such
as public ownership, evenly applied fiscal or regulatory policies,
or discretionary policies, and how effectively governments cooperate
internationally and/or domestically in applying these policies.
Our expectation is that there is a significant period ahead when
the use of discretionary powers will be prevalent, when rules of
the game are unclear, and when intergovernmental harmonization
of policies or agreement will be minimal. Our expectation is
that this phase, once played out (hopefully with minimal damage
to countries and to firms) will lead to a more stable period with
clearer rules in some key areas. This might be expected to occur
in the domestic policy of a country to facilitate administration of
basically discretionary policies. Experience with the discretionary
authority should tend to advance understanding of what is most
important and what is attainable in dealing with foreign investors.
In addition, if there are strong unilateral policies in many countries,
there would be costs seen to all participants in confrontation and
retaliation, and pressures would emerge for greater clarity in
domestic policies and for international accord. With regard to
international agreement on the rules for government dealings with
multinationals—or for the activities of multinationals within each
jurisdiction—the prospect would seem to be less promising. There
are far more technical and ideological problems in resolving different
government approaches to the large corporations than there are, for
example, in reaching agreement on trade policy—and perhaps a
greater diversity of interests among governments depending upon
their stake in the activities of multinational enterprises.

The appeal of discretionary policies is not hard to see and
follows directly from experience of governments in dealing with

domestic industrial institutions and policy where they have had
to turn increasingly to discretionary techniques. With the variation
in industry and firm experience, and the suspicion of market
approaches in those markets that are distorted, general policies
applicable to all firms are not likely to yield satisfactory outcomes
at minimal cost. Unlike across-the-board approaches, however,
such discretionary approaches put a maximum continuing demand
on the government's greatest skills if the policies are to work.

The Canadian tradition of discretionary regulation reveals a
penchant for defining the scope of discretion in law in order both
to provide for greater predictability and to limit the power of the
delegated authority. Consequently, even the discretionary approach
involves a good deal of attention to legal technicalities and potentially costly proceedings that reduce the ostensible focus on the
purposes of the regulation and the anticipated flexibility of its
implementation.

One consequence of such discretionary policies in Canada
will be that businessmen will become much more astute as students
of the government process. In some quarters they are already
credited with a great deal of success in this regard, of course.
The increased use of discretionary powers is leading to a far
more technocratic approach by business, partly because government
itself has a better-equipped technostructure and partly because of
the increase in regulating agencies.

Many multinational firms might have to make internal changes
to accommodate these developments. Authority within the firm
might have to be more decentralized—despite the centralizing
trends that technology supports through transportation and communication developments—if national objectives are pursued with vigor.
The criteria of international investment allocation will have to
account more fully for government attitudes, with large international
firms having to develop miniature state departments to deal with
their need to reconcile international political pressures. Better
facilities are likely to be developed for understanding the domestic
political issues and process in host countries and for public relations
efforts to satisfy various interests of the "fairness" of the effects
of the firm's activities.

It perhaps bears mentioning that the failure of governments
and businesses to work out a viable procedure could lead in some
cases to direct dealings between governments that either largely
circumvent the corporate institutions or set the terms of their
activities by government fiat. The current interest in government-
to-government dealings on petroleum might well alter the role of
the major oil companies as intermediaries between producing and
consuming interests. These developments may be short-lived—
or may be localized to the petroleum industry because of its critical
and quasi-public utility role where security of supply considerations

dominate. Nevertheless, there is some evidence of a preparedness by governments of widely differing political persuasions to consider adopting new methods in international commercial dealings if their economic or political objectives cannot be easily met through multinational firms.

If, on the other hand, governments concentrate on diminishing foreign ownership by encouraging domestic participation in foreign-controlled firms, rather than on regulation, we expect that this may not diminish or prevent control. There are many techniques to assert control without ownership rights in the firm, techniques such as contracts on sales or highly restrictive licenses. One outcome will be that governments will then be driven to monitor these other arrangements. One danger in focusing on kinds of arrangements rather than the aims of the policy is that both governments and firms lose sight of their respective performance objectives or find them more costly to achieve with losses to the rest of the community.

If the approach is by regulation rather than ownership we can expect increasingly to see a dichotomy of shareholder and management control on the one hand and public control and sharing of ownership on the other. Canadians are accustomed to a significant degree of public ownership in some industries and might not find its extension to some others unpalatable. Nevertheless, it seems unfortunate that corporations so often seem unwilling to contemplate anything but 100 percent share ownership and governments and corporations alike have given so little thought to viable alternatives in at least some sectors, alternatives that minimize the political and economic risks for both governments and firms. Joint ventures and dynamic licensing agreements are two such forms that deserve more consideration, and we expect that firms will and should experiment more with these and other forms in response to the circumstances noted.

One other matter that multinational firms might consider is the stance that some of them or their proponents take about the political and economic effects of their spreading activities. On the economic side it is often implied or stated that an open-door policy to foreign business investment is a sufficient guarantee of economic development. Virtually all of the literature on economic development of both high-income and low-income countries suggests that it is a great exaggeration at best. Important social characteristics outside the firm and varying degrees of government support and intervention are critical to the process. Much the same can be said about those views that see the spread of the multinational enterprise as nothing less than the herald of a new world political order. We believe that claims of this kind, inconsistent with both theory and the evidence about us, raise expectations that are bound to be disappointed and that form the basis of part of the criticism of multinational enterprise activity. Any institution that

attempts to carry the burden of both international economic development and political order on its shoulders will have to tread softly
in this nationalist age, or better still accept only a realistic part
of that burden.

INTERNAL GOVERNMENT RELATIONS
IN A FEDERAL STATE

A federal structure involves the presence of regional governments—
with claims to elected political legitimacy equal to that of the central
government—to actively argue the regional and to some extent other
group differences that exist in any state. The jurisdiction of such
regional governments includes varying degrees of capacity to use
their own policies to challenge the decisions of the central government in balancing competing domestic interests.

Thus, in decentralized federal systems such as Canada's there
are important consequences and some important constraints to take
into account in considering policies regarding multinational enterprises. The federal government has jurisdiction over international
affairs, interprovincial trade and commerce, competition policy,
and a number of industries, but the provinces have the proprietary
right in natural resources within their boundaries and significant
regulatory powers with respect to many other industries. Both
levels of government have substantial jurisdiction via tax and subsidy
to stimulate industrial development. This complicates the negotiation
and settlement of some actual or potential policies on multinational
firms, for the federal government may hesitate to act without provincial agreement given both the internal political costs or given the
common interest that both levels of government have in the outcome.
More bluntly, there is less likelihood of a strong policy with regard
to foreign-owned firms in Canada given this constitutional position,
given the differing perceptions of the issues, and given the ability
of firms to move within the Canadian common market. This is true
despite the intentions of the federal government to discuss cases
under the review process with the interested provinces without
allowing them a veto. How you regard this depends on your view
of the issues posed by foreign ownership. Within the context of
a review mechanism we are less likely to fully exploit our bargaining
power and, conversely, less likely also to make demands that will
cause firms to operate inefficiently.

INTERNATIONAL GOVERNMENT RELATIONS

The changing relations between national governments and the
implications for multinational business are even more difficult to

consider in a brief context. Ideally, as we conceive it, three objectives should be aimed at on this level: first, to make it possible for multinational firms to contribute to national and international economic well-being; second, to realize and share in an acceptable way among nations any net social benefits associated with or derived through such firms—such as tax benefits or the upgrading of the community's labor skills; and third, to achieve a reasonable degree of domestic control over the forces that determine domestic effects. What we have instead of internationally accepted rules for this purpose is an attempt by governments to capture (or repatriate) more of the gains nationally, in the United States by such techniques as the Domestic International Solar Corporation (DISC), investment tax credits, "Buy American" policies, and the Burke-Hartke proposals, and in Canada by techniques that are equally well known.

Theory suggests that where two parties have a mutuality of interests in some respects and conflicting interests in others, both will gain by cooperation rather than confrontation or a battle. Indeed, the kinds of techniques used by governments to both attract and constrain multinational firms sometimes look like the largest nontariff barrier of all, with consequences for an efficient and productive distribution of resources and improved real incomes nationally and internationally, which are most unfortunate. Yet the prospects for harmonizing some policies that affect multinational firms or of agreements on others are not encouraging, much as we would like to believe otherwise. Perhaps we shall have to await the passing of the host of protectionist measures unleashed in recent years and the preparedness and capacity to develop mechanisms to deal with the underlying problems before more can be done here.

Developing policies in this area are even more difficult than with regard to international policies constraining certain trade practices and adjudicating others. Since important parts of the tax, subsidy, and regulatory process with regard to the firm and hence with regard to the domestic industrial structure and performance may be involved in such agreements, governments will be even more loathe to surrender sovereignty in such cases than in the comparatively simple case of exchange of goods between firms and countries. In addition, there are wide differences in the views of how much freedom of decision making firms should have in any case. In the extreme case of a worldwide code, if the criteria could be defined, some of the ingredients and some of the institutions of a very loosely defined federal state would be necessary in principle to deal with the problems raised by differing national laws and by multinational firm policies—including a court to adjudicate differences. That, we suggest, is some way off. Perhaps a useful interim step would be a set of voluntary guidelines on performance of the firm and treatment by governments, but experience within countries suggests these would have to be very general in order to accommodate the differences in ideas and in interests involved.

In the meantime, despite the difficulties, we would urge that intergovernmental attempts be instituted to achieve harmonization of policies or other collective agreements in certain specific areas that are less all-encompassing in substance. One such area could be some minimum degree of harmonization of tax and subsidy policies with reference especially to those used to attract foreign investment. Competition among nations on this account is a nontariff barrier in some respects and would thus tie in with the current international trade negotiations. Such competition reduces the net return to the public sector for each dollar of public subsidy and also leads to retaliatory measures between states. The firms would lose some subsidies if harmonization occurs on some items, but would gain through more stability of policies affecting them. Establishment rights and antitrust laws are other possible areas to be explored.

We believe international agreements would be desirable for two reasons. One, often cited by the firms, is to give them certain minimum guarantees on the treatment they can expect within different jurisdictions, so that their decisions can be made with less uncertainty. The other reason is the interest of national governments representing the interests of the nation. That interest requires assurance that other governments will not be asked by multinationals, and will not in fact intervene or retaliate in their efforts, to operate their foreign investment policies. We do not have sufficient definition of the parameters in both cases to generate such an overall agreement at the present time. Nevertheless, we suggest a start be made in some negotiable areas. The alternative is national approaches to multinational firms with negotiation on specific issues as particularly difficult situations arise; or perhaps bilateral negotiation, although this is probably not acceptable in the Canada-U. S. context given the preponderance of investment from the United States. It may well be that public opinion and government are not prepared to go further than this at present given the desire for national policies now and the difficulties of international or regional agreement. Difficult technical issues, philosophical differences as to the role of government and of the corporation, reluctance to surrender jurisdiction, and a desire to assert control of national policy all point to national approaches for the time being. Unilateral national actions that invite retaliation, however, are likely to lead increasingly to situations unfavorable to some national and firm interests where there are overlapping interests of the scope involved in multinational operations. Pursuit of both national policies and attempts at international agreement in selective areas would appear the most likely outcome for some time.

Agreements on specific issues might well have only marginal effects on the net distribution of benefits between countries, given the complexity of government policy issues involved. Nevertheless, such efforts are likely to be pursued as governments search for a balance between domestic control of their economies in furtherance of their economic and social goals and also a more efficient international allocation of resources.

NOTES

1. Section 2 of "An Act to provide for the review and assessment of acquisitions of control of Canadian business enterprises by certain persons and of the establishment of new businesses in Canada by certain persons," Bill C-132, before the First Session of the Twenty-Ninth Parliament, 1973.

2. The broader welfare effects of foreign direct investment and related policy issues are discussed in detail in Government of Canada, Foreign Direct Investment in Canada (Ottawa, 1972), and A. E. Safarian, "Perspectives on Foreign Direct Investment From the Viewpoint of a Capital Receiving Country," Journal of Finance, May 1973.

III

NATIONAL TRADE
POLICIES AND
MULTINATIONAL
BUSINESS
ACTIVITIES

8

TRADE OF MULTINATIONAL
FIRMS AND NATIONS'
COMPARATIVE
ADVANTAGE

Robert A. Cornell

Much of the current debate about the impact of multinational firms on international trade—especially debate on the questions of interest to government policy makers—centers on "mercantilist" issues. Both home and host countries focus their attention on the trade balance, with critics of the MNCs alleging that foreign direct investors are prone to produce trade deficits and friends of the companies (plus the companies themselves) arguing the reverse. As a result, the bulk of the serious, policy-oriented research in this field has stressed the balance of trade, balance of payments questions.[1]

MNCs AND INTERNATIONAL ECONOMIC POLICY

When a trade surplus is the prize, international economic policy toward the MNCs is a kind of zero-sum game. If multinational business generates a trade surplus for the home country, then it follows that a deficit is in store for the host countries (ignoring third-country trade effects). In most of the key countries studied by the U. S. Tariff Commission (1973),* this is exactly the case with respect to the U. S.-based MNCs' bilateral trade flows: a surplus for the United States, a deficit for the host country. Games of this type are easily understood, and they make possible easy

Robert A. Cornell is Deputy Director, Office of Economic Research, U. S. Tariff Commission. The views expressed in this chapter are not necessarily those of the Commission.

*See References section at the end of this chapter for full titles and publishers of references cited in the text.

identification of the winners and losers. In one location or another
the MNCs can be branded as culprits and subjected to appropriate
policy constraints to correct "disequilibrium" that they have caused.
To forestall this kind of exercise of sovereign power against them,
many firms themselves adopt policies—which may be uneconomic—
to adjust "their" balances of trade in various countries in which
they operate, through sourcing or transfer-pricing decisions, so
as to minimize big, adverse flows that might not sit well with the
local finance ministries.

It is, of course, axiomatic that the realities of international
economic relations demand governments' attention to balance of
trade and balance of payments questions. However, it is equally
axiomatic that these are not the only questions. Fundamentally,
most modern nations adhere, however imperfectly, to notions of
comparative advantage; they perceive their long-run interest in
exporting those things they produce with some competitive edge
and importing the ones in which their local productive expertise
is (in relative terms) less adequate. On these grounds, the questions
about the MNCs' role in international trade change. Now, it is
important to ask whether the patterns of MNC-generated trade do
or do not conform to the patterns that policy makers identify as
consistent with the international "competitiveness" of their nations'
industries.

Questions of this sort crop up in odd ways. For example,
concerns in the United States about technology transfers abroad
really are questions about whether the United States is somehow
"exporting" a recognized source of its comparative advantage
rather than the exportable goods that such an advantage should
generate. A more specific question in the same vein is whether
the MNCs somehow prefer more to export their technology than the
products that could be made with it—competitively—in plants
at home. More broadly, is there something perverse about the
internationally footloose behavior of capital, technology, and
management skills in the hands of the MNCs that causes the
patterns of a nation's trade to move away from where comparative
advantage is perceived to lie?

Policy strategies designed to move toward trade along the lines
suggested by comparative advantage no longer need be the strategies
of zero-sum games. The goal for all countries is to trade internationally at the least cost in terms of resources. If all countries
move toward this goal—and if the MNCs conform to the trade
patterns that it implies—then, because trade is more efficient,
everyone ought to be better off. An important subsidiary goal of
public policy becomes that of easing the burden on formerly
protected industries that may be seriously and abruptly damaged by
passage to a world of efficiency and that should not necessarily be
asked to perish in bankruptcy and unemployment on the altar of the

general national welfare. Beyond this, the trade balance can
be regarded with benign neglect, as long as it doesn't egregiously
threaten the current exchange rate.

The main issue for this chapter is whether or not the MNCs
based in the United States conduct their trade along lines that
seem consistent with what we know about the patterns of U. S.
comparative advantage. To make the same study for other countries
would represent a major effort well beyond the scope of the chapter.
However, the techniques involved are appropriate for any country
on which the requisite data are available so that, in principle at
least, this is a study applicable to all countries.

The analysis does not mention the size of the trade balance
even once. This does not mean that the trade balance is unimpor-
tant; it means only that a different question is under review. In
discussing the question, however, it is well to bear an overall
context in mind. The context is as follows: With respect to the
MNCs' direct effects on U. S. trade in manufactures in 1970, they
accounted for 62 percent of total U. S. exports and only 34 percent
of total imports. Between 1966 and 1970 they generated a total of
$3.4 billion in net "new" exports (new exports less new imports)
of manufactured goods, while non-MNC firms increased their
net "new" imports by even more—$3.6 billion.[2] Thus the MNCs'
contribution to the U. S. trade balance appears to have been
decidedly positive.

DETERMINANTS OF RELATIVE COST
AND COMPARATIVE ADVANTAGE

Economic theory never has abandoned the eminently sensible
idea that trade patterns ultimately are determined by relative costs
of production in different countries. It has, however—especially
since about 1960—gone through a period of great doubt about exactly
what are the most crucial determinants of relative costs in international trade. Older theories associated with the Marshallian-
Walrasian tradition stressed differences in national factor endowments
as the basic determinants of trade patterns. The basic notion here
is that countries relatively rich in certain productive factors will
have lower costs in making goods that use those factors most heavily
and (assuming that lower-cost producers have the market advantage)
will therefore be exporters of those kinds of goods. "Factors" may
be resources or inputs of any sort to productive processes, but
they are often simplified to the dual elements "capital" and "labor."
More recent formulations, recognizing that this duality of factors
seemed to have less empirical explanatory power than was hoped
for, have stressed the concept of "human capital," defined as the
skill-level of the labor force, in which training and education have

been invested. The concept of human capital is a relatively new one but, in its application to trade theory, it sits squarely within the neoclassical tradition.

Many other new theories have sprung up in the past 10 or 15 years, but they really are not challenges to the traditional approach in the sense of attempts to replace it. They stand beside it as nonexclusive new explanations. Notable among them are the theories of S. B. Linder (1961), stressing product differentiation, and of Raymond Vernon (1966), focusing on product life cycles. Linder argues that, more relevant than resource endowments, are differences (real or advertized) in basically very similar products that arise in response to different national demand patterns and industrial development paths. These minute differences among products then form the basis for international trade as domestic markets become relatively saturated. The Vernon hypothesis notes that the producer of a new product will have a competitive edge— and will export—until his product ages enough to be imitatable abroad, at which point "new" new products will enter trade. Nations can maintain their comparative advantage to the extent that they can stay ahead in the race to develop new products.

The analysis of this chapter takes an eclectic approach with respect to all theoretical points of view—an approach that was found to have great usefulness in an earlier Tariff Commission study (1972), and that is now being developed further in the Commission's current work on analyzing the "competitiveness" of U. S. industries in international trade. The approach is simply to collect a lot of different numbers describing industry characteristics, with no predilection to accept any particular theoretical explanation for the determinants of relative costs, and then to see which of the characteristics analyzed pop up as the most useful. In particular, 13 different series of industry characteristics are used as possible keys to understanding U. S. trade performance with respect to manufactured goods. The different series—and the results theory says they "ought" to show—are described in the following paragraphs.

Capital-Labor Ratio. Different industries use different amounts of capital per worker. According to traditional theory, which notes that the United States is among the world's capital-rich nations, industries that have the higher capital/labor ratios should be the stronger export industries, while those with lower ratios should be less able to withstand import competition.

Labor Intensity Ratio. Taking the ratio of payroll to value added in an industry provides a measure of the amount of labor input embodied in a productive process. This measure abstracts from capital endowments, and thus it is different from the capital-labor ratio that in its upside-down version would take account of an industry's richness in labor relative to its capital stock. In any case, high wages in the United States are thought to attest to relative labor scarcity. Hence, industries with high labor intensity ratios (that is, industries that use the scarce factor, labor, relatively intensively in production) should be among the poorer export performers and the less viable competitors against imports.

Human Skills. Inasmuch as human capital appears to be an especially important factor in explanations of the patterns of U. S. foreign trade, this study uses two related, but not identical, proxy variables to measure the stock of such capital. The first (labeled "Human skills (A)" in later sections) amounts, for each industry, to the annual wage of nonproduction workers in that industry, capitalized at an arbitrarily chosen 8 percent. It is an attempt to measure the value of human capital engaged in those industrial tasks in which such capital is supposed to count most heavily—scientific and technical services (including R&D) and marketing.[3]

The second measure—"Human skills (B)"—is simply the percentage of nonproduction labor in total employment in each industry. It is to be hoped that this measure captures the effects on competitiveness of varying the "mix" between production and technical manpower in different industries.

In both human skills series the relationships to be anticipated are straightforward. Industries with the greater inputs of skilled labor—human capital—should show up as the better export performers, and vice versa for those industries using lesser amounts of human capital. The underlying assumed reason for such results would be the empirical fact that human capital is the preeminently abundant factor in the United States, the world's richest country in skilled labor.

Productivity. This series really represents an explicit admission that we may not truly know the basic sources of competitiveness. Perhaps physical and human capital, plus certain poorly understood kinds of ordinary production labor inputs, all combine in some industries to spell "performance" in a complicated manner that the preceding series do not successfully unravel. The result should be high rates of productivity, or value added in production per production worker man-hour, in those industries. Industries that have higher productivity rates will be competitive in export markets; those with lower rates not only will do poorly abroad but will have trouble meeting import competition at home.

Scale Economies. One widely noted characteristic of the U. S. economy is that the vast size of its domestic market allows the full realization of economies of scale for industries in which such economies are important. If so, then it follows that the economy is peculiarly well-adapted to nurturing industries with low relative costs associated with the savings in unit costs that come from production on a large scale—and that these industries will possess a competitive advantage in international trade. Industries in which scale economies are not important, on the other hand, will not fare so well in the international marketplace.

Concentration Ratios. Beyond economies of scale, firm size
and the degree of market dominance together constitute a factor
that could govern the ability to compete successfully in export
markets or against imports at home. This series measures the
percentage of total output in each industry accounted for by its
eight largest firms. High concentration ratios should be associated
with strong competitiveness, and low ratios with poorer competitive
performance.

Product Differentiation. A measure of product differentiation
is aimed at a direct test of the Linder hypothesis. Industries that
show higher levels of product differentiation should make better
showings in export markets and should at the same time be most
competitive against imports.

First Trade Dates. Vernon's product life cycle hypothesis
stresses the competitive ability of industries producing a flow of
new products, as against the lesser effectiveness in international
markets of industries marketing older, easily imitatable products
in which foreigners have equal advantages with domestic producers.
This series is an indirect approach to evaluating the hypothesis.
It is derived from an examination of U. S. export data to discover
when an industry's products first became important enough in trade
to warrant separate entries in the statistical schedules. The first
trade dates of "old product" industries will be early ones; those
of "new product" industries will be more recent. The latter should
be associated with superior competitive performance in international
trade.

Profitability, Growth Rates of Shipments, Value Added, and
Employment. Once again, these four series represent a kind of
tacit admission that our knowledge of the determinants of trade
may not be as complete as one would like. All four are visible
evidences of the dynamism—or lack of it—that an industry may
possess; all four beg the question of what the roots of that dynamism
may be. However, all four also point toward the plausible hypothesis
that the more profitable, faster-gorwing industries will be revealing
successful competitive performance in the domestic market and
therefore should be making the best showing both in export markets
and in competition with imports. The slower-growing, less profitable
industries ought to be the poorer performers in international trade.

METHOD OF ANALYSIS

Suppose that the United States possessed only two industries,
both of which sell in the domestic market as well as exporting and
importing. Concentrating for a moment on the amounts of capital
per worker required for production in each industry, it is almost
certain that these amounts will differ because of differences in the

technical nature of the production processes involved. Now, for each dollar's worth of national output, it will be possible to construct a weighted average amount of capital per worker required for production of that output in the two industries together. Separating that output into domestic shipments and exports, similar weighted average capital-per-worker input values can be calculated for each. The same can be done for imports, with the strong proviso that one should realize that he is measuring the capital-per-worker requirements of imports as if they were produced under domestic production conditions. These will be the requirements of import replacements rather than of the imports themselves.

Now, consider a simple case, where domestic shipments are identical in size for both industries, but one industry is a strong exporter facing little import competition, while the other is a weak exporter with serious import competition. These performance characteristics will show up in the weighted average factor input calculations. If the strong export industry happens to have a high capital-labor ratio, then the weighted average capital-per-worker input for total exports will be larger than the weighted averages for either domestic shipments or imports. The three weighted average factor input calculations—for domestic shipments, exports, and imports—thus can be easily compared, without a profusion of numbers, by using ratios. One can quickly ascertain the capital requirements for producing exports relative to those for making import replacements; or for exports relative to domestic shipments; or for imports relative to domestic shipments.

These are precisely the sorts of ratios that are presented in Tables 8.1 and 8.2 which display the main results of this study. Separate sets of ratios are calculated on the basis of the weighted average "content"—in exports, imports, and domestic shipments of manufactured goods—of each of the 13 characteristics described in the preceding section. These weighted average characteristic content values are calculated across 31 industry groups that together account for all manufacturing output, exports, and imports, and the values are compared in ratio form.

The figures show the characteristic content comparisons in two ways. In the top half of each table the characteristic contents of exports, imports, and domestic shipments are compared for the values of inbound and outbound trade and domestic sales in a single year, 1970. These comparisons illustrate the industry characteristics of traded and domestically sold goods as "photograph-ed" in a given recent period. However, the analyst also should be interested in changes in the patterns of output and trade. Hence, in the bottom half of each table the characteristic contents of "new" exports, imports, and domestic shipments are compared—"new" being defined as the changes in the values of the trade and shipments variables between 1966 and 1970.

PART A: RATIOS BASED ON VALUES FOR 1970

Embodied Industry Characteristics	Characteristic Content of Exports Relative to Content of:	
	Imports	Domestic Shipments
Capital per worker	0.712	0.957
Labor intensity	0.982	1.007
Human skills (A)	1.028	1.045
Human skills (B)	1.068	1.061
Productivity	1.040	1.013
Scale economics	1.556	1.276
Concentration ratios	1.013	1.081
Product differentiation	1.245	1.163
First trade date	1.033	1.037
Profitability	1.125	1.176
Growth: Shipments	1.077	1.101
Growth: Value added	1.060	1.073
Growth: Employment	1.360	1.388

PART B: RATIOS BASED ON CHANGES IN VALUES, 1966-70

Embodied Industry Characteristics	Characteristic Content of New Exports Relative to Content of:	
	New Imports	New Domestic Shipments
Capital per worker	1.074	0.899
Labor intensity	0.967	1.046
Human skills (A)	1.020	1.098
Human skills (B)	1.035	1.006
Productivity	1.036	0.935
Scale economies	1.235	0.970
Concentration ratios	1.008	1.147
Product differentiation	1.292	1.124
First trade date	1.037	1.047
Profitability	1.083	1.203
Growth: Shipments	1.065	1.098
Growth: Value added	1.039	1.030
Growth: Employment	1.291	1.276

Sources and note: Compiled from data in Appendix Tables A.1 and
A.2. See Appendix A for descriptions of industry characteristics and
methods of derivation.

TABLE 8.2

Performance Ratios for MNC Trade vs. Aggregate U. S. Trade,
1970, and for Changes in the Trade Variables, 1966–70

PART A: RATIOS BASED ON VALUES FOR 1970				
	Characteristic Content of MNC Exports Relative to Content of:			
Embodied Industry Characteristics	U. S. Imports	Domestic Shipments	U. S. Exports	MNC Imports
Capital per worker	0.957	1.286	1.344	1.247
Labor intensity	0.984	1.010	1.003	0.991
Human skills (A)	1.037	1.054	1.009	1.007
Human skills (B)	1.081	1.073	1.012	1.043
Productivity	1.062	1.034	1.021	1.026
Scale economies	1.778	1.458	1.143	0.965
Concentration Ratios	1.031	1.099	1.017	0.998
Product differentiation	1.187	1.109	0.953	1.152
First trade date	1.032	1.036	0.999	1.022
Profitability	1.121	1.171	0.996	1.026
Growth: Shipments	1.042	1.065	0.966	1.053
Growth: Value added	1.016	1.029	0.959	1.033
Growth: Employment	1.196	1.220	0.879	1.202

PART B: RATIOS BASED ON CHANGES IN VALUES, 1966–70				
	Characteristic Content of New MNC Exports Relative to Content of:			
Embodied Industry Characteristics	New U. S. Imports	New Domestic Shipments	New U. S. Exports	New MNC Imports
Capital per worker	1.102	0.923	1.026	1.029
Labor intensity	0.993	1.074	1.027	0.990
Human skills (A)	1.027	1.105	1.006	0.987
Human skills (B)	0.993	0.965	0.959	1.000
Productivity	1.027	0.927	0.991	0.964
Scale economies	1.117	0.930	0.959	0.753
Concentration ratios	0.991	1.127	0.984	0.968
Product differentiation	1.189	1.034	0.920	1.114
First trade date	1.016	1.026	0.980	0.986
Profitability	1.011	1.123	0.933	0.975
Growth: Shipments	0.988	1.018	0.927	1.016
Growth: Value added	0.973	0.965	0.937	0.991
Growth: Employment	0.977	0.966	0.757	1.036

Sources and note: Compiled from data in Appendix Tables A.1 and A.2. See Appendix A for descriptions of industry characteristics and methods of derivation.

Table 8.1 is designed to show the basic characteristic content patterns of trade and domestic shipments for aggregate U. S. trade. It thus establishes what might be called "standard" values of the ratios, against which the trade performance of the MNCs can be measured. In Table 8.2, the appropriate comparisons for the MNCs vs. all traders are made. The characteristic content values for the MNCs are calculated as weighted averages across the industrial spectrum in exactly the same way as are the values for aggregate trade. They are possible as a result of the availability of the most highly disaggregated breakdown of MNC trade figures yet made for a recent period—namely the numbers provided to the U. S. Tariff Commission for its recent study (1973) by the Bureau of Economic Analysis of the U. S. Department of Commerce. Figures for 1966 are based on a full census of U. S.-based foreign direct investors; those for 1970 are estimates based on a sample survey taken for that year.

THE RESULTS

The "standard" performance ratios for aggregate U. S. trade, as displayed in Table 8.1, hold few surprises. These results are generally consistent with those derived from a much more disaggregated study of U. S. industrial trade performance conducted by the U. S. Tariff Commission (1972).

Although theory would lead to the opposite expectations, U. S. exports show up in Part A of the table as significantly less capital intensive than either import replacements or domestic shipments. This is yet another demonstration of the famous "paradox" first uncovered by Wassily Leontief (1953) and later reconfirmed many times, recently by R. E. Baldwin (1971). With respect to new trade, however, Part B of the table produces a somewhat odd result. Relative to new domestic shipments, new exports in the 1966-70 period were a good deal less capital intensive than the values for Part A show for 1970, indicating that, if anything, the tendency for domestic shipments to exceed exports in capital intensity must have become more pronounced over the period. However, relative to new imports, new exports emerge as 7.4 percent more capital intensive. Given the relation between new exports and new domestic shipments, it would appear that this result apparently derived from a significant decline in the capital intensity of new imports—meaning that new imports over the 1966-70 period were significantly more "like" new U. S. exports in terms of capital intensity than has traditionally been the case. This change, however, clearly was not serious enough to alter the basic character of the Leontief Paradox, as revealed in Part A in the exports/imports ratio for capital per worker for the end year 1970.

With respect to labor intensity, both parts of the table indicate 1970 exports and 1966-70 new exports to be slightly less labor intensive than either 1970 imports or 1966-70 new imports. At the same time, exports in 1970 almost exactly mirrored the labor content of domestic production in general, although new exports showed a somewhat greater labor intensity than did new domestic shipments.

As for all the other series—the ones that should reflect the newer, more exotic explanations of where U. S. comparative advantage lies—the results are very much of a piece. In each case, 1970 exports are more intensive in the characteristic at issue than are 1970 imports or, for that matter, domestic shipments in that year. Clearly, human skills, productivity, scale economies, industrial concentration, highly differentiated product lines, flows of new products, and whatever are the factors causing industrial dynamism all represent a package of rather powerful factors helping the analyst to understand where U. S. comparative advantage lies. Scale economies and product differentiation stand out as producing the starkest comparisons between 1970 exports and imports, with exports 55.6 percent more "intensive" in scale economies than imports, and with exports showing a 24.5 percent greater tendency toward product differentiation than imports. Among the "dynamism" indicators, profitability and the growth rate of employment appear to produce the sharpest differences between exports and imports.

Generally the same results emerge in the comparisons for "new" trade between 1966 and 1970. However, the values of the individual ratios, while they point in the same direction, are generally lower than the comparable values in the top half of the table. In the cases of new exports relative to new domestic shipments they slip below 1.000 for both the productivity and scale economies series. All these figures may suggest that, with respect to recent changes in trade, the factors contributing to strong U. S. positions of comparative advantage, although still strongly present, may be weakening slightly. Our exports may be becoming more like our imports in terms of characteristic content—or vice versa.

Moving to Table 8.2, in which the trade performance of the MNCs is brought specifically into the comparisons, several interesting results need comment. First, as compared with aggregate U. S. imports, MNC exports exhibit virtually the same kinds of characteristic content as do aggregate U. S. exports for 1970. That is, they are less capital intensive, slightly less labor intensive, and considerably more possessed of all the other characteristics measured. However, it would seem that MNC exports are surprisingly more capital intensive than domestic shipments, MNC imports, and U. S. exports in general. Continuing down through the top half of the table, one finds also that, while scale economies appear to characterize MNC exports to an even greater extent than aggregate

exports, the outbound shipments of the MNCs seem to embody <u>fewer</u>
scale economies than MNC imports. Equally striking are the three
growth series ratios at the bottom of the third column in Part A
of the table; clearly, MNC exports arise in slower-growing industries—
no matter how growth is measured—than do U. S. exports in general.

In Part B of Table 8.2, still more surprises are revealed. In a
real sense, the third column of the table, which compares new MNC
exports with new U. S. exports in general, is the "tip-off" to
divergences in performance patterns between the MNCs and exporters
in general. If the MNCs matched the performance of exporters in
general, all the values in this column would differ only insignifi-
cantly from 1.000. Values higher than 1.000 would indicate a
more significant presence in MNC exports of the characteristics
measured; values less than 1.000 would indicate a less important
content of these characteristics in the goods traded by the MNCs.

Most of the values in this third column are less than unity,
and several of them are quite divergent in the downward direction
from 1.000. With respect to "new" export trade generated between
1966 and 1970, it must be concluded that the MNCs' exports embodied
significantly fewer of the characteristics that appear to govern the
basic elements of comparative advantage of aggregate new U. S.
exports in international trade. The various values in the first
two columns of the table, in turn, reflect the differences uncovered
in column three, in the sense that the column three figures "explain"
why the first two columns of Table 8.2 differ from the two columns
of Table 8.1—that is, why the characteristic contents of MNC
exports relative to both aggregate imports and aggregate domestic
shipments differ from the same ratios calculated with aggregate
U. S. exports in the numerator.

Other differences between MNC trade and aggregate trade are
pointed up—especially in the ratios for "new" trade—when one
compares column four of Table 8.2 with the first column of Table 8.1.
How do the characteristic contents of new MNC exports relative to
new MNC imports stack up against those of aggregate exports
relative to aggregate imports? The answer is twofold: In some
cases (the human skills series, for example) the divergences
between characteristic contents of exports and imports that "explain"
the aggregate trade flows disappear in trade generated by the MNCs;
and in other cases (scale economies, concentration ratios, first
trade dates, and profitability, for example) the relationships
actually flip over! Those characteristics that would "explain"
aggregate export performance relative to aggregate import performance
now purport to work in the opposite direction, signifying, for the
MNCs, that their new imports are more like aggregate new exports—
and their new exports are more like aggregate new imports.

The foregoing represents rather gloomy evidence for the MNCs
and their friends, anxious to defend the MNCs' contributions to the

U. S. trade accounts. However, it is the kind of evidence that
one must be careful not to cite out of the context of an overall
interpretation of what the figures in Tables 8.1 and 8.2 mean.
The remainder of this chapter proceeds to such interpretation.

CONCLUSIONS

Considered as a group, the ratios presented in Tables 8.1 and
8.2 lead to the fairly unambiguous conclusion that the patterns of
MNC trade, in terms of the characteristic content of traded goods,
do indeed match the patterns of aggregate U. S. trade. Aggregate
exports and MNC exports look more or less alike when their
characteristic contents are compared with those of aggregate U. S.
imports. A quick comparison of the ratio values in the first columns
of Tables 8.1 and 8.2 will confirm this, both for the levels of
trade in 1970 and for "new" trade generated between 1966 and 1970.
With some exceptions, moreover, the same conclusions emerge when
the characteristic content ratios of aggregate exports relative to
aggregate imports are compared with those of MNC exports relative
to MNC imports (column 1 of Table 8.1 vs. column 4 of Table 8.2).
In general, therefore, the patterns of MNC trade reflect the patterns
of U. S. comparative advantage as measured by the characteristic
contents of traded goods.

There are a number of exceptions to this generalization, however,
and these show up especially strongly in the various ratios measuring
performance in terms of "new" trade. They suggest that in some
cases MNC trade flows move counter to the patterns of comparative
advantage in aggregate trade as revealed by the industry characteristic data. Since these exceptions are concentrated in the "new"
trade ratios, they also suggest that, at the margin, the impact of
MNC trade on U. S. trade in general may indeed look like an
"erosion" of what are perceived to be the traditional sources of
U. S. competitiveness in international trade.

Appearances can be deceiving, however. Another way of looking
at the exceptions cited in the preceding paragraph is to note that
the MNCs' trade may really reflect the departure to foreign production locations of firms that are not particularly well-endowed with
the characteristics that suggest strong performance in export and
import markets. Thus, the trade of the MNCs is not "erosion"
of U. S. competitiveness in international trade, but validation of
it. The analysis conducted here may merely have been an exercise
in drawing from the ranks of U. S. exporters and importers in
general a specific sample of less-competitive firms—labeled "MNCs"—
whose trade performance would of course suggest a less competitive
characteristic content than that of traders in general. This sort
of interpretation is heretical only in the context of the popular myth

that "multinational firm" is a phrase to be equated with the epitome of super performance in the home country, the host country, and international trade. Perhaps our understanding of the phenomenon of multinational business would be much assisted by bringing back to earth our perceptions of the MNCs as somehow acting beyond the rules of normal economic behavior.

There are many ways in which further research along the lines conducted here may help to resolve some of the questions raised so far. It would be particularly interesting and not especially difficult to analyze non-MNC trade patterns in the same manner as the trade patterns of the MNCs have been examined. Another important bit of work would be to gather the necessary characteristics data for a group of foreign economies in which foreign direct investment by U. S. firms is heavy, proceeding to analyze MNC trade vs. aggregate trade in each of them in the fashion followed here. One could raise the fascinating hypothesis that the multinational firm is one that migrates to places where it can most easily adapt its own array of industrial characteristics to local conditions— in which case the exports of the MNCs from host countries would tend closely to reflect the arrays of characteristics that contribute to strong trade performance in those economies. In other words, perhaps XYZ Company Inc. is "un-American" but only in the sense that the array of characteristics that define its trading performance look more like those that define the performance of, say, a British firm. If so, it ultimately makes sense for XYZ Company Inc. to become XYZ Ltd., to the benefit of both itself and the two economies concerned.

NOTES

1. Good examples of fine work in this area are the Reddaway Reports (1967 and 1968) produced in the United Kingdom, as well as the Hufbauer-Adler study (1968) commissioned by the U. S. Treasury Department. Less theoretically rigorous, but advantaged by the emergence of more complete data, was the recent Tariff Commission study (1973). Chapters II and III of that study addressed balance of payments and balance of trade questions, respectively, and concluded that, on balance, the MNCs provide a substantial prop to the U. S. external accounts.

2. See Tariff Commission (1973), Chapter III, for details and for an analysis of "indirect" effects that may have sprung from foreign affiliates' erosion of markets traditionally served by exports from the United States.

3. This general type of measurement is suggested by Kenen (1965). However, the series used differs from the Kenen suggestion in that it capitalizes the total nonproduction wage rather than the

wage differential between production and nonproduction workers.
The underlying idea is that it may be more important to consider
the relative amounts of total nonproduction manpower used in
different productive processes independently of whatever relations
may hold between the proportions of production and nonproduction
manpower inputs in particular industries. If the input of educated,
highly-skilled manpower really is a key factor in international
competitiveness, then its effect should show up strictly on the
basis of the volume of such input applied, rather than in the ratio
between the amounts of that kind of labor used and the amounts
of ordinary production labor used.

REFERENCES

Baldwin, R. E. "Determinants of the Commodity Structure of U. S.
    Trade." American Economic Review 61 (1971):126-46.

Hufbauer, G. "The Impact of National Characteristics and Technology
    on the Commodity Composition of Trade in Manufactured Goods."
    The Technology Factor in International Trade, ed. R. Vernon.
    New York: National Bureau of Economic Research, 1970,
    pp. 145-231.

_____ and F. M. Adler. Overseas Manufacturing Investment and the
    Balance of Payments. Tax Policy Research Study No. One.
    Washington, D. C.: U. S. Treasury Department, 1968.

Kenen, Peter B. "Nature, Capital, and Trade." Journal of Political
    Economy. October 1965.

Leontief, W. "Domestic Production and Foreign Trade: The American
    Capital Position Re-examined." Proceedings of the American
    Philosophical Society 97 (1953):332-49.

Linder, S. B. An Essay on Trade and Transformation. New York:
    John Wiley, 1961.

Reddaway, W. B., et al. Effects of United Kingdom Direct Investment
    Overseas; Interim and Final Reports. Cambridge: Cambridge
    University Press, 1967 and 1968.

U. S. Bureau of the Census. Annual Survey of Manufactures, Industry
    Profiles. Washington, D. C., 1972 (publication no. M70 [AS]-10).

U. S. Internal Revenue Service. Corporation Income Tax Returns,
    Statistics of Income, 1968. Washington, D. C., 1972
    (publication no. 16-3-72).

U. S. Tariff Commission. Competitiveness of U. S. Industries. Report to the President on Investigation No. 332–65 under section 332 of the Tariff Act of 1930. Washington, D. C., 1972 (TC publication no. 473).

_____, Implications of Multinational Firms for World Trade and Investment and for U. S. Trade and Labor. Report to the Committee on Finance of the U. S. Senate and to its Subcommittee on International Trade on Investigation no. 332–69 under section 332 of the Tariff Act of 1930. Washington, D. C., 1973 (TC publication no. 537).

Vernon, R. "International Trade and International Investment in the Product Cycle." Quarterly Journal of Economics 80 (1966):190–207.

PART

IV

**ANTITRUST
POLICIES AND
ISSUES**

9

THE ANTITRUST
ISSUE AND
MULTINATIONAL
BUSINESS
Howard J. Aibel

Perhaps it would put my treatment of the assigned topic in the proper perspective if at the outset I made three rather obvious points: (1) "the antitrust issue" is only one aspect of overall national policy—primarily economic policy, but also political and social policy; (2) "the antitrust issue" is itself a multinational one; and (3) "the antitrust issues" for multinational businesses are national, transnational, and international in character.

THE WIDER MEANING OF ANTITRUST

When considering the antitrust issue we should realize that what we are really dealing with is any governmental intervention that seeks to alter entrepreneurial behavior or alter the balance of market forces in order to achieve perceived policy aims. Hopefully in this context it is helpful to think of the antitrust issue in terms less parochial to the United States by rendering it as "governmental policy regarding regulation of business activity." Perhaps this rubric makes it easier to see how in some countries the issue could translate to a policy of free trade and be stated in terms whose reference point is the promotion of competition through the lowering of all barriers to trade, whether governmental or private, while in other countries the issue translates differently.

Some countries prohibit restrictive business practices with laws and regulations that are as specific as those of the United States but that they, nevertheless, enforce more flexibly, in the hope of furthering policy aims accorded a higher priority than the per se elimination of restrictive business practices. Thus, I am

Howard J. Aibel is General Counsel, International Telephone & Telegraph Corporation.

told that in certain member countries of the EEC businesses are encouraged to cooperate in loose federations that agree on prices and production rationalizations, in furtherance of the policy aim of developing economic units thought to be more efficient and, hence, more capable of competing for business in those countries as well as in the rest of the European Community.

Again, in the mid-1960s in the United Kingdom, regulatory authorities permitted Rolls-Royce to become the sole producer of aircraft engines in that country when acquisition by Rolls of Bristol Motors was approved. The aim was to make Rolls more competitive in world markets, principally in the United States.

The EEC Commission recently exempted a so-called specialization agreement, pursuant to which German and Belgian needle-producing firms combined manufacturing operations despite the fact that the Commission found that the agreement had the object and effect of restricting competition within the Common Market on a showing that greater efficiency resulted with the effect of lowering costs and improving quality. On the other hand, in some countries the issue could be stated in protectionist terms whose reference point is the promotion of local development, by foreign as well as domestic interests, where the barriers to competition from abroad established by the government are sometimes an inducement to the entry of foreign investment.

Looking beyond national borders, exporting nations may be willing to allow trade restraints privately agreed upon by domestic competitors in the export trade (as the United States does under the Webb-Pomerene Act) while importing countries inveigh against such cartel activities for increasing their domestic costs for imports (as the United States did in the recent case of the international quinine cartel).* However, government policy will almost always seek to expand the opportunity for local enterprises to increase domestic employment and the level of industrial activity and to improve the home-country balance of payments. Complicated? Yes, but it is the task of multinational businesses to fit into the often overlapping and conflicting regulatory schemes of the countries in which they do business.

CHARACTERISTICS OF U. S. POLICY

It is probably one of the strengths of the United States that among the developed countries this nation is one of the few that does not have a clearly defined mode for the formulation and implementation of a unified national economic policy. We tend to react

---

*See Chapter 10, section entitled "The Quinine Case."

to particular felt policy needs and situations in ad hoc ways. Of course the basic general policy may be established by legislation such as the Sherman Act, or at least as the Sherman Act has been interpreted by the courts. The courts have characterized the Sherman Act as "a charter of freedom" that "has a generality and adaptability comparable to that found to be desirable in constitutional provisions." Policy may also be established by legislation as specific as the Glass-Steagall Act, which permanently divorced commercial banking from investment banking.

The United States has other legislation that creates regulatory commissions to establish policy for specific sectors of our economy such as transportation and communications. And we have an executive department, the Department of Transportation, and a presidential office, the Office of Telecommunications Management, which are also charged with the same functions. Moreover, the Antitrust Division of the Department of Justice attacks, through court action, not only the conduct of private parties thought to be contrary to the antitrust policy, but also the regulatory policies and programs of administrative agencies such as the Interstate Commerce Commission and the Federal Communications Commission for which the maintenance or establishment of competition may be only one of several conflicting policy aims sought to be served.

We also see the numerous U. S. federal district courts entertaining antitrust challenges to executive branch action designed to effectuate domestic economic desires, such as the private lawsuit challenging the agreements reached by the State Department with foreign steel producers limiting exports of steel to the United States. As another example, where else but in the United States would the courts be asked to direct a major restructuring of whole industries by private parties as in the case of the litigation brought against General Telephone and Electronics by ITT and against IBM by Telex and others?

Personally, I don't think I would have it otherwise. However, at any particular time a coherent national economic policy is not always easy to discern. Indeed, our regulatory policy varies from one sector of the economy to another, from one enforcement agency to another, and from one time to another as politics and policies change. This is certainly the case with respect to transnational activities of U. S.-based companies.

TRENDS IN ANTITRUST

Looking only at U. S. government antitrust enforcement for a moment, I would like to venture a personal observation, based on some 20 years of active participation in the antitrust field (and as counsel for both plaintiffs and defendants), that there are definite periodic trends or "fads" in antitrust enforcement. As soon as one antitrust dragon has been perceived and routed, someone always promptly finds another one worthy of the attention of a knight errant.

For example, not too long ago the U. S. antitrust focus was on mergers among actual large competitors. But now that such mergers no longer occur in the United States, we have seen a remarkable development of the abstract theories of "potential" competition, and "foothold" mergers, and even "toehold" mergers. After elimination of the last toehold, there wouldn't appear to be much left to work with, but experience indicates that the ingenuity of the antitrust ideologists will develop something.

Similarly we have seen the attack on the practice of actual reciprocity between buying and selling business turn later into an attack on purely theoretical "possible" or "potential" reciprocity.

We have observed the recent crusade against certain large conglomerate mergers conducted under the frightening banner of "aggregate concentration," which utilized a misleading statistical mix of foreign and domestic manufacturing and nonmanufacturing business activities in an attempt to convince the public that concentration of aggregate manufacturing assets in the United States was rapidly increasing. Fortunately, in November 1972, the Bureau of the Census demonstrated that the "share of total value added by manufacture" accounted for by the largest 50 companies was 25 percent in 1963 and 24 percent in 1970; and the share accounted for by the largest 100 companies was 33 percent in 1963 and still 33 percent in 1970.

Perhaps even more significantly, the Bureau of the Census report shows that there were significant changes in the identity of the companies that were in the group of the top 50 manufacturing companies in 1963 as compared to 1970—and that the particular top 50 companies that had a 25 percent share of "value added" in 1963 had actually dropped to 23 percent by 1970, while the particular top 100 companies that had a 33 percent share of "value added" in 1963 had dropped to 31 percent by 1970. So much for the well-publicized spectre of "aggregate concentration in U. S. manufacturing assets."

I've burdened you with this detail because, with the changing cycles of antitrust theory, it is quite possible that we may see similar misapprehensions regarding "aggregate concentration" emerging again in the multinational context. Since the Census Bureau report and other rebuttals to the claims of increasing aggregate concentration have not received nearly the same amount of publicity as the original misleading contentions, there is a danger that the original charges will become part of the world's economic folklore.

THE UNCTAD REPORT

For instance, in a recent Report on Restrictive Business Practices by the Ad Hoc Group of Experts organized by the United Nations Conference on Trade and Development (UNCTAD), the following is said with respect to multinational corporations:

> Their significant power was evident from the fact that the total sales of a number of the multinational corporations exceeded the gross national products of most developing countries and the rate of growth in sales of multinational corporations exceeded the rate of growth in the gross national products of most developing countries. In addition the large and growing proportion of world trade concentrated in their hands added to their significance. . . .

The U. S. Census Bureau statistical data to which I referred, which debunks the ideologically inspired and erroneous theory of increasing aggregate concentration in the United States, suggests that the assertions in the UNCTAD report regarding rates of growth and increasing concentration of world trade in the hands of multinational corporations similarly will not withstand critical analysis.

The UNCTAD group went on to assert that the behavior of multinational corporations was not always in line with government policies in host countries and that cooperative action is required to achieve harmony. What the UNCTAD group was concerned with is what they characterized as "restrictions imposed" upon subsidiaries of developed country-based multinational enterprises. But these "imposed restrictions" may rather, in the parent and subsidiary context, be actually the operational working out of the overall business plan of the multinational enterprise by defining the mission of the subsidiary in carrying out that plan, with the aim of achieving the efficient allocation of resources available to the overall enterprise. For instance, the UNCTAD group cited as an invidious practice the arrangements and understandings that restrict subsidiaries from exporting from host countries raw materials in processed and semiprocessed forms to firms not in its own multinational enterprise grouping. Another example cited was what were characterized as "territorial market allocation arrangements" involving exports of manufacturing and distributing subsidiaries. This certainly is the traditional antitrust rhetoric if one overlooks the fact that subsidiaries are involved.

If an enterprise is to be run in as rational and economic way as possible, one can see decisions regarding the efficient development of raw materials resources producing limitations on sales outside the enterprise group. But these are actions taken in light of overall corporate business strategy and of the long-term needs of the multinational business for the raw materials and the capital required to serve expanding markets. Again, the carrying out of effective marketing and customer service programs on a multi-national basis may well produce sourcing plans that appear to be "restrictions" on the subsidiary, but that may in fact represent an effort by the multinational business to achieve the most efficient allocation of resources in serving customers effectively. But in any event, it is important to note that these are changing arrangements, changing as economic realities change and certainly not immutable. Regulations very often are immutable regardless of economic changes.

It is perhaps appropriate to note that one of the UNCTAD experts was reported as being of the view that "the views [of the group as to restrictions on subsidiaries of multinationals] were too broad and too sweeping. In his opinion it would not be in the interest of the developing countries themselves if the multinational corporation were totally denied the possibility to implement a consistent corporate strategy of their own."

Clearly the restrictions cited by the group are for internal regulation in each host country, perhaps acting within the framework of regional economic groupings. However, the desirability of such regulation must be seen in the overall context of the policy desires of developing countries to industrialize, to attract foreign capital and foreign-developed technology to their borders so as to create employment, develop export markets for manufactured goods, and thereby increase the general level of welfare of the population while improving their balance of payments.

THE ANDEAN COMMUNITY

Consider for a moment the impact upon foreign investors of the approach toward solving these problems taken by the countries of the Andean community. Generally speaking, the days when foreign companies could come to the Andean community countries seeking markets via direct foreign investment and were permitted relatively free entry appear to be over. The approach now is for the nations of the community to select the foreign inputs according to the needs of an overall development scheme and thereafter to control foreign enterprises domiciled in the community to assure that they fulfill a beneficial role. Moreover, over a defined number of years the foreign enterprise that wishes to export to other nations in the community must be transformed into a mixed ownership enterprise, one in which national investors own and control from 51 to 80 percent of the company. In addition, not only must the foreign company divest ownership rights, but it must also relinquish a corresponding amount of effective control of the enterprise.

If a foreign parent company transfers technology to its subsidiary, arrangements designed to bind the subsidiary into the overall worldwide business plan of the parent (in the use by the subsidiary of the transferred technology) are greatly restricted. These new laws and regulations also have application, of course, to preexisting enterprises and foreign-owned or controlled units of multinational businesses that are in the countries of the Andean community. They must conform.

As to the multinational or foreign national enterprise not already present in the host Andean community country, it has at least two choices: the first is to come in, subject to the existing and future regulations of its conduct that the host country may adopt; the second is to stay out. The decision as to what to do will to some extent depend upon an appraisal as to whether current import markets may be lost if a competitor is accepted as a foreign investor in the host country, and the borders are, in practical effect, closed to imports. But the big issue will be control of the subsidiary and the transferred technology.

So far, it appears that most potential newcomers have elected to stay out, since the reported new foreign investments in the countries of the Andean community since 1969 have been insignificant, with the exception of investments related to natural resources.

How this will work out for these countries is problematical. Certainly the experience to date does not indicate that prospective foreign investors in the Andean community nations have found that the climate is favorable for the making of investments and the transfer of technology to the community. While this may change, it would appear that the host country may not secure desired foreign investment when the regulatory scheme into which foreign enterprises must fit has costs for them that are judged to be too high or are too unpredictable to permit a rational appraisal.

Perhaps you now understand why one must appreciate that the antitrust issue, or as we agreed the idea would be restated, the governmental policy toward regulation of business activity, is only one aspect of overall national economic policy.

Obviously, there are some traditional antitrust problems to be found in international trade, as is illustrated by the classic international cartel cases involving price fixing and allocations of market and customers. Recent decisions by the Common Market antitrust authorities, and by the German Cartel Office, indicate that restrictive agreements among competitors continue to be formed and challenged in Europe, just as in the United States. Some multinationals may find that their subsidiaries are, unfortunately, involved in such arrangements.

MULTINATIONALS AND COMPETITION

But if one puts aside the thought, unrealistically held by some theoreticians, that subsidiaries of multinationals should be required to act as though they were not part of such a multinational enterprise, multinationalism in business does not in itself necessarily lead to restraints on competition, or inevitably have any anticompetitive effects. Rather, it should be readily apparent from even a cursory examination of the retail consumer marketplaces of most of the world that the development of multinational business investments in expanding productive capacity and in expanding exporting and trading activities across national boundaries has had the effect of dramatically increasing the amount and effectiveness of competition in pricing, styling, and quality among multinationals as well as between multinationals and local enterprises.

Thus from the point of view of generalized antitrust analysis, multinationalism in business tends to broaden the size of the markets that are available or open to competition, while at the same time tending to increase the amount of worldwide productive capacity that is available to serve that larger market. It seems clear that this effective opening of international markets is a highly desirable goal for those of us who profess to advocate greater competition for the benefit of consumers.

In the unlikely event that a single producer does achieve an effective dominance or control over one of these newly expanded worldwide markets, in the sense of achieving real power unilaterally to raise prices or exclude competitors, or a worldwide cartel of competing producers achieves the same result, that will certainly present a conventional antitrust issue. This would be the problem of monopoly power or horizontal conspiracy. At the present time this possibility would appear to arise on an international market basis primarily in such well-known areas as (1) relatively scarce basic natural resources such as nickel and chromium and diamonds—and perhaps French wine; (2) in rapidly changing very high technology products such as large computers, air frame manufacturing, and nuclear reactor equipment; and (3) in true invention and patent monopoly situations such as new drugs and xerography.

I believe the only truly significant public policy arguments that can be raised against the opening of international markets through multinationalism and international trade are not antitrust issues, but are rather, as I see it, other politically potent issues: first, a desire to protect against loss of jobs and to prevent unemployment in inefficient local industries; second, national defense fears against undue reliance on foreign suppliers of raw materials or products essential for national security; and third (and perhaps most basic), concern that foreign control of industry will deprive the host nation of control of its destiny.

It is vitally important that these important issues that translate into a nationalistic economic policy leading to subsidization of local industry, protective tariffs, and "dumping" should be squarely faced and fought openly on their own merits and should not be concealed behind a false facade of contrived and irrelevant antitrust rhetoric.

Contrary to the popular mythology, the multinational and international businessmen are not "above and beyond the reach" of the various national laws regulating business activity. Instead they are subject to each of those national laws whenever they engage in any significant amount of business within a particular country, and at the same time may also be subject to the broad reach of the U. S. antitrust laws if U. S. imports or exports are affected, or to the Common Market regulations, and so on.

From the multinationals' point of view, the problem is not one of being above the law. Rather, the problem is that of complying with a multitude of vastly different regulatory systems, each of which is inspired by different aims and goals. It is a basic fact of life that the multinational is a citizen of each of the countries in which it operates and must conduct itself accordingly. As I said at the outset, the antitrust issues for multinational businesses are national, transnational, and international. But because multinationals move across national borders, and operate in a multitude of jurisdictions, the basic thrust of their development is and will be the establishment of a more open system of trade and commerce.

10

MERCANTILISM AND MONOPOLY— ALTERNATIVES TO A COMPETITIVE AMERICA

Donald I. Baker

These are not times that encourage sound public policy. We live in the shadow of the sheiks—and amid great public skepticism engendered by events in Washington. Yet, despite the distractions and aggravations, we must all try hard to think calmly and clearly about where we are and where we want to get. Only by asking the right questions can we ever hope to come up with the right answers.

This is particularly true of international trade policy which vitally affects not only American business, but the American consumer. We must compete abroad but also protect the consumer at home. Antitrust is vital to both these goals.

DOMESTIC COMPETITION AND INTERNATIONAL TRADE

Peter Peterson's 1971 report, The United States and the Changing World Economy, is a good place to start. He looks at many things— including the new competition brought into our own markets by foreign industrial firms in Europe and East Asia; he looks at our difficulties in competing abroad; and he asks us to look at our future. In essence, he says we have two choices. One is the road to mercantilism—"of erecting a variety of new restrictions . . . against the products of our trade partners." He rejects this choice as "a prescription for defeat and an admission of failure." Instead, he takes a second alternative, looking in the opposite direction: that is

to meet head-on the essential—if demanding—task of improving our productivity and our competitiveness in

Donald I. Baker is Deputy Assistant Attorney General, Antitrust Division, U. S. Department of Justice.

an increasingly competitive world, to seize the initiative
in designing a new, comprehensive program designed to
build on America's strengths, and to encourage a competitive world trading system with the confidence that comes
with having a sense of our future. [He adds that] the basis
for this confidence must be a strong domestic economy, . . .
stimulated by . . . the technological advances which will
both increase our international competitiveness and help
our society fulfill its promise of a better life and productive work for its citizens.[1]

Strong competition at home is vital to this mission. A firm
that has trouble competing in Columbus or Cleveland is going to have
an even harder time in Munich or Milan.
    Competition is particularly vital to the high-technology products
that have been America's strongest suit. To invent and develop a
new product requires skill, imagination, capital, and hard work.
A sleepy, dominant firm can go on practicing the art of the past,
while opportunities are missed and consumer demands go unmet.
The situation is made even worse for the consumer and for the
country if the sleepy giant is protected by government against more
enterprising foreign competitors.
    Let me take but one highly topical example. For years,
Detroit resisted the small car because the industry leaders felt
that "mini cars mean mini profits." The small car market—then small—
was left to the Europeans, and later the Japanese. They found that
at first a few and gradually many more Americans wanted small cars
in preference to the great gas guzzlers so favored by Detroit. And
in time Detroit could not resist the tide; it too had to develop
small cars and advertise their gas mileage rather than their horse-
power. Of course, we still have too many great gas guzzlers on
the road to serve our national need in a time of a great energy
shortage, but think how much worse it would be today if we had
nothing but giants on the road. And this might well have been the
case but for the important role played by foreign competition in
the domestic market. (One might add for the record here that the
large Detroit cars have never done very well in foreign markets,
where people generally had poorer roads, shorter distances, and
much higher fuel costs.)
    This is not an isolated example. One might look at steel
as another case where the dominant American firms have been slow
to innovate and are now hard pressed in the world. Our dominant
American firms did not develop or promptly deploy the basic oxygen
process. Rather, it was developed abroad and first introduced into
this country by a small manufacturer. Of course, in the end, the
dominant American steel makers had to come around to the new
process, despite their heavy fixed investments in the old technology—

but they did so only reluctantly, only under pressure. Meanwhile, they pleaded, increasingly loudly, for government protection against imports; and ultimately they received such protection in the form of voluntary steel quotas negotiated with government assistance. This in turn led—not surprisingly—to domestic price increases that Walter Adams has described as "electrifying." Within three years, steel industry prices rose at almost ten times their prior rates; and some key products, such as cold rolled sheet, rose over 30 percent.[2] These increases were passed on not only to the American consumer—but to American firms seeking to sell finished steel products abroad.

What is disturbing is not only the increases in prices paid by American customers, but the implications of protection for the firms protected. It seems highly unlikely that a firm artificially protected at home this year will be better able on that account to compete abroad next year. There may be a few exceptions, but a general rule seems to be that those who live off protection need ever more of it; and those who must buy from a protected industry need ever more outside competition.

U. S. ANTITRUST—A HANDICAP TO U. S. TRADE?

There are some who point to antitrust law and enforcement (rather than business and labor inefficiency) as a main source of our trade problems. For example, last April, former Governor Connally of Texas spoke to the spring meeting of the Antitrust Section of the American Bar Association. He treated antitrust as a historic relic, left over from the horse and buggy days of the 1890s. "The world is changing, and we must change with it." These changes, he argued, "dictate substantial amendment to our antitrust laws today."[3] He saw American firms as being inhibited by a too vigorous application of what he regarded as outdated laws. The governor did not propose any precise reforms, but he clearly seemed to favor broad authority in American firms to enter into agreements that would in any way promote exports, and he opposed any antitrust monopoly or merger cases that might limit exports in any way.

Of course, legal questions cannot be resolved on such an abstract plane. Nor can sound economic policies. Rather, we must ask the hard questions. Do we want less competitive domestic markets on the theory that American consumers should subsidize export opportunities? Do we want export cartels even if they have a substantial anticompetitive spillover into the domestic market? Do we really think that America will lead the world in developing new products, services, and delivery systems if our large and vital national market is walled off from the rest of the world?

Unless we are willing to answer those questions in the affirmative—
which I am not—we must look to antitrust as an affirmative tool,
rather than a drag. Maintaining our competitiveness here is vital
to our place in the world.

And, after all, antitrust is not some archaic set of legal rules,
beloved by the lawyer but unknown to the layman. Rather, it is
a sensible economic policy embodied in law that can—and indeed
must—be understood by us all. In a sense, one might say the
matter is too important to be left to the lawyers.

Nor is antitrust an exclusively American product (even if it
has had a longer history here than abroad). Other industrial
countries are looking increasingly to antitrust to protect their
consumers and stimulate their domestic industries. And, in some
areas, such as resale price maintenance in Britain, they have gone
well beyond our law. Indeed, from the standpoint of international
business planning, foreign antitrust liability is something that
increasingly must be reckoned with (as it should be). This reality
is underscored by the fact that the EEC can, and has, levied
fines that are very much higher than those available to us under the
Sherman Act.

COMPETITION AT HOME—
THE FIRST PRIORITY

The Justice Department's main antitrust mission is to assure
competition in our domestic economy. So far as international trade
is concerned, the antitrust commitment is to allow foreign products
to compete in our markets free of private restraints, and to allow
American products to compete abroad free of private restraints
imposed by those subject to our jurisdiction. Antitrust does not
prevent American firms from getting together to sell abroad where
their efforts do not raise prices in our domestic market. Nor does
antitrust prevent American firms from getting together to buy abroad
where their efforts produce lower prices in our domestic market.

We do not start with a fully competitive domestic economy.
Rather, a few industries are dominated by a single firm, and a
good many other industries are dominated by such a small number
of firms that they can behave in some vital respects as if they
were monopolists. As I have already noted, such conditions can
have an important adverse effect on the industry's ability to serve
the public at home or compete abroad. Our existing legal tools are
not really satisfactory to deal with this structural problem on a
broad scale, nor do we really have adequate enforcement resources.[4]
In these circumstances the government has tended to rely mostly
on strict antimerger enforcement to prevent bad conditions from
getting worse, or to prevent them from being created in the first place.

This effort has been broadly successful, especially in preventing mergers between direct competitors.

We have also relied, as a country, upon foreign firms to apply the spur of competition to dominant American enterprise. Antitrust enforcement has sought to preserve that spur (as has Antitrust Division participation before the Treasury and the Tariff Commission in dumping cases).

The government's main antitrust enforcement effort has been against what I shall call the classic international cartels. Such a cartel normally involves leading firms in two different countries agreeing with each other that they would not poach on each other's "home" markets.[5] The evil of such a cartel is clear: It denies the American consumer the benefit of competitive foreign products, and it denies the American firm the opportunity to export and compete abroad. Clearly, such agreements are not designed to serve the interests of the American public—or the interests of the United States as an exporting nation. Rather, they serve the private interests of the parties—the basic private interest in having a quiet life.

A similar problem can be seen where a leading American firm seeks to merge with a leading foreign competitor, for, like the cartel, such an agreement limits the foreign firm as a potential entrant, or an independent competitor, in the American market.[6] If the American market is dominated by a very few firms, and the foreign firm is one of a relatively few potential entrants, then its elimination by merger may have serious anticompetitive results. Imagine—going back to my earlier discussion on automobiles—how different our domestic situation might have been had General Motors in the early 1950s bought up Volkswagen, Fiat, and Renault. What turned out to have been an important spur on domestic competition would have been eliminated as an independent factor. (Of course, the international mergers that raise serious antitrust problems are relatively few in the real world, and therefore American firms have generally had little antitrust difficulty in making acquisitions abroad, nor have foreign firms had difficulty making acquisitions in the United States.)

THE QUININE CASE

The domestic interest in antitrust enforcement against cartels is particularly critical where the primary production of a particular product is abroad. Here, we will be vitally concerned that any appropriate action be taken to deal with any foreign cartel in such a situation. The international quinine cartel offers the best example. It involved foreign firms and some foreign subsidiaries of American firms engaged in a long-term and broadly successful effort to control the world prices in quinine—a product of which

America consumes about a third of the world's supply. The government filed indictments in New York and was able to bring enough of the malefactors into court to put a stop to the cartel and bring down the price of quinine, while recovering substantial damages for the government.[7] (You should also note that the EEC brought a parallel action, after the Justice Department had sued, and imposed very substantial fines.)

In broad outline, the Justice Department's concern is with any private cartel arrangement that adversely affects the American market. Private parties who can be reached should be if they engage in activities designed to raise prices or exclude products from American markets. This should apply whether the agreements are actually made in New York, London, or Hong Kong. As the Supreme Court has stressed, "A conspiracy to monopolize or restrain the domestic or foreign commerce of the United States is not outside the reach of the Sherman Act just because part of the conduct complained of occurs in foreign countries."[8]

Even parties that are beyond the reach of our jurisdiction may be dealt with directly if they engage in cartel practices that injure our domestic markets. This can be done by means of remedies against their goods and their American importers under the Wilson Tariff Act (15 U. S. C. Secs. 8-11) or through exclusion of their goods under the procedures provided in Section 337 of the Trade Adjustment Act (19 U. S. C. Sec. 1337).

Of course, what is sauce for the goose is also sauce for the gander. We treat antitrust primarily as a consumer protection statute for American consumers. We must concede that foreign countries may do the same thing—that they may protect their consumers against the actions of foreign firms that limit competition in their markets. Of course, this does not put American firms at a special disadvantage, since all sellers would have to qualify under the same antitrust rules in a particular country. It simply means our American exporters' agreements among themselves may raise serious antitrust questions abroad, even if they do not do so here.

COMPETITIVE EXPORTS ABROAD

This brings me to the second part of the antitrust enforcement mission—namely to protect American exports of goods, services, and capital against privately imposed restraints barring them from foreign markets. In other words, we want our goods to be able to compete abroad on their merits. Cartels can prevent this.

In general, American firms are permitted to collaborate in selling abroad, so long as they avoid anticompetitive spillovers into the domestic market. Thus in general they can collectively agree on prices and markets that they will serve, since the purpose of the Sherman Act does not extend to the protection of foreign buyers against such horizontal restraints. (As I have already indicated, that is a matter for foreign law.)

The Webb-Pomerene Act specifically authorizes such arrangements, where "goods, wares and merchandise" are involved and where certain safeguards are met.[9] In fact, Webb-Pomerene has proven to be of little practical importance because most joint export arrangements could be carried on under the Sherman Act, and because American firms selling highly differentiated products have generally not wanted to merge sales efforts with their competitors. To eliminate any doubt, however, the Nixon administration has proposed to expand Webb-Pomerene to cover various types of services.[10]

However, in considering other legislative proposals, Congress should not allow export promotion to be used as a device for eliminating competition in the domestic market. The American consumer should not be asked to subsidize the exports of our firms by paying noncompetitive prices here in the United States. I suppose one could say that if we allowed a company to make a monopoly profit in the United States it _might_ use that profit to subsidize export sales. On the other hand, it might not. But in any event, this would be bad policy for the United States—costly to our consumers, and deadening to our firms. Do we really think they would be better off in the world without the spur of competition here at home?

There are, of course, several kinds of situations in which private arrangements may foreclose export and investment opportunities for American firms abroad, and they may therefore be subject to our antitrust laws. One is the classic cartel, already discussed, where the American firm enters into an agreement to limit its own exports into a foreign competitor's markets as part of an international market allocation scheme.[11]

Another example would be where an American firm gangs up with others to drive another American firm out of an export market. This has occurred on a few occasions.[12]

Still another example would be where an American firm—particularly a leading one—enters into an exclusive, long-term arrangement with a foreign customer—an arrangement that has the effect of preventing any other American firms from competing for the customer's business. This would have to be looked at in terms of its competitive effect, particularly with regard to how important the foreign buyer was in the total market for U. S. exports.[13]

A final example would be the foreign buying cartel: If a group of foreign firms get together and allocate their purchases between various American sources, they are necessarily limiting competition within our domestic economy for goods that will be exported. Such buying cartels are of direct interest to our government and should be subject to American antitrust scrutiny to the extent that we can assert jurisdiction over the parties.

To summarize, the American antitrust interest with respect to export restraints is generally more limited than with respect to domestic restraints or import restraints. We are not generally talking about protecting American consumers, but only about protecting firms from being victimized by others subject to our jurisdiction.

THE AWKWARD PRESENCE OF GOVERNMENTS

The antitrust laws deal with private action, not government action. Yet around the world we see some governments increasingly involved as actors. We see this in the Middle East, where the oil-producing countries have put together a big cartel. We see this in Eastern Europe, where state trading monopolies are a way of life. And we see it in a variety of government-imposed restraints designed to limit competition to protect their own national firms. Of course, there is very little that antitrust enforcement can do about all this, for the obvious reason that one sovereign cannot prosecute another.

At the same time, some would go a step farther and argue that antitrust prevents American firms from operating effectively in the presence of foreign government cartels. I do not think this argument will stand up to careful analysis.

In fact, the Justice Department has authorized—and the Sherman Act permits—necessary cooperation among American firms to deal with a foreign government buying or selling cartel, provided that that cooperation does not spill over into the domestic market.

Moreover, antitrust permits any firm to comply with the command of a foreign government, even if its conduct would otherwise be offensive under our antitrust laws.[14] Of course, antitrust problems will come up when the firm, rather than the foreign government, has been the moving force in imposing anticompetitive restraints. Thus, for example, the Supreme Court found that an American firm had used authority delegated to it by the Canadian government to extend its own position in Canada and squeeze another American firm out of the Canadian market;[15] this was discretionary action, not something required by the Canadian government.

While speaking of governments, I should also say something about our own. This is hardly a novel subject given the temper of the times in Washington and around the country. Foreign firms and foreign governments have sometimes said that American antitrust enforcement discriminates against them. This view sometimes even appears in the press. For example, a February 1973 Wall Street Journal article commented on the disparity between the large U. S. investment abroad and the relatively small foreign investment in the United States. It stated: "The most frequently mentioned deterrent to more foreign subsidiaries in the U. S., though, is clearly the

belief that the Justice Department will go gunning for them while
winking at anti-trust infractions by American companies."[16] This
just isn't so. The suggestion that we "go gunning" for foreign
firms because they are foreign is just as disturbing—and just as
erroneous—as the suggestion that we "lay off" domestic firms because
they make campaign contributions.

Nor is it supported by the record. In fact, our enforcement of
the antimerger statute has led directly to opportunities for foreign
firms to enter the United States with sizable acquisitions. This
was true of British Petroleum (BP)—which in 1969 entered retail
marketing on the Gulf Coast by buying properties put up for sale
because of a government challenge to the Atlantic-Richfield-Sinclair
merger.[17] It is also true of Lloyds' Bank—one of Britain's largest—
which has entered California through acquisition of the billion-dollar
First Western bank which the Justice Department had prevented from
being sold to Wells Fargo in 1972.[18] In sum, the Justice Department's
policy has consistently been to welcome foreign firms, such as
British Petroleum and Lloyds' Bank, as sources of new competition
in our domestic markets. Once here, such firms can expect, and
will receive, the same antitrust enforcement that U. S. firms get.

This is the truth, yet what the foreign firms think may be at
least as important. If they believe—however inaccurately—that we
will "go gunning" for them, and therefore stay away, then we are
all the losers. This underscores a general point of vital importance:
that law enforcement must be fair-minded and even-handed; and,
more than that, it must be perceived by those affected as being
carried on in this way.

NOTES

1. Peter Peterson, The United States in the Changing World
Economy, Vol. 1, (Washington, D. C.: Government Printing Office,
1971), p. iv.

2. Walter Adams in Competitive Measures and Competitive
Facts, Conference Board Report No. 549 (New York, 1972), pp. 5-6.

3. Bureau of National Affairs, Antitrust and Trade Regulation
Report No. 609, April 17, 1973, A-4 to A-5.

4. See Donald I. Baker, Section 2 Enforcement—The View From
The Trench, 41 Antitrust Law Journal 613 (1972).

5. See, for example, United States v. National Lead Co.,
63 F. Supp. 513 (SDNY 1945), aff'd 332 U. S. 319 (1947); United
States v. Imperial Chemical Industries, Ltd., 100 F. Supp. 504
(SDNY 1951). Cf. United States v. Westinghouse Electric Corp.,
C. A. No. C-70-852-SAW (N. D. Cal. 1970).

6. United States v. Jos. Schlitz Brewing Co., 253 F. Supp.
129 (N. D. Calif. 1966); United States v. Gillette Co., C. A.
No. 68-141 (D. Mass. 1968).

7. United States v. N. V. Nederlandsche Combinatie Voor Chemische Industrie, 1970 Trade Cases para. 73,181 (S. D. N. Y. 1970).

8. Continental Ore Co. v. Union Carbide & Carbon Corp. 370 U. S. 690, 704 (1962).

9. 15 U. S. C. Secs. 61-65.

10. S. 1774. See also testimony of Assistant Attorney General Thomas E. Kauper, September 6, 1973, on this bill and S. 1483.

11. See, for example, Timken Roller Bearing Co. v. United States, 341 U. S. 533 (1951).

12. See especially Pacific Seafarers, Inc. v. Pacific Far East Lines, Inc., 404 F. 2d 804 (D. C. Cir. 1968), where a group of steamships by predatory pricing drove the plaintiff off a market reserved to American flag carriers (that is, an export market for U. S. services).

13. Cf. Tampa Electric Co. v. Nashville Coal Co., 365 U. S. 320 (1961).

14. Interamerican Refinery Corp. v. Texaco Maracaibo Inc., 307 F. Supp. 1291 (D. C. Del. 1970); cf. Parker v. Brown, 317 U. S. 341 (1943).

15. Continental Ore Co. v. Union Carbide & Carbon Corp., 370 U. S. 690 (1970).

16. Wall Street Journal, February 26, 1973.

17. United States v. Atlantic Richfield Co., C. A. No. 69-Civ.-162 (S. D. N. Y. filed January 15, 1969). Subsequently, BP itself was sued for buying the leading gasoline marketer in Ohio, United States v. British Petroleum Co., Civ. No. 69-954 (N. D. Ohio 1969), settled by consent decree, 1970 Trade Case para. 72,988. Here it was treated in "precisely the same way we would have analyzed a proposal to unite Schio with another American company in the position of BP's American subsidiary." Assistant Attorney General Richard W. McLaren, "Antitrust Policy Today," New York, N. Y., March 5, 1970, p. 7.

18. United States v. Wells Fargo Bank, C. A. No. CT-2-98-RHS (N. D. Cal. filed January 17, 1972).

V

**MULTINATIONAL
FIRMS AND
DEVELOPING
COUNTRIES**

11

MULTINATIONAL ENTERPRISES IN DEVELOPING COUNTRIES: SOME ISSUES IN THE MANUFACTURING SECTOR

Walter A. Chudson

It is risky to draw sharp distinctions between sectors of economic activity or categories of countries, whatever may be the subject of discussion. However one interprets reports of the death of Adam Smith, or of Karl Marx for that matter, we have grown accustomed to economic policies that acknowledge a mixture of "market forces" and public intervention for various ends. This applies to policies affecting the multinational enterprise or—more broadly— to various forms of foreign business participation in production in so-called host countries. And we see that in a world of rapidly changing national and international economic policies, labels change their significance with surprising speed. We see, for example, that some socialist countries of Eastern Europe welcome joint equity investments; and we see a few—admittedly rare—specimens in which such countries enter into partnership on an equity basis with local public enterprises in developing countries. In the developing world, certainly, many shades of gray is the dominant color of fashion.

Nevertheless, I submit that there is some use in drawing certain distinctions implied in the title of this chapter:

1. The issues posed by the interaction of multinational enterprises with developing countries are different in nature and severity from the more balanced relationships typical of the developed or industrial countries.

2. The involvement of a manufacturing affiliate of a multinational firm raises a number of issues that are sufficiently different from those raised by a comparable involvement in mineral development as to warrant separate attention.

Walter A. Chudson is Adviser on Foreign Investment, Department of Economic Affairs, United Nations, New York. The views expressed do not necessarily represent those of the Secretary-General of the United Nations.

129

THE SPECIAL PROBLEMS
OF DEVELOPING COUNTRIES

With regard to the first point, it would be misleading to imply that relations among sovereign states in the industrial world in regard to the penetration of multinational firms are untroubled. And as the barriers to trade are, hopefully, further lowered, the impact of national industrial policies will surely touch many tender spots and give rise to pain and anguish to many parent firms operating within this group of countries. Yet one has only to think of the kind of issues preoccupying the EEC or OECD membership to realize that these are not in general likely to lead to major confrontations—unless they should be used as pawns in a larger game of international economic policy. I refer to such matters as tax evasion and tax duplication; disparities in subsidy policy; disparities in antitrust policies; problems of disclosure of corporate information; the assertion of extraterritorial jurisdiction; adjustment of the impact on labor of production and investment decisions within the group of countries, and the like. Sensitive as these issues are, the growing interpenetration of industrial investment (the reduced dominance of U. S. firms) and the apparent narrowing of the technological gap as compared with the technological chasm faced by the developing countries suggest that among the countries of Europe, North America, Japan, and the OECD membership generally, the advantage of avoiding a bellum omnium contra omnes will be appreciated and in due course form the basis for some form of multilateral system of common policy.

I do not suggest that the developing countries do not see problems with multinational enterprises and vice-versa that may lend themselves to some sort of international action. But those that rank high, notably the settlement of investment disputes, offer little likelihood of near-term action, while a number of those listed above appear to be of second priority. Between various types of forums that may serve as the scene of international action on the one hand, and measures strictly under the control of the developing host country on the other, there is quite a range of possibilities. But the preoccupations of the developing countries with the phenomenon of external control and the inherent tendency to judge the performance of the multinational enterprise—at least in its nonpolitical dimension—in terms of the economic impact on the host country, in the context of major structural change, directs their attention to the goal of maximizing the benefit-cost balance as best they can judge it. Pie-baking and pie-slicing are the predominant concerns that underlie their policy toward foreign business participation.

First, however, a word about minerals vs. manufacturing as the focus for host-country policy.* It seems safe to say that direct investment in mineral development (and in plantation agriculture) has been the most contentious and unstable of all those involving multinational operations. Apart from the mystique of depleting assets and the political and economic impact of enclave operations of typically large-scale projects, reinforced by the insecurity of dependency on a single export sold often in an unstable world market, the development of tension in minerals seems to reflect the inescapable dynamics of mineral exploration, discovery, and exploitation.

Studies have shown that concession agreements in large natural resource projects have tended to go through a predictable evolution, reflecting changes in the relative bargaining positions of the foreign investors and the host governments.† The typical history has involved overgenerous concessions to induce exploration and initial investment, followed by demands for renegotiation or expropriation once the reserves are located and the heavy investments completed. After the fact, all large natural resource concessions appear to have been written in terms highly favorable to the foreign investor.

What is needed and is being increasingly arranged is a formula that provides compensation to the foreign firm for the initial risk and then, in the event of successful exploitation, a formula for sharing the benefits on a long-term basis. This may take the form of a procedure for renegotiating a concession agreement or of a variety of contractual arrangements in which the foreign firm is essentially an agent rather than a principal (as in petroleum). But the point is that initial bargaining for terms that would be in theory applicable for 20 or 40 or more years is unrealistic.

These transformations are not lacking in manufacturing projects, but the shifting of the balance occurs over a longer time and the element of uncertainty is generally so much less as to change the climate of negotiation and balance between the ex-ante and ex-post relations. To be sure, there is some parallel in the local disenchantment that sets in when a manufacturing project has been established behind a high wall of protection and remits large profits derived from sheltered production for the local market.

----

*The rest of this chapter concentrates on manufactures, but many of the points would apply to certain service industries; and it is, of course, understood that sometimes excluded sectors (banking, insurance, publications, etc.) and agricultural projects have special features.

†I am indebted particularly to the work of Theodore H. Moran, Louis T. Wells, Jr., and Raymond Mikesell.

INDUSTRIAL POLICY AND FOREIGN INVESTMENT

The current preoccupation of host countries about foreign investment in manufacturing can be better understood by a brief backward look. The rather frenzied days of extreme import-substitution in the 1950s and early 1960s have passed and governments are in a better position to face the question: How can the multinational enterprise or—more broadly—various forms of foreign business participation fit into the framework of the national industrial policy?

Putting it in other terms, how can the social cost-benefit balance of foreign participation be measured so as to determine the optimal degree, form, and conditions of foreign participation? And how can the operations of the foreign enterprise, once established, be controlled so as to extract the maximum benefit for the host country? Implicitly, of course, this assumes a nonzero-sum game that confers benefits on both host country and investor while minimizing the tensions that may be generated in the process.

A major question is whether the inputs that are combined in a direct investment (capital, technology, management, and marketing links) can be obtained more cheaply and with greater net benefit through some alternative arrangement—through licensing, management contracts, hiring of expatriate personnel, engineering contracts for "turnkey" plants, or equipment purchase. Considerable stimulus has been given to this inquiry by the precedent of new contractual arrangements for organizing mineral projects. The object in that case was to find formulas that supplied scarce foreign talent in such a way that many of the tensions of foreign ownership, foreign control, subsoil rights, and threats to sovereignty did not arise. This led to extensive use of management contracts, service contracts, and joint ventures designed to reduce political tension while providing the lacking inputs.

FOREIGN INVESTMENT AND THE ACQUISITION OF TECHNOLOGY

The fact that direct investment, the predominant form of multinational enterprise, supplies technology as a major ingredient has come increasingly to the fore. The origin and nature of this technology and its economic implications occupies a central position in the complex of policy issues arising between the multinational firm and the host country.

The juxtaposition of those two Hellenic words—technology and oligopoly—in fact, provides an effective handle by which to grasp many of the issues arising between host countries and foreign business participants. Together they explain the love-hate relationship between host country and foreign business participant.

Technology is the key that promises to unlock the door to development; but the key is seen to be held in the hands of the oligopolistic multi-national firm offering a Faustian bargain at the expense of the continued dependence of the structurally weak host country. When to this mixture is added a touch of economic development planning, a pinch or more of nationalism, and a soupcon of vertically integrated or horizontally organized international production, the cauldron is not unlikely to reach a lively bubble.

Capital is also not typically in short supply, but in a wide range of manufacturing activities the active ingredient, as the pharmacologists say, is not capital but technology in the broad sense—let us call it managed technology. From this arises the dependency of the host country and its obverse, the external control that underlies so much of the negotiating and regulatory policies increasingly practiced by developing countries.

Numerous efforts have been made to establish a rough typology of foreign investments in order to distinguish the degree of dependence, the motivations, and the interaction between investors and host governments. Such classification should assist in defining potential cost-benefit balances of specific projects and in helping the host country to conduct an efficient negotiating policy before entry and an optimum policy of ensuring the maximum benefits from the subsequent operation of the enterprise. The division of enterprises into export-oriented and import-substituting has obvious use; and within exported-oriented projects, it seems significant to distinguish an affiliate in a worldwide vertically integrated system based on high technology (electronics, pharmaceuticals, automobiles) from an industry primarily engaged in processing local raw material for export.

The nature of the industrial sector is obviously an important variable in determining external dependence and also the feasible alternative forms of foreign business participation. Iron and steel, textiles, cement—these are not industries in which one encounters the problems that fill the catalog of complaints of external dependence and control expressed by host countries.

In brief, one dimension of a national policy toward foreign investment in developing countries should be an awareness of the supply conditions in the world market for technology in the broad sense. Naturally, this knowledge—call it consumers' intelligence if you will—must be interpreted against the background of the host country's industrial potential and policies. In the remainder of this chapter I propose to deal with a few aspects of interaction between the demand and supply side of this market for technology. At this stage, however, I think it is useful to state the major issue, as I see it: To what extent can these matters best be settled by policies applicable generally to all incoming investments or at least broad categories of investments, or to what extent is case-by-case negotiation of incoming investments useful in order to secure the optimum social benefit for the host country?

The question of bargaining for tariff protection is discussed separately below. Clearly the level of protection should be related to the country's general commercial and industrial policy, not to the question of foreign ownership per se. The same could be said of tax policies, access to local credit, and similar broad issues. But there is the fact that the relationship between the parties is subject to the oligopolistic pressures deriving from proprietary technology and product differentiation. How wide a bargaining range is produced by this situation will vary greatly with several factors. But the point is that there are monopoly rents to be squeezed and that the squeezing relates not just to sharing profits (otherwise the matter could be regulated by limiting the bargaining to royalty rates and a few other stipulations) but to a variety of conditions of production, with numerous side effects and independent long-term values from the point of view of the host country. Just how far to go in this barking-at-the-heels approach to the multinational enterprise remains a question of art for which no objective guidelines are discernible. Certainly, there is a danger that host governments will become excessively distracted with petty issues and lose the vision of the whole.

PROJECT APPRAISAL AND
FOREIGN INVESTMENT POLICY

Because the calculation of the private rate of return on an investment is a satisfactory indicator of its real contribution to economic output only if market prices of inputs and outputs reflect their true opportunity cost, government authorities are increasingly turning to some form of systematic project appraisal as a means of combining in a single calculation various economic criteria that indicate those projects that can increase output as much as possible, using abundant resources (such as labor) intensively and economizing on scarce resources (such as financial and skilled human capital and foreign exchange). This analysis should properly take account of alternative technologies, scale of operation, and other alternative conditions of production and marketing. The calculation should, of course, include the foreign cost of capital and technology compared with the local opportunity cost or "shadow price."

Granted that an agreed system of project appraisal is an essential ingredient of long-term industrial strategy, the question remains what weight to give to political, social, and even cultural considerations—the impact on income distribution, regional location, externalities of various kinds, including displacement or stimulus of local entrepreneurship, savings, and investment. These matters are not amenable to the planner's calculus; ranking projects according to their contribution to objectively measurable economic criteria is quite different from introducing highly arbitrary assumptions about the relative importance of political and other values. Such matters must therefore be left for political decision.

After much trial and not a little error, the role of industrialization in the development process is being seen more clearly in developing countries. There seems to be a convergence in academic and government thinking—sometimes ominously labeled "the new orthodoxy."

One lesson has been learned but applied more in the breach: the importance of enlarging markets by regional cooperation in order to achieve economics of scale. Another lesson learned at heavy cost has been the dead or bitter end of excessive import-substitution. With this has come a new vision: export-oriented industrialization. But this vision is not without some growing apprehension that the early success stories may be harder to repeat in a protectionist world and, more relevant here, not without skepticism that the lion's share of the gains (oligopoly rents) from the new international division of labor represented by this form of vertically integrated production will be reaped by the scarce cooperant factors—the technology, capital, management—supplied by the multinational enterprise, while the superabundant local labor embodied in the exported subassemblies and consumers' goods will be rewarded at the competitive price. This is essentially an issue of collective bargaining with an international dimension, which will have to be left for another discussion.

Project appraisal or cost-benefit analysis is a preliminary step to the analysis of bargaining scope and final negotiation with the foreign investor. The former determines whether the project is at all worth bargaining about. The latter seeks a more advantageous division of the gain for the host country within a perceived bargaining range.

In many developing countries the most crucial aspect in evaluating foreign investment projects is the country's commercial policy together with its foreign exchange policy as expressed in a typically overvalued exchange rate. These two elements provide in effect a subsidy to firms manufacturing for the domestic market, which must be paid for by the rest of the economy; putting it otherwise, they frustrate the policy of generating foreign exchange at minimal social cost. Excessive protection provides a subsidy from which foreign firms frequently benefit most because they account for the major part of industrial production in many countries; they are followed in this respect by the local capitalist and the wage earner in the manufacturing sector—all enjoying monopoly rents at the expense of agricultural producers. In other words, the profits earned in manufacturing are enhanced by providing imported inputs at low cost (through overvaluation of the exchange rate and through duty-free importation) while sales prices are protected behind extremely high import barriers. When profits are repatriated, the real loss to the national income attributable to the project is even greater than it would be if the same "sick" industry were locally owned.

This circumstance also tends to make imported capital equipment abnormally cheap and to reduce the private incentive to adopt labor-intensive technology.

Much of the criticism of foreign investment in a number of developing countries is traceable to the commercial policy described. In a large portion of cases studied by UNCTAD recently a negative contribution to national income by specific foreign investments is simply explained by this one factor.

The solution to the problem is, of course, a reform of commercial policy, not of policy toward foreign investment as such. Adoption of a more uniform level of duties and the equivalent (including imposition of duties on intermediate goods) and a parallel incentive to exports would have the salutary effect of screening out socially unproductive foreign investment and encouraging socially productive investments now unprofitable. This step would mean a substantial convergence between the market profitability and the social profitability of investments, including foreign investments. Of particular importance, the need for a special system of project appraisal to "screen" foreign investments in terms of their social cost-benefit would be much less.

If countries are not prepared to introduce such reforms, the next best solution is to appraise projects using a shadow price for foreign exchange, as well as for capital, unskilled labor, skilled labor and managers, and selected domestic outputs. However complex this may seem, it is far more efficient than the pragmatic tests often applied by governments to foreign investments in terms of their net contribution to foreign exchange, employment, and domestic value added. If made with even roughly accurate shadow prices, this appraisal should ensure the rejection of all projects that do not give a return to national resources at least equal to the opportunity cost of domestic capital. By incorporating the actual cost of foreign inputs, the net benefit of foreign participation can be compared with the alternative of using domestic inputs (socially valued at their opportunity cost).

CHOICE OF TECHNOLOGY

Preoccupation with unemployment in developing countries continues to attract attention to the classical issue of choice of technology in relation to factor prices. The industrialist, particularly the foreign industrialist, is accused of selecting manufacturing processes that are excessively capital-intensive, reflecting factor prices in the industrialized world.

Technological constraints on factor substitution vary greatly from one industrial process to another and among sectors, such as manufacturing, earth moving, and construction. Also, additional problems arise from differences in scale. Some industries in developing countries contain plants of a suboptimal scale, sheltered behind tariff walls and operating at high social cost. Nevertheless, these plants may be more labor-intensive than their counterparts in larger markets as a result of the technology associated with small plants, not as a response to factor-price differentials.

But we are interested here not in the nature of the firm's behavior but in the performance of the multinational enterprise as such. Still scarce evidence suggests that the predominant factors influencing choice of technology by the multinational firm are scale of operations and competitiveness of environment. Removal of the influence of scale and of the ability to avoid price competition tend to leave the multinational and local firms with similar technologies in comparable industries. Some evidence also indicates that the multinational enterprise tends to use more labor-intensive second-hand machinery than a domestic firm in a developing country because of procurement capacity. Also, case studies reveal the apparent paradox that foreign firms use more labor-intensive methods in ancillary functions of manufacturing (packaging, materials, handling) because of more efficient management.

If the above diagnosis is correct, the implication is that many developing host countries are not likely to influence technology simply by changing factor costs (through subsidies, tariff changes, taxation, or other general policy instruments). To the extent that technical conditions would make factor-substitution economic, bringing differences in factor-price relations to bear on technological adaptation seems to require a number of steps: a strengthened competitive climate to exert pressure on the multinational as well as the local firm; encouraging the acquisition of second-hand machinery; modifying labor laws that tend to raise relative labor costs unduly. But given such conditions, attention should then be paid to the effectiveness of different approaches to influencing the private costs to the firm of labor and capital.

NEW PRODUCTS AND THE PRODUCT MIX

It is not realistic to expect that relieving unemployment in developing countries can be carried out by the growth of manufacturing or that the industrial sector will absorb the full increase in the labor force or all the existing unemployed. Nor is it to be expected that a large part of the burden of relieving unemployment in developing countries can be carried out by technological change in the modern sector of manufacturing. Nevertheless, there is evidence of a response by multinational enterprises to develop products that fit the markets and relative factor prices of the developing countries.

But the basic motivation of such action understandably has been the existence of a large or attractive prospective market and the related fear of competitive action by rival firms. The question of why multinational firms do not decentralize research and development more than they do remains an issue of contention. Stated in its sharpest terms, the failure to develop a local R&D capacity in the developing countries is seen as evidence that the phrase "transfer of technology" is a sham, since the capability for independent technical action remains generally so limited. This ultimately must be seen as a question of national science and technology policy, and of the educational system and other types of institution-building in developing countries. To refer the problem to the multinational corporation seems to direct it to the wrong address.

HIDDEN COSTS OF TECHNOLOGY

In the developing countries the concept of the cost of foreign investment to the host country and of the technological component in particular has long since left the realm of conventional corporate accounting. One category of such "costs" is macro-economic in character, seen by some analysts as the obverse of the conventionally praised positive macro-economic effects of direct investment. The list is long; the multinational enterprise provides capital but may discourage domestic savings (if savings are limited by investment opportunities and these themselves are limited); the contribution to public revenue may be partially offset by tax concessions; it may stifle local entrepreneurs (infant entrepreneur theory); it may be the vehicle for setting wage levels at even higher than usual disequilibrium levels; it is the vehicle for introducing tastes that affect the product mix in an undesirable way. The list could be extended. The list of complaints is as long as any list that might be drawn against oligopoly behavior in any country plus the concerns about displacement by foreign affiliates of local resources, actual or potential. They may be exaggerated, but a system of project appraisal must either confront them in some way when measuring the externalities of the project or take the position that the social cost-benefit analysis will take care of the most important part of the impact of foreign investment on the host economy.

Aside from these macro-economic concerns, there are some more specific problems of which a few deserve mention.

The effort of developing countries to evaluate proposals for the supply of technology through whatever transfer mechanism and the attempt of host governments to administer customs, tax, and exchange regulations are both complicated by the nature of the transactions between the foreign firm and the recipient enterprise in the host country. Transactions such as the pricing of goods and services exchanged between the foreign parent and its domestic affiliate, the provision of financing by the parent in the form of debt, and charges for royalties are particularly contentious issues because of problems of disclosure, measurement, and regulation.

Of all these, perhaps the issue of transfer pricing proves the most contentious, particularly in the event of presumptive over-invoicing of imports by local manufacturing affiliates. While the understanding of the motivation for such practices by multinational enterprises has grown, there has not been a parallel growth of evidence on the extent of such practices. There has, however, been some development of thinking and action about national or international action to defuse this issue.

Several developing countries have instituted systems of monitoring invoice prices of a substantial part of their imports and some of their exports. In some cases the primary object has been the policing of capital exports by residents, but the policing of intrafirm transactions of multinational firms has been included. An obvious problem is the determination of the "arm's length" or reference price by which the extent of overinvoicing is to be judged. Some countries are monitoring prices at the port of embarkation using the services of a worldwide cargo inspection agency, for which they pay a substantial price, incidentally. The knowledge that such a check will be made and that shipments may be blocked unless satisfactory justification of deviations from arm's length prices is furnished should serve as a healthy deterrent.

Other procedures at the national level are possible and a few have been instituted. The checking of invoices can be done by national customs authorities—subject admittedly to all the vagaries and pitfalls of regulatory action in such circumstances. The income tax authorities of the host country can require an audit of intrafirm transactions perhaps on a sample basis. In some cases where imported intermediate inputs are fairly standardized the reference price or a price-formula might be prearranged.

The incentive to shift profits from the normal profit account to an overinvoiced imported input is less when the level of import duties is higher. If a developing country raises duties on intermediate imports to introduce a more uniform treatment among all categories of imports (primarily in order to reduce exploitation of the farm population), one by-product should be a lessened tendency by multinational firms to overinvoice imports. This has been paralleled in a number of countries by tightening concessions in the form of duty-free imports by such firms. A similar tendency is the introduction or imposition of higher withholding taxes on royalties, management fees, and similar charges by parent enterprises. The logic of all these actions—apart from the allocation of national resources to their most productive use at the margin—is to obtain the maximum local share of profits in a situation of bilateral monopoly.

Other issues in the category of hidden costs are the territorial allocation of export markets and restrictive business practices involving such matters as tied purchases, price and production restrictions on licensees, and so on. Short of international action outlawing or regulating such practices (a possibility that can hardly be regarded as imminent), the strongest defense a host country can erect against such practices is the enforcement of antitrust measures and the monitoring of contracts and performance by government agencies.

THE EVOLUTION OF NATIONAL POLICY TOWARD
FOREIGN BUSINESS PARTICIPATION

During recent years the role of foreign business participation in developing countries has been scrutinized and appraised with an intensity that is unprecedented. Despite a number of conflicts, nationalizations, expropriations, and other traumatic incidents, it seems that the intensity of the scrutiny should be interpreted as a genuine concern, for the most part, to devise ways and means by which foreign business participation can be integrated into a national policy of industrial development with maximum benefit to the host country.

It would be unrealistic to eliminate from this seemingly rationalist approach the political, social, cultural, and even ideological dimensions. But at least there is some reason to expect that the price of pursuing the noneconomic objectives can be more clearly seen against the background of objective appraisals of the economics of foreign investment projects. And it may be hoped that the intense—some might even say fanatic—explorations that are being pursued into all the nooks and crannies of oligopolistic behavior will in the end result in eliminating some of the mystery and awe with which the operations of multinational corporations are regarded.

There is, of course, another view—which one may perhaps label Galbraithian—that proceeds from the notion that the multinational corporation, being simply the international extension of big business and its technostructure, must be judged to have all the shortcomings of its national progenitor plus a few other unpleasant attributes resulting from its partial escape from national sovereignty. Worse still, these attributes become even more unappetizing when the relationship is between the multinational enterprise and a developing country seen as occupying a status of peripheral tutelage. Thus, the multinational corporation in its present form is judged unsafe at any speed. Short of a radical transformation of the national economy of the home country, there is no acceptable alternative revealed by the diagnosticians of this school. In other words, the blueprint for the international economic structure of a world of socialist nation-states (not, be it noted, a world federation with principles of international equity built in) has been left for the future to define.

Such visions aside, for most developing countries, sufficient unto the day is the foreign oligopoly thereof. It is this reality that must be coped with to obtain the inputs of capital, technology, management, and marketing whose value is being judged in specific terms. For such countries the modus vivendi is expressed in several ways. Perhaps the most general is bargaining power or negotiating capability. Related to this is the concept of exploring ways and means by which the desired foreign inputs can with advantage be obtained in forms that reduce the cost and enhance certain national objectives, particularly a higher degree of local control, however that rather mysterious word may be defined.

The outcome of this probing by host countries is not likely to be a uniform pattern of policy and regulations, no matter how enticing such formulas as the Andean Pact may seem. The significance of such formulae as Article 24 is probably not so much in the specifics but in the spirit of negotiation and control it implies. Countries with a strong administration of the "commanding heights" of public policy are likely to be less inclined to negotiate over such a long list of items when settling the terms of foreign participation in a new project. Their reasoning will presumably be that the optimum sharing of the pie will accrue through taxation, growth of output, employment, training, and the like without an attempt to define too thoroughly specific performance by the enterprise in question.

The execution of this kind of policy calls for two important instruments. One is information. The other is the capability to use this information in judging the costs and benefits of alternative ways of acquiring the desired foreign inputs.

It would be rash to say that getting information about foreign inputs presents no problem to developing countries. But it is the sort of problem at which a government can work singly or collectively with a prospect of accomplishment. Increasingly, therefore, we find developing countries seeking to learn as much as possible about the costs and benefits of joint ventures, management contracts, licensing, and turnkey projects. In this process they are learning that whatever the transfer mechanism may be, the international market for technology is an imperfect one, both in the sense of the price (including the hidden costs) and the quality of the technology supplied, including various externalities. They are learning also that the competitive conditions under which technology can be obtained from commercial sources varies with the branch of industry and changes over time not only with the increased number of sources throughout the world but also with the absorptive capacity of the host country.

In other terms, the developing countries are seeking to improve their ability to measure the net social benefit of individual projects (when social and private costs and benefits diverge) and to strengthen their capacity to deal with oligopolistic enterprises. At the same time, they are facing the problem of improving their capacity to absorb technology and, if conditions warrant, to displace foreign inputs by local resources at lower social cost.

The above appraisal ignores the role of international action in two senses, both of which are currently being explored by an ad hoc United Nations group, under a mandate to report its recommendations to the General Assembly.

One is what might be called international action pure and simple. This refers to various agreed rules, guidelines, GATT-like codes, or, even at the lowest level, rules of procedure to discuss problems of mutual interest in an international forum. Apart from the willingness of governments to meet in an international forum with a certain input of information to consider ("the lowest common forum"), there seem to be a few topics that lend themselves to politically acceptable treatment in the foreseeable future. One is the subject of international taxation. In this matter both developed and developing countries may have sufficient mutuality of interest to support the formulation of commonly agreed principles and a mechanism for information gathering and cooperation among national tax authorities. Some contribution might be made in this way to the definition of taxable income in the various national jurisdictions and thus to the solution of the transfer-price problem.

Another subject that may lend itself to international surveillance of some sort is restrictive business practices. More difficult is the prospect of a procedure for the settlement of investment disputes. To go beyond the existing rather weak machinery for voluntary submission to arbitration provided by the International Centre for the Settlement of Investment Disputes, one would probably need some balanced commitment by the industrial countries—acceptance of the Calvo doctrine, for example—as a quid pro quo for agreement on the part of host countries to abide by some principles of minimum rights for the local subsidiary.

I pass by other visions of international cooperation, such as that advocated by Jack Behrman, proposing a form of coordinated international investment planning by governments utilizing the multinational enterprise as its chosen instrument.

My conclusion is that the focus of action, for some time, will remain largely with the national measures that can be taken by host countries (at the national or perhaps regional level). The main burden will fall upon the host countries themselves. But such action can be substantially supported by information, research, technical assistance, and advisory services from neutral agencies, of which the United Nations is the major example.

12

MANAGEMENT PRACTICES
OF MULTINATIONAL
CORPORATIONS AND
HOST GOVERNMENT
POLICIES

Anant R. Negandhi

In recent years increasing attention is being directed on the issue of the impact of multinational corporations on national economy, employment, balance of payments, antitrust provisions, security regulations, national identity, and social and economic development plans of host countries.

The multinational corporation also has been recognized by many as the most efficient and enlightened entity for generating economic and industrial growth and providing advanced technology and management know-how in developing countries. However, as Emile Benoit has remarked:

> These are unhappy days for U. S. multinational companies. Widely criticized at home for "exporting jobs" and undermining the U. S. balance of payments, they are criticized just as severely abroad for exploiting underpaid foreign labor, using monopoly power and preferential access to cheap or costless capital to crush or buy out local competitors.[1]

Although the arguments on the positive and negative impact of the multinational corporation have generated a rather voluminous literature, few systematic studies seem to be forthcoming that will enable one to examine the specific impact of the multinational corporation on the various issues raised above. Particularly, the studies examining the micro or organizational practices of the multinational corporation in host countries are largely lacking.

Anant R. Negandhi is Professor of Administrative Sciences and International Business, Kent State University.

It is true that many of the controversial issues concerning the impact of the MNC are at the policy level. However, the policies are merely guidelines to decision making and provide a framework for organizational practices at the micro level. The examination of organizational practices of the subsidiaries thus can be helpful to explore the implications of various corporate policies on host countries.

CONFLICTS BETWEEN MNCs AND NATION-STATES

The purpose of this chapter is, therefore, to explore the potential and actual conflict that may exist between the objectives and aspirations of the nation-states and the multinational corporations. As stated earlier, this will be done through the examination of organizational practices of the subsidiaries operating overseas. A large-scale cross-cultural management study undertaken in six developing countries (Argentina, Brazil, India, the Phillipines, Taiwan, and Uruguay) provided some data to explore a few of the issues raised above. Specifically, the following aspects have been examined in some detail:

- The overall "behavior" of multinational corporations
- The impact of multinational corporations in transferring advanced management practices to developing countries
- The role of the multinational corporation in increasing research and development (R&D) activities in developing countries
- The impact of multinational corporations in developing human resources (managerial personnel in particular) in the host countries

A total of 56 U. S. subsidiaries and 55 local firms as well as 15 U. S. parent companies were examined with respect to their policies, practices, and effectiveness.[2] The background data on these companies were obtained from published records. The information on management policies, practices, and effectiveness was gathered through personal interviews with executives and other employees. A 40-page interview guide was utilized. On an average, 15 persons in each firm were interviewed. One to three days were spent in each firm. Group interviews were held in preliminary sessions, followed by an intensive interview with each individual executive. The persons interviewed held these positions: chairman or president, board of directors, general manager, directors of marketing, sales, production, finance, and personnel, and chief accountant or controller. These interviews were conducted during the period of January 1966 to December 1970.

THE BEHAVIOR OF MULTINATIONAL
CORPORATIONS ABROAD

One of the main issues of conflict involving the nation-states and the multinational corporations is concerning their behavior in the host countries. The most challenging charges made by some of the developing countries is that the U. S.-based corporations are the agents of the U. S. government and are working against the goals and objectives of the host countries. It also is being argued that the multinational corporations are not "behaving" as good citizens. Frank Shaker, for example, seems to have reflected the sentiments of many developing countries:

However zealously the advocates of the multinational corporation may promote its virtues, there is basically no such thing as a truly international corporation. The subsidiary owes its allegiance to corporate headquarters in the United States from whom it takes its orders and by which it is guided accordingly. While the corporation itself wields powerful political influence, it is at the same time an instrument of U. S. foreign policy. Nation-states will not long tolerate foreign control and domination of their industries and other economic institutions. Developing nations are seeking their own patterns of development for their society and are reassessing their positions vis-a-vis the international corporation.[3]

As we are witnessing the cases of ITT and other utility and mining companies in Latin America, the above charges are not entirely without foundation. However, these instances seem to be exceptions rather than the rule. Our intensive interviews with executives of both U. S. and local firms, community leaders, and government officials in the six developing countries indicated that the executives of U. S. subsidiaries were largely apolitical in nature. The executives themselves felt that the U. S. government was helping them least in their plight against host-government policies. In this respect our findings concur with those of Claude McMillan et al. in Brazil. Almost a decade ago they observed

that the U. S. government is the tool of U. S. business seems incredible to the American corporation manager whose complaints receive little more than polite attention in the U. S. State Department. At no other time in history has a government been so indifferent to how its private sector fared abroad, and in no other part of the free world today is a nation's private business used so sparingly to gain political objectives.[4]

Concerning the citizenry issue, we made some attempts to examine the nature of attitudes and perceptions of executives of the U. S. subsidiaries toward various important "publics." These include employees, consumers, suppliers, distributors, stockholders, government, and the community.

To examine these attitudes and perceptions, we first consulted the published documents and manuals of the companies studied. Then we interviewed 15 to 20 executives of each company. This was followed up by interviews with selected "publics" or the task agents themselves. In all of these interviews we sought to obtain the actual "feelings" of the executives toward the various publics mentioned above.

To evaluate the overall attitudes of the companies toward their publics, we assigned numerical values with respect to the intensity of concern shown by the executives. This is shown in Figure 12.1. The following three descriptive categories were created to group the companies studied:

Category	Total Score
High concern toward publics	75-100
Some concern toward publics	40-74
Low concern toward publics	0-39

As shown in Table 12.1, U. S. subsidiaries in developing countries were no worse than their local counterparts with respect to their attitudes toward publics. In fact, they were somewhat better. Only three U. S. subsidiaries exhibited a negative attitude toward publics. There were ten comparable local companies in this category.

ORGANIZATIONAL PRACTICES
OF U. S. SUBSIDIARIES

In this section the nature of management practices and effectiveness of U. S. subsidiaries in developing countries will be reviewed briefly. Our aim of so doing is to examine whether the U. S. subsidiaries are becoming the agent for transferring advanced management practices to those countries. The detailed analyses of results obtained in this study are reported elsewhere.[5] In the main, the managerial practices concerning planning, controlling, organizing, leading, and staffing will be studied.

Long-range planning of a five- to ten-year duration was a common practice of U. S. subsidiaries in the six developing countries. The typical U. S. subsidiary also formulated its long-range plans in full detail and involved all levels of managerial, technical, and supervisory personnel in the planning process. The policy-making

FIGURE 12.1

Ranking Scale for Concern toward
Task Environmental Agents

	Much or Very	Mild	Little or No
Employee	Much Concern	Concern	Concern
	20	10	0
Consumer	Consumer, The King	Consumer, A Necessary Agent	Consumer, Passive Agent
	20	10	0
Community	Much or Very Much Concern	Some Concern	Little or No Concern
	10	5	0
Government	Good Partner	A Necessary Evil	Government Be Damned
	15	5	0
Supplier	Good Relationship Absolutely Necessary	Good Relationship Helpful	Relationship A Necessary Evil
	15	7.5	0
Distributor	Good Relationship Absolutely Necessary	Relationship Helpful	Relationship A Necessary Evil
	15	7.5	0
Stockholder	Owners, Masters, Good Public Relation Personnel	Owners, Masters Only	Profit-eaters
	10	5	0

Two persons were involved in interviewing and evaluating published documents. Each of them independently evaluated the information collected to rank each firm's concern toward its task groups. The greatest difference between the two interviewers did not exceed eight points out of a possible 100 points. The two interviewers' scores were averaged to obtain the final score for each firm.

For details on methodology and scaling, see A. R. Negandhi and S. B. Prasad, Comparative Management (New York: Appleton-Century-Crofts, 1971), pp. 19-33.

TABLE 12.1

Organizational Concern of U. S. Subsidiaries
and Local Firms in Six Developing Countries

Organizational Concern toward Publics	U. S. Subsidiaries (n = 56)	Local Firms (n = 55)
High concern	14	12
Some concern	39	33
Low concern	3	10

Source: Compiled by the author.

task was taken quite seriously by this type of firm. Efforts were
made to use major policies effectively, both as guidelines and as
instruments of an overall control to achieve the firm's objectives.
Major policies were made by top-level executives, but, in their
formulation, all levels of managerial and technical personnel were
consulted and their views considered. These policies were generally
concentrated in the areas of pricing, personnel selection, plant
investment, and salary and wage standards.

Employee training, employee relations, purchasing, acquisition,
and expansion received much less emphasis, however. Other control
devices used by the U. S. subsidiary included cost and budgetary
controls, quality control, the maintenance of equipment, and
setting of work standards for the blue-collar, supervisory, clerical,
and managerial personnel. Such techniques as periodic management
audit systems, however, were only used by a few of the U. S.
subsidiaries.

The U. S. subsidiary was organized on the basis of major
business functions: production, sales, accounting, and finance.
A typical firm had five to seven departments. Specialized staff
personnel were found frequently. Service and maintenance departments
were well organized.

Authority definition was clear for each position in the organization.
The degree of decentralization in decision making was greater in the
U. S. subsidiaries. Attitudes of the U. S. subsidiary's executives
regarding decentralization were only partially consistent with their
practices.

Leadership style used in the U. S. subsidiary can best be
characterized as democratic or consultative. Executives of the
U. S. subsidiary manifested a great deal of trust and confidence in
their subordinates. The attitudes of the executives of the U. S.
subsidiary were not totally consistent with their leadership styles.

Manpower management practices were well developed. The
personnel department was organized as a separate unit with a
specialized, trained personnel manager. Manpower management
policies were formally stated. Such personnel techniques as job
evaluation, development of selection, and promotion criteria for
managerial and technical personnel, and training programs for the
blue-collar employees were widely utilized. However, there was
not much sophistication in compensation and motivational techniques
and practices.

Managerial effectiveness, in terms of handling human resources,
was found "excellent" in some aspects and "poor" in others. For
example, while the typical U. S. subsidiary did not find it difficult
to attain high employee morale, it experienced some difficulties in
motivating its employees. Particularly, absenteeism was a problem.
Employee productivity was average and scrap loss was higher as
compared to the U. S. parent companies.

With regard to high-level manpower, the U. S. subsidiary
was able to attract and retain trained managerial and technical
personnel and was able to achieve cooperative departmental
relationships. It was also able to utilize effectively its high-level
manpower and adopt and respond to environmental changes without
much difficulty. By and large, the U. S. subsidiary made good
profits and was expanding its sales considerably (three- to fivefold
on average).

The overall profile of management practices and effectiveness
of the U. S. subsidiary as well as the local firm is outlined in
Table 12.2.

Although this overall profile of management practices and
effectiveness represents a dominant picture of the actual situation
in those developing countries, it does cover up many significant
interfirm differences.

UTILIZATION OF ADVANCED
MANAGEMENT PRACTICES

Table 12.3 indicates the proportions of the U. S. subsidiaries
and local firms that are able to utilize certain elements of advanced
management practices. For example, data presented in this table
show that 70 percent of the U. S. subsidiaries, versus 33 percent
of the counterpart local firms, in the two regions are undertaking
comprehensive planning. Similarly, 58 percent of the former
companies, as against 25 percent of the latter firms, have introduced
formalized quality control for all or major products manufactured
by them. Manpower planning, however, has received the most
cursory treatment even in the U. S. subsidiaries. Merely 14 percent

TABLE 12.2

Profiles of Management Practices and
Effectiveness of the U. S. Subsidiary
and the Local Firm

Elements of Management Practices and Effectiveness	U. S. Subsidiary	Local Firm
1. Recruitment of potential managers	Formally and systematically done. Openminded on all potential sources for managerial personnel.	Done on ad hoc basis. Restricted to small group of family members or relatives and friends.
2. Recruitment of middle and senior managers	Formally and systematically done. Provided opportunity for advancement within the firm.	Done on ad hoc basis. No systematic attempt at providing opportunity for advancement within the firm.
3. Management education	Formally done. Regularly using outside training courses or personnel.	Done on irregular or ad hoc basis.
4. Attitudes toward management development	Visualized as necessary element in company's growth and survival.	Considered as unnecessary expenses.
5. Treatment of existing management	Continuous evaluation. Ready to demote or fire second-rate and promote young and qualified.	Little or no evaluation. Adherence to seniority.
6. Delegation by senior management	Delegate authority to subordinates.	Unwilling to delegate authority.
7. Management structure	Decentralized. Individual positions are well defined and specified. Organization charts and manuals are used.	Centralized. Individual positions are not well defined and authority line diffused. Organization charts not used widely.
8. Management communication	Free flow of communication encouraged and demanded.	A great deal of secrecy and hoarding of information at all levels.

(continued)

(Table 12.2 continued)

Elements of Management Practices and Effectiveness	U. S. Subsidiary	Local Firm
9. Use of management consultants	Used frequently.	Not used.
10. Interfirm comparison at home and overseas	Done on regular basis.	Not done at all or done on ad hoc basis.
11. Market share	Constant awareness of market share.	Not much concern.
12. Objective of firm	Growth and profits	Profits
13. Assessment of performance	Measured in terms of growth, long-term potential, human resources, profits, assets, and sales.	Measured in terms of short-term profits.
14. Diversification	Considered as desired objectives.	Undertaken as necessary evil.
15. Future of firm	Evaluated on long-term basis.	Evaluated on short-term or medium-term basis.
16. Long-range planning	Five- to ten-year duration. Systematic and formulized.	One- to two-year duration. Done on ad hoc basis.
17. Use of budgetary control	Used with considerable emphasis on its importance to the firm.	Done haphazardly with less emphasis on its importance for the firm.
18. Reviewing of operations	Regularly undertaken with feedback mechanism well developed.	Done on ad hoc basis with no feedback mechanism.
19. Capital budgeting	Regularly done.	Done on ad hoc basis or not done at all.
20. Policy making	Formally stated; utilized as guidelines and control measures.	Formally not stated; not utilized as guidelines and control measures.
21. Other control devices used	Quality control, cost and budgetary control, maintenance, setting of standards	Quality control, maintenance
22. Grouping of activities	On functional-area basis	On functional-area basis

Elements of Management Practices and Effectiveness	U. S. Subsidiary	Local Firm
23. Number of departments	Five to seven	Five to seven
24. Use of specialized staff	Some	None
25. Use of service department	Considerable	Some
26. Authority definition	Clear	Unclear
27. Degree of decentralization	High	Low
28. Leadership style	Consultative	Paternalistic-autocratic
29. Trust and confidence in subordinates	High	Low
30. Managers' attitudes toward leadership style and delegation	Would prefer autocratic style; authority should be held tight at the top	Would prefer consultative type
31. Manpower policies	Formally stated	Not formally stated
32. Organization of personnel department	Separate unit	Not separate unit
33. Job evaluation	Done	Done by very few
34. Development and selection of promotion criteria	Formally done	Done by some
35. Compensation and motivation	Monetary and nonmonetary	Mostly monetary
36. Employee morale	High	Moderate
37. Absenteeism	Average	High
38. Turnover	Low	Low
39. Productivity	Average to high	Low
40. Ability to attract trained personnel	Able to do so.	Somewhat able to do so.
41. Interdepartmental relationships	Very cooperative.	Somewhat cooperative to poor.

(continued)

(Table 12.2 continued)

Elements of Manage-ment Practices and Effectiveness	U. S. Subsidiary	Local Firm
42. Executives' perception of of the firm's overall objectives	Systems optimization as an important goal.	Subsystems optimization as an important goal.
43. Utilization of high-level manpower	Effectively utilized.	Poor utilization.
44. Adapting to environmental changes	Able to adapt with-out much difficulty.	Able to adapt with some difficulty.
45. Growth in sales	Phenomenal	Considerable to low
46. Relationship of sales to pro-duction	Production facilities are planned on cre-ating greater demands for the goods.	Production is based on serving short-supply market conditions (seller's market).
47. Advertising and public relations	Seen as useful in creating public image of the company.	Used only as a neces-sary evil.
48. Capacity, effi-ciency, and productivity	Assessed on regular basis.	No regular assessment.
49. Plant capacity	Utilized at the fullest possible level; regu-lar maintenance.	Utilized as seems appro-priate by top man without objective assessment. Irregular maintenance.
50. Buying function	Conceived as mana-gerial function.	Conceived as clerical function.
51. Suppliers	Conceived as part-ners in progress.	Conceived as a necessary evil.
52. Operational research techniques	Uses various tech-niques to optimize plant capacity.	Regards various techniques as status symbols rather than optimizing devices.
53. Creation of positive labor relations	Conceived as management responsibility.	Conceived as govern-ment/labor union responsibility
54. Assessment of good labor relations	Done on regular and systematic basis.	Done on ad hoc basis.
55. Grievance procedure	Carefully worked out, agreed by all parties and adhered to.	Roughly drawn up and not always followed.

Elements of Management Practices and Effectiveness	U. S. Subsidiary	Local Firm
56. Unions	Conceived as having constructive role to play.	Conceived as nuisance.
57. Workers' output	Belief that employees will give their best when treated as being responsible.	Belief that employees are lazy.
58. Personnel function	Conceived as top priority.	Conceived as clerical chaos.
59. Training and education of workforce	Conceived as necessary element of organizational activities; variety of training.	Conceived as a necessary evil. Mostly on-the-job training for the blue-collar employee.
60. Shortage of skilled labor and/or other labor	Not taken for granted. Action to train up semiskilled and unskilled personnel.	Acceptance of shortage of skilled employees as limiting factor.
61. Method of payment	Based on objective criteria. Attempts to pay higher than market rate.	Based on what they can get by with the minimum.
62. Employees	Conceived as resource.	Conceived as a necessary evil.
63. Relationship of research department to production	Close cooperation between two units.	Research department usually nonexistent, or if exists, operating as separate unit.
64. Problems of firm	Conceived as an opportunity to undertake cost-efficiency measures.	Conceived as fault of others: government, labor union, competition.
65. Unprofitable products	Ready to drop unless found useful for the long-range growth.	Unable to find out in the first place.
66. Competition	Conceived as healthy and necessary.	Conceived as unfair and destructive.

Source: The format of this table was adapted from A. Gater et al., Attitudes in British Management (Middlesex, England: Penguin Books Limited, 1964), pp. 207-13. For striking similarities in our findings with respect to the U. S. subsidiaries and local firms and their findings concerning "Thruster" and "Sleeper" firms, see ibid., pp. 207-30.

TABLE 12.3

Utilization of Advanced Management Practices in
U. S. Subsidiaries and Local Firms in the Two Regions:
Summary of Findings
(in percentages)

Elements of Advanced Management Practices and Effectiveness	Both Regions		Latin America		Far East		Firms With High Concern		Firms With Some and Low Concern	
	U. S. n = 56	Local n = 55	U. S. n = 20	Local n = 17	U. S. n = 36	Local n = 38	U. S. n = 14	Local n = 12	U. S. n = 42	Local n = 43
Planning Function										
Comprehensive planning	70	33	65	18	75	40	94	43	64	31
Long-range planning (5- to 10-year duration)	66	33	75	6	62	45	95	60	57	26
Considerable participation in planning process	66	35	55	36	71	40	76	60	60	28
Formalized and documented major policies	48	22	25	18	65	23	71	57	45	16

Elements of Advanced Management Practices and Effectiveness	Both Regions		Latin America		Far East		Firms With High Concern		Firms With Some and Low Concern	
	U.S. n = 56	Local n = 55	U.S. n = 20	Local n = 17	U.S. n = 36	Local n = 38	U.S. n = 14	Local n = 12	U.S. n = 42	Local n = 43
Formalized standard settings for production employees	73	52	60	52	83	57	82	92	73	44
Formalized standard settings for clerical and supervisory personnel	40	24	15	18	48	28	65	50	31	17
Formalized and systematic quality control for all or major products	58	25	60	26	57	27	80	75	50	12
Formalized and systematic cost control for all or major products	62	37	65	36	61	36	96	97	50	17
Formalized budgetary controls	52	37	30	23	64	45	97	97	39	24

(continued)

157

(Table 12.3 continued)

Elements of Advanced Management Practices and Effectiveness	Both Regions		Latin America		Far East		Firms With High Concern		Firms With Some and Low Concern	
	U.S. n = 56	Local n = 55	U.S. n = 20	Local n = 17	U.S. n = 36	Local n = 38	U.S. n = 14	Local n = 12	U.S. n = 42	Local n = 43
Formalized and systematic manpower planning	14	09	05	0	19	13	57	33	0	02
Formalized personnel policies	36	40	20	29	44	45	86	67	19	33
High "status" of personnel department	54	47	40	47	61	47	79	58	45	44
Formalized selection process	68	38	70	41	67	37	93	68	60	30
Formalized and systematic appraisal system	68	42	60	29	72	47	100	83	57	30
Formalized training programs for the blue-collar employees	50	65	NA	NA	50	95	79	92	41	58
Formalized training programs—supervisory personnel	52	53	NA	NA	81	76	86	92	41	42

Elements of Advanced Management Practices and Effectiveness	Both Regions		Latin America		Far East		Firms With High Concern		Firms With Some and Low Concern	
	U.S. n = 56	Local n = 55	U.S. n = 20	Local n = 17	U.S. n = 36	Local n = 38	U.S. n = 14	Local n = 12	U.S. n = 42	Local n = 43
Formalized training programs—managerial personnel	41	38	NA	NA	64	55	71	83	31	26
Formalized managerial succession programs	48	18	60	18	42	18	79	42	38	12
Formalized and systematic means of determining wages—blue-collar employee	39	29	55	47	31	21	29	08	43	35
—Clerical employee	50	51	55	47	47	54	64	50	45	51
—Supervisory and managerial personnel	18	18	30	41	11	08	21	–	17	26
Use of both monetary and nonmonetary incentives	54	38	70	41	44	37	79	68	45	30
Institutionalized participation programs	56	33	50	24	58	37	100	83	40	19

(continued)

159

(Table 12.3 continued)

Elements of Advanced Management Practices and Effectiveness	Both Regions		Latin America		Far East		Firms With High Concern		Firms With Some and Low Concern	
	U.S. n=56	Local n=55	U.S. n=20	Local n=17	U.S. n=36	Local n=38	U.S. n=14	Local n=12	U.S. n=42	Local n=43
Behavioral Measure of Effectiveness										
High employee morale	30	18	20	24	36	16	71	50	18	12
Cooperative interpersonnel relationship	09	09	–	–	14	13	21	33	05	–
Able to hire and retain highly trained personnel	48	18	40	18	53	19	86	67	36	20
Cooperative interdepartmental relationships	52	25	25	12	67	32	93	83	38	9
Firm's overall objectives were perceived as important	59	33	30	12	75	42	86	83	50	19
Executives spent their time on policy making and future planning	39	16	15	12	53	18	93	67	21	23

Table 1. Elements of Advanced Management Practices and Effectiveness

Elements of Advanced Management Practices and Effectiveness	Both Regions		Latin America		Far East		Firms With High Concern		Firms With Some and Low Concern	
	U.S. n = 56	Local n = 55	U.S. n = 20	Local n = 17	U.S. n = 36	Local n = 38	U.S. n = 14	Local n = 12	U.S. n = 42	Local n = 43
High degree of drive and enthusiasm on the part of executives	32	27	30	29	33	26	79	83	17	12
Able to adapt to environmental changes without much difficulty	43	27	45	18	42	32	93	92	33	26

Table 2.

Elements of Advanced Management Practices and Effectiveness	Region/Ownership				Organizational Concern toward Task Agents		
	Latin America		Far East		High	Some	Low
	U.S. n = 20	Local n = 17	U.S. n = 36	Local n = 38	n = 26	n = 72	n = 13
Consultative type of decision making regarding:							
Major policies	25	18	65	23	65	30	0
Selection and promoting of executives	35	52	33	40	58	37	18
Long-range planning	55	36	71	40	70	52	0
Standard-settings for blue-collar employees	60	52	83	57	85	54	24
Standard-settings for clerical and supervisory personnel	15	18	48	28	60	28	0
Leadership Style							
Democratic or participative as perceived by the subordinates	65	35	48	25	75	35	8

Source: Compiled by the author.

of these companies have paid attention to this aspect. The proportion of the local firms undertaking manpower planning is still smaller, only 9 percent.

By and large, a higher proportion of the U. S. subsidiaries has attempted to decentralize decision-making aspects with respect to major and functional policies.[6] Also, many of these companies have used democratic leadership style. In the same vein, a greater number of the U. S. subsidiaries have paid considerable attention to selection, promotion, training, and development of their employees.

REGIONAL DIFFERENCES

Notwithstanding such overall patterns, we were also able to detect considerable differences in certain practices between the firms in Latin America and the Far East. Data for long-range planning, for example, show that merely 6 percent of the local firms in the Latin American region were undertaking long-range planning of a duration of five to ten years. The comparable proportion of the local firms in the Far Eastern region was 45 percent. In the same manner, approximately two-thirds of the U. S. subsidiaries in the Far Eastern region formalized and documented their major policies and utilized them as control measures, as against merely one-fourth of those in Latin America. Standard setting for the clerical and supervisory personnel received greater attention in the U. S. subsidiaries in the Far East than in Latin America. The same was true with respect to budgetary controls, personnel policies, decentralization in decision making, and employee appraisal systems. Only in the matter of compensation a larger number of firms, both U. S. and local, in the Latin American region adapted formalized practices and procedures.

In summing up, the following picture seems to emerge:

1. Relatively a greater number of the U. S. subsidiaries in both regions are able to utilize advanced management practices than their counterpart local firms.

2. Relatively a greater number of both the U. S. subsidiaries and the local firms in the Far East region are able to utilize advanced management practices than those in the Latin American region.

Judging from these data, it is clear that the U. S. subsidiaries are transferring advanced management practices to the developing countries. However, their impact on local companies seems to be minimal. Why so? one would ask. Our inquiry in this respect revealed two main factors that seemed to be inhibiting the utilization of advanced management practices by the local enterprises: lack of interfirm mobility and the seller's market conditions.

There has been very little mobility of executive and supervisory personnel between the U. S. subsidiaries and the local firms in those countries. Generally, U. S. subsidiaries not only pay twice the pay scales of local counterparts, but also provide considerable opportunities to their employees for advancement and training. As a result, once employed and trained, the employees are very reluctant to leave the U. S. subsidiaries. Although few of the U. S. subsidiaries in these countries provide their trained personnel and other resources to management institutions, their impact has been very marginal. Coupled with the above factors, the prevailing seller's market conditions in developing countries provide very little. incentives or urge to local enterprises to utilize advanced management practices. Under such a market situation, the enterprise can make large profits regardless of the quality and cost of its product. And large proportions of the local enterprises seem to be operating with this so-called short-term management philosophy.[7]

To summarize, we find that although the U. S. subsidiaries are in a position to transfer advanced management practices to developing countries—and they do for their own operations—by and large, their impact has been minimal. Lack of "extra" and concerted efforts on the part of U. S. subsidiaries can and has been sighted as the main reason behind this. Our findings, however, indicate that the surroundings and circumstances that encourage the utilization of advanced management practices are themselves lacking in the developing countries. In other words, developing countries have not assumed proper responsibility to create an atmosphere where the higher level of management can become a necessity.

IMPACT OF MULTINATIONAL CORPORATIONS ON RESEARCH AND DEVELOPMENT ACTIVITIES

Although the present dialogue on the adverse impact of multinational corporations on both home and host countries has been concentrated on the issues of transfer pricing, export of jobs, balance of payments, antitrust provisions, trading with the "enemy" countries, and the like, no issue has consumed more energies and displayed higher emotions than the issue of the MNC impact on research and development activities. Particularly, in developing countries, this has become a national concern. As Ray Matthews has observed, developing countries invite multinational corporations "to promote science-based industries at home in the hope that they may ultimately become centers of technological innovation with international standing."[8]

However, multinational corporations have generally centralized their research and development activities either in their home countries or in some developed countries. The developing countries, as a result, have remained dependent upon developed countries for their technological innovations and advancements.

Our inquiry with the 56 U. S. subsidiaries in the six developing countries revealed that the majority of these companies relied on their parent companies for research and development activities. Less than 10 percent of the subsidiaries studied expended some resources to these activities in their overseas operations. Even with respect to product development and modifications, the subsidiaries relied on their parent companies.

Almost a decade ago a study by the National Science Foundation in India indicated that "the industrial sector of the economy has relied mainly on imported technical know-how, [and] research in private industry is negligible."[9] This situation has not changed much during the last ten years.

However, the developing countries seem determined to change this situation. Many of them now realize that they are endowed with many natural resources that have remained thus far unexploited. For example, Brazil has about one-third of the world's known iron ore reserves, yet its share of the world iron ore market is only 1 percent. Many such instances can be cited.

It is true that the availability of scientific and technical personnel, laboratory facilities, and the presence of an overall scientific atmosphere make industrialized countries more attractive places for R&D activities. Slowly, this is being recognized by some progressive leaders of developing countries. Accordingly, some of these countries have been making concerted efforts to increase their supply of scientific and technical personnel. They also have been spending increasing amounts of money for developing research laboratories. For example, the Indian government increased its expenditure on research threefold during the last ten years, and the supply of trained scientists and engineers has increased fourfold during the last decade. At the present time there seems to be oversupply of trained scientists and engineers in many of the developing countries and this is reflected in the so-called brain-drain phenomenon. Thus, in coming years, the multinational corporation will be increasingly challenged by the host countries concerning their research and development activities. In other words, as Matthews has predicted, tremendous pressure from host countries will move the multinational corporation from an ethnocentric to a geocentric behavior with respect to research and development activities.[10]

IMPACT OF MULTINATIONAL CORPORATIONS
IN DEVELOPING HUMAN RESOURCES

It is argued that the multinational corporation, besides providing advanced technology and managerial know-how, is an efficient machine to train and develop human resources, particularly managerial and technical personnel. Realizing this fact, many developing countries in recent years are making demands on foreign subsidiaries to increase their employment of local personnel in top-level managerial positions. This political pressure as well as the high cost of employing expatriates have induced subsidiaries to place nationals in top positions. For example, in the 56 U. S. subsidiaries that we visited, only less than a dozen U. S. citizens were holding permanent positions in overseas operations.

However, this level of effort on the part of the U. S. subsidiaries has not satisfied entirely either government officials or the local executives themselves. Many local executives interviewed indicated that the so-called localization is carried out in letter only and the spirit behind it is lacking. Some of these top-level executives bitterly complained about the erosion of their decision-making power. For example, the general manager of a U. S. subsidiary in Taiwan echoed the feelings of many local managers when he told us: "We cannot decide anything: we are not allowed to do so. We do what they [meaning executives in the parent companies] tell us to do. It is fair to say we live like a king, but work like an educated peon."

As Stephen Hymer has observed, the multinational corporation would tend to centralize strategic decisions in regional coordinating centers and in corporate headquarters in the advanced countries. As a result, he predicts, "Latin Americans, Asians, and Africans would at best be able to aspire to a management position in the intermediate coordinating centers at the continental level. Very few would be able to get much higher, for the closer to the top, the more important was a common North Atlantic cultural heritage.[11]

Our interviews with the top-level local executives in the U. S. subsidiaries indicate an even more pessimistic outlook than what Hymer predicts, and we expect a greater tension developing between the multinational corporation and the developing countries in this respect.

SUMMARY

The purpose of this chapter was to examine the potential and actual conflict between the multinational corporation and the developing countries. It was argued that the examination of micro-level practices of subsidiaries may provide some insights in understanding the implications of policy-level conflicts between them and the host countries.

The study utilized data collected for a large-scale cross-cultural study undertaken in Argentina, Brazil, India, the Philippines, Taiwan, and Uruguay. The following aspects were examined in some detail:

- The overall "behavior" of multinational corporations in host countries
- The impact of multinational corporations in transferring advanced management practices to developing countries
- The role of multinational corporations in increasing R&D activities in developing countries
- The impact of multinational corporations in developing human resources, particularly managerial personnel

The findings indicate that the large majority of executives of the U. S. subsidiaries were apolitical in nature and their overall behavior as "citizen," as reflected in their attitudes toward major publics, was no worse than in their counterpart local firms.

With respect to transferring advanced management practices into developing countries, the impact of the U. S. subsidiaries was minimal, although the subsidiaries were able to utilize advanced practices for their own internal operations.

The MNCs, through their subsidiaries, did very little R&D work and one would expect a greater tension being developed between the MNC and the host government.

The impact of the MNC on developing human resources in developing countries seems to be ambivalent. On the one hand, the subsidiaries have replaced the majority of expatriate managers with the local nationals. On the other hand, however, their decision-making power is severely limited.

NOTES

1. Emile Benoit, "The Attack on the Multinationals," Columbia Journal of World Business, November–December 1972, p. 15.

2. See A. R. Negandhi and S. B. Prasad, Comparative Management (New York: Appleton–Century–Crofts, 1971) and A. R. Negandhi, Organization Theory in an Open System Perspective (New York: Dunellen, 1975).

3. Frank Shaker, "The Multinational Corporation: The New Imperialism," Columbia Journal of World Business, November–December 1970, p. 84.

4. Claude McMillan, Jr., R. F. Gonzalez, with Leo G. Erickson, International Enterprise in a Developing Economy: A Study of U. S. Business in Brazil (East Lansing, Mich.: Bureau of Business and Economic Research, 1964) p. 221.

5. Negandhi and Prasad and Negandhi, op. cit.

6. For details see: A. R. Negandhi and B. D. Reimann, "A Contingency Theory of Organization Re-Examined in the Context of a Developing Country," Academy of Management Journal 15, no. 2 (June 1972):137–46; "Task Environment Decentralization and Organi-

zational Effectiveness," Human Relations 26, no. 2 (1973):203-14; "Correlates of Decentralization: Closed and Open Systems Perspectives," Academy of Management Journal, forthcoming.

7. A. R. Negandhi, "Advanced Management Know-How in Developing Countries," California Management Review 10, no. 3 (Spring 1968):53-60.

8. Roy A. Matthews "The International Economy and the Nation State," Columbia Journal of World Business, November-December 1971, p. 58.

9. National Science Foundation, "Expenditure for Research and Development in Various Countries: India," (mimeo) 1966, p. 1.

10. Matthews, op. cit.

11. Quoted from Richard L. Barovick, "Congress Looks at the Multinational Corporation," Columbia Journal of World Business, November-December 1970, p. 78.

13

SOME ASPECTS OF PRIVATE DIRECT INVESTMENT IN DEVELOPING COUNTRIES

Grant L. Reuber

The subject of private foreign investment in developing countries is vast, complicated, and controversial. It is also a subject that, although evoking much speculation over the years, has received less sustained and systematic attention in terms of data collection and analysis than many other aspects of economic development. This study is principally concerned with describing and evaluating some of the main characteristics and economic effects of private direct investment in manufacturing industries. So that these central features may be seen in perspective, considerable attention is also given to the supply characteristics of direct investment, to alternative sources of capital, and to the auxiliary factors and market access associated with direct investment.

The empirical information on which the study is based has been obtained from four general sources: evidence scattered through a variety of earlier studies, data collected by national governments and international agencies; figures assembled by the OECD, including statistics on the stock of private foreign direct investment found in various countries; and data on approximately 80 private investment projects located in the developing countries, collected from the head offices of investors in North America, Europe, and Japan by means of a direct survey conducted by personal interview.

Little will be said here about this survey evidence. Stated briefly, we attempted to collect firm data on a series of manufacturing projects undertaken during the decade of the 1960s. Projects were defined as investments that represent a separate and discrete step-up in the firms' activities rather than a routine and marginal

Grant L. Reuber is Professor of Economics, University of Western Ontario. This chapter is part of a larger study that was completed under the auspices of the OECD Development Centre.[1]

extension of activities already underway. Each firm was visited twice: once to indicate the information being requested and to select the project on which data would be provided, and the second time to collect and review the data provided. Information of this kind is obviously open to many qualifications and needs to be interpreted with caution. On the other hand, this approach provided one way of obtaining evidence on some of the questions at issue.

The study, after a general review of the subject, considers the determinants of investment and the relationship and relative cost of various forms of portfolio and direct investment. It then goes on to consider the determinants of direct investment. After that, consideration is given to the effects on host countries: on production and trade, on employment and income, on productivity and costs, on the transfer of knowledge, on the structure of the economy, and on the distribution of income. In addition, an appendix based on the OECD figures on the outstanding stock of private direct investment describes the structure and distribution of direct investment in the developing countries as it was at the end of the 1960s.*

TAX BENEFITS TO THE HOST COUNTRY

So much by way of background. I now turn to the question of tax benefits to the host country. It is generally accepted that one of the distinguishing features of direct investment under existing tax treaty legislation is the opportunity it affords the host country to tax foreign capital and the rents arising from the auxiliary factors associated with such capital. Thus, if the home and the host country have a common income tax rate of 50 percent and the firm in the host country makes a profit of $1,000, half the profit accrues to the host country as taxes and half to the firm as its return on investment. Moreover, since the tax rate at home and in the host country is the same the tax is neutral as far as the allocation of investment between the two countries is concerned.

At the end of 1970 the total stock of direct investment outstanding in the developing countries was approximately $40 billion, of which some $12 billion was in the manufacturing sector. On the basis of reported after-tax earnings and current income and withholding taxes, one may reasonably assume a tax of some 8 to 10 percent on foreign equity that accrues to the developing countries. This implies a gain via taxes to host developing countries of between $3.2 and $4.0 billion per year—an amount equal to 40 to 50 percent of all official flows to the developing countries in 1970 and approximating 1 percent of the combined GNP of these countries.

---

*See Appendix B at the back of this book.

Such an estimate and the whole notion that host countries effectively tax foreign equity is subject to many qualifications based on differences between nominal and effective tax rates. Some of these qualifications arise because of differences in the tax rates and the existence of tax havens, others because of intricacies in the details of tax laws and tax administration and still others because of intracompany pricing policies whereby profits are transferred from country to country for purposes of minimizing total tax payments. These complications are widely recognized though their empirical importance remains very much in doubt. I should, however, like to draw attention to another kind of complication that, so far as I am aware, has been largely ignored in the literature and that I believe may be much more important, especially for the developing countries. This complication arises because of price distortions in the developing countries and the wide variety of subsidies in one form or another that enhance the profits of foreign subsidiaries. The empirical importance of such distortions is evident from two general sets of evidence. First, cost-benefit studies on particular projects, such as those conducted by I. Little, Tibor Scitovsky, and M. Scott, indicate that price distortions give rise to wide and unsystematic disparities between private and social rates of return. Secondly, the estimates of effective protection made by Bela Balassa and others suggest very high and widely different subsidies on value added in many areas of manufacturing.

How price distortions and subsidies affect the real return to host countries from taxing foreign equity depends to an important degree upon what one assumes about alternatives as well as other considerations. Assume first that the investment will either be undertaken by the foreign investor or not at all. Assume also that the project is uneconomic by international standards and will only be undertaken if the host country provides sufficient protection and subsidies to bring the after-tax rate of return up to the point where it conforms with the international supply price of capital. The investment can be attracted from abroad in this situation and the gain to the community (B) will be equal to the tax paid by the investor (T) <u>minus</u> the difference in the unit real resource cost if the product is produced locally rather than imported (c) <u>times</u> the number of units (q) produced by the project: $B = T - cq$. In this situation it is quite possible that the real resource cost of having the project exceeds the tax paid, and the benefit, in any event, will be less than the tax if there is a real resource cost of local production exceeding that of imports.

Suppose, however, that the alternative is an identical project financed by local capital. Assume also that the difference in relative efficiency between the next best alternative locally and this locally financed project is measured by c, the difference in the subsidy required to make both projects competitive at international levels. Then the social loss of undertaking this locally financed project locally will be cq. And the difference in the social loss between undertaking the project with foreign or local financing will be $(T - cq + cq) = T$. In other words, there is a common loss cq no matter how the project is undertaken and if undertaken by foreign investors the host country gains the full amount of the tax on foreign equity.

Extending this example, one may make the further assumption that the supplies of foreign capital, as well as other critical inputs, are considerably more elastic then the supply of these inputs domestically, if only because the developing countries absorb a small share of world capital flows and associated auxiliary factors. In this situation providing a subsidy to an industry may result in a larger expansion in the industry under foreign financing than under domestic financing with the consequence that there will be a greater misallocation of domestic resources. Suppose that with foreign financing $q + q'$ units are produced. Then the gain to the host country of relying on foreign rather than domestic financing will be $T - c (q + q') + cq = T - cq'$. In this case the real resource cost of the misallocation of resources due to the additional output resulting from foreign financing may conceivably be greater than the real resource gain of being able to tax foreign capital; and the net gain to the host country will necessarily be less than the tax paid.

A third possibility is that all production activity is subsidized in one form or another. If the degree of subsidy is everywhere the same, presumably the subsidies simply cancel each other out and no allocative effects result. More realistically, however, one may assume that the degree of subsidy differs among various industries and that the incentives thus provided lead to economic inefficiency. Assume also that all of these industries have access to both domestic and foreign capital resources. The opportunity cost of using foreign capital in one industry rather than another will reflect the <u>difference</u> in the tax collectable on the foreign capital in the two projects (T') <u>plus</u> the <u>difference</u> in the real resource cost of the two projects (c') <u>times</u> the <u>difference</u> in amount of uneconomic output (q'). In these terms the benefit of foreign financing is $T' - c'q'$. For domestic financing, the cost is $c'q'$ assuming the same amount of uneconomic production in each industry irrespective of the source of finance. Thus the difference between foreign and domestic financing $T' - c'q' + c'q' = T'$, which may be either positive or negative.

So far the same level of efficiency has been assumed among the alternatives considered. Assume that foreign financed projects are x percent more efficient than the alternatives defined in the foregoing examples. If the unit cost of foreign financed projects is c, then the unit cost of production for the alternative is $(1 + x)c$. In the second example this means that the social gain derived from the project is $T - cq + (1 + x)cq = T + xcq$, that is, the gain is greater than the tax payment by the saving in domestic resources due to the greater efficiency of the foreign firm. In the third example the gain becomes $T - c(q' + xq)$, which is greater than before making the assumption of difference in efficiency. In other words, for the foreign financed project, the positive effect of higher production efficiency tends to offset to some extent the negative scale effects on resource allocation. In the third example the gain remains T' if one assumes a constant differential in relative efficiency between foreign and domestic projects in both sets of projects.

This analysis can obviously be made enormously more complicated by introducing additional assumptions such as differences in the input and in the output mix depending on whether the project is financed by foreign or domestic capital. Enough has been said however to emphasize several points. First, the ability to tax foreign capital evidently plays an important role in the analysis, as has long been recognized. Second, once a system of subsidies and regulations that influences resource allocations is taken into account, it is difficult to conclude on a priori grounds or on the basis of macro analysis whether foreign investment is beneficial or not. Reaching such a conclusion requires detailed project analysis in which the many assumptions realistically relating to particular projects can be spelled out and taken into account explicitly. It is particularly important to specify the alternative assumed in the absence of foreign investment—a specification that is missing in most of the work of which I am aware on this subject. In the absence of such detailed specification, it is doubtful whether anything can be said about tax benefits from macro calculations. Third, the complications arising from price distortions are likely to be especially great as far as foreign investment in manufacturing is concerned since in most developing countries protectionist policies, discriminatory tax and subsidy measures, and direct controls of various kinds have been especially prominent in the manufacturing sector.

TYPES OF INVESTMENT

The second aspect of private direct investment that I wish to discuss concerns the relationship between the characteristics and effects of direct investment on the one hand, and the type of investment on the other. The most revealing discussion of this question of which I am aware is in a paper by Richard Caves.[2] In this paper he emphasizes the distinction between horizontal and vertical foreign investment. Vertical investment is associated with oligopoly and the incentives to reduce uncertainty and competition. Horizontal investment requires that that investing firm have some special advantage in the form of knowledge, production, and marketing skills, access to market or access to inputs that (1) can be drawn upon the new location and offer sufficient advantage to overcome the extra cost of producing in a foreign location and (2) is tied to the actual process of production and distribution, thereby implying a higher return via direct investment than through licensing or some other form of exploiting the asset.

In my study a distinction is drawn between export-oriented projects and those oriented toward local sales. Although the categories are not completely parallel, export-oriented projects consist principally of vertical investments and locally oriented projects of horizontal investments. About a third of the projects in our sample were classified as export-oriented projects on the criterion that over 10 percent of the output was exported. A relatively low ratio was deliberately chosen to identify these projects because of the bimodal distribution of the sample when classified on this basis: export-oriented projects, on average, sold 87 percent of their output abroad; the remainder sold an average of 3 percent of their output abroad.

The evidence suggests some important differences between these two types of investment. These differences were reflected not only in qualitative evidence collected during the interviews but also in a statistical analysis of the data collected. The latter consists of a series of simple regressions in which some characteristic or effect of investment, C_i, is regressed on the percentage of total sales made up by export sales, S_i. This equation was expanded to include as well a series of dummy variables to pick up any systematic differences between host country areas or the home country of the investor.

$$C_i = a_o + a_1 S_i + a_2 \begin{bmatrix} \text{host country dummies} \\ \text{or} \\ \text{home country dummies} \end{bmatrix}$$

For present purposes I shall ignore the dummy variables and concentrate on some of the relationships between C and S. It is convenient to consider these under three general headings: how firms invest, why firms invest, and the effects of the investment on the host country.

As for the first category—how firms invest—the evidence sheds some light on three characteristics that I shall consider in turn. The first concerns ownership structure. The degree of foreign control was highest in export-oriented investment. Presumably this reflects in part the power of the investor vis-a-vis the host country because of the investor's unique access to international markets. Moreover, in a closely integrated operation direct control is more important from the standpoint of avoiding risk and uncertainty. In the case of locally oriented projects, the host country's control over the market and the investor's monopolistic market positions encouraged firms to impose local participation. Further, such projects probably have more to gain from local partners in the form of political accepta- bility, access to knowledge about local circumstances, and access to additional local resources. When a simple regression was run a highly significant and positive coefficient for S_1 is indicated. At the same time the value of R_2 is very low, suggesting that many other factors also enter into the picture.

A second characteristic of how firms invest concerns the initial financial structure of the project. The share of total capital invested brought from abroad is positively and very significantly related to the export share of sales. The evidence also seems to suggest that the share of total financing provided by foreign equity is approxi- mately one third irrespective of the orientation of the project: The difference in financing arises mainly in the relative amount of initial financing raised abroad in the form of debt: Debt raised abroad is positively and very significantly related to export shares. This probably reflects differences in the relative ease in making external payments in the form of interest rather than in the form of dividends, given existing currency restrictions. The figures also indicate a strong negative association between the share of exports and the share of total initial financing done through equity sales, which is consistent with the positive association between local ownership participation and the share of local sales.

The third characteristic to be considered concerns rates of return. The evidence collected for this study on this question is weak. Moreover, it emerges sometimes in the form of profit rates and sometimes in the form of payback period. Nevertheless, the evidence does suggest fairly clearly that realized profits are positively related to the export share of sales. Moreover, export-oriented profits are very high—averaging some 30 percent on equity compared to locally oriented projects where profits averaged some 20 percent— and write-off periods are very rapid. Turning from the level of earnings to the disposal of earnings, one finds that a substantially larger share of earnings are reinvested for locally oriented projects. The biggest differences arise in two other categories, however. Earnings in the form of royalties and fees are of only minor importance for export-oriented projects but of substantial importance for locally oriented projects. By contrast, a substantial part of the earnings to the firm of export-oriented projects is derived in the form of lower cost components that are absorbed in production outside the country.

Some of the evidence collected on profits is summarized in Tables 13.1 and 13.2. (In the larger study, locally oriented projects are subdivided into those that were actively initiated by the host- country government and the rest, designated as "market-development" projects.)

Profitability of Sample Projects
by Home Country of Investor, by Type of Investment, and by Host Country

	Average percent Return on Equity (after tax)[a]	Internal Pay-back Period (years)[b]		Repatriation Period (years)[c]	
		Current Estimate	Originally Expected	Current Estimate	Originally Expected
Home country of investor					
Europe	15.1 (17)	9.0 (23)	8.4 (23)	8.0 (18)	10.1 (17)
North America	23.0 (6)	4.5 (13)	4.0 (13)	7.3 (8)	8.5 (10)
Japan	33.1 (14)	6.5 (10)	6.1 (10)	5.3 (12)	8.3 (16)
Type of investment					
Export-oriented	32.0 (10)	6.3 (16)	5.9 (16)	5.9 (14)	8.2 (17)
Market-development	14.7 (16)	7.9 (20)	6.6 (22)	9.6 (13)	9.9 (12)
Government-initiated	27.4 (11)	7.3 (10)	8.1 (8)	5.4 (11)	9.3 (14)
Host-country area					
Latin America	15.3 (12)	8.8 (13)	7.3 (13)	6.8 (10)	7.7 (11)
India	15.7 (6)	8.1 (9)	6.3 (9)	9.0 (8)	9.4 (9)
Far East	30.8 (10)	5.2 (12)	5.4 (13)	5.5 (11)	7.6 (14)
Other	30.2 (9)	6.8 (12)	7.6 (11)	7.3 (9)	12.4 (9)
Total	23.2 (37)	7.2 (46)	6.7 (46)	7.0 (38)	9.1 (43)

[a]The mean average of the rates of return (total accounting profits after tax relative to total equity) calculated project by project.

[b]The number of years required to earn back the total equity invested (accounting profits [after tax] plus depreciation).

[c]The number of years required to repatriate the total foreign capital: share of dividends plus interest, royalties, fees and related profits. Estimates of "related profits" are based on estimates by firms of (1) the marginal profit on inputs supplied to the project and (2) the differential between the cost of production at home and the price at which output is purchased from the project in the host country.

Source: Compiled by the author.

175

TABLE 13.2

Application of Sample Project Earnings
by Home Country of Investor, Type of Investment,
and Host Country

	Percent Reinvested	Percent Dividends	Percent Royalties and Fees	Percent Other[a]
Home country investor				
Europe (20)[b]	47.7	28.2	19.1	5.0
North America (16)	34.7	24.6	8.3	32.4
Japan (14)	57.8	21.6	3.4	17.2
Type of Investment				
Export-oriented (14)	34.0	25.4	1.4	39.2
Market-development (19)	45.7	30.1	12.8	11.4
Government-				
initiated (17)	57.3	19.6	17.6	5.5
Host Country Area				
Latin America (15)	56.7	17.4	7.8	18.1
India (9)	43.2	30.9	22.0	3.9
Far East (13)	34.3	21.3	7.1	34.3
Other (13)	45.6	34.1	11.9	8.0
Total (50)	46.4	25.2	11.2	17.2

[a]Figures in parentheses indicate number of projects in sample.
[b]Includes savings on production costs and profits on input sales.

Source: Compiled by the author.

    Why firms invest abroad is a complicated question on which,
at least as I read the literature, there are many hypotheses that
available evidence to date has failed to narrow down very clearly.
One set of hypotheses is found in the literature on the determinants
of domestic investment and emphasizes liquidity, rates of return,
and output-capacity relationships, all of which may be seen as
factors influencing short-term variations in investment. A second
set of hypotheses emanate from the literature on industrial organization and emphasize longer-term strategic factors such as the economics
of new product development, the economics of product-differentiated
oligopoly, and competition for market shares. A third set of questions arises from the influence of government policies on foreign
investment flows. Although an attempt is made to examine these
influences on an aggregative basis in the larger study, in this
study I refer only to the relationship between the type of investment
and investment determinants.

For export-oriented projects, local market considerations are of little or no consequence. Investment of this type is mainly propelled by competitive pressure to seek out low-cost sources of inputs. And firms make it a practice to shop among various developing countries for the lowest cost source of such inputs. In addition to the level of wages, consideration is given to the availability of labor, land, and basic infrastructure, the terms on which countries permit imports, the absence of host-government control and interference, and the extent of tax allowances and other financial incentives provided by host-country governments.

For locally oriented projects the size and future prospects of the local market are of central importance. A key factor is usually the degree of protection against foreign imports that is provided. In many cases the firms are not so much searching out profitable opportunities but rather are responding to specific threats to their existing activities; financial incentives are of less importance. Longer-term strategic considerations, associated with horizontal investment in industries characterized by product differentiation and oligopoly play an important role.

Turning to the effects on host-country economies, one finds that the dichotomy between export-oriented and locally oriented projects is generally evident in a variety of effects such as in the degree of integration of the project into the local economy, its effect on foreign trade flows, and several aspects of the transfer of knowledge in the form of technology, skills, and training. One particularly important manifestation is the relative level of production costs by international standards in export-oriented as opposed to locally oriented projects. For the projects in our sample the mean cost of producing in the home country the same product as in the host country was a third more for export-oriented projects and roughly a third less for locally oriented projects.

STATISTICAL ASSOCIATIONS

Before examining these relationships in greater detail, I should like to digress briefly to report on some simple attempts made to examine what if any statistical association exists between the stock or flow of direct investment on the one hand, and the level of GNP per head or the growth in GNP or in GNP per head on the other. This relationship has, of course, been examined before by others such as Robinson, Hollis Chenery, as well as others including a recent paper by Gustav Papanek.[3] The only novelty I can claim is that I had access to a new set of figures on the stock of private direct investment in over 100 developing countries at the end of 1967. This is a substantially larger sample than is usual in earlier work of this kind.

As shown in Table 13.3 a highly significant statistical association exists between the stock of private investment per capita and GNP per capita for the entire sample of developing countries as well as for each subsample. There are two major difficulties, however, in interpreting any evidence of this kind. The first arises because foreign investment may simply be displacing local savings. Although the evidence available from a number of other studies suggests that this happens to some degree, it also suggests that foreign capital inflows nevertheless do add to the total stock of capital. A more serious difficulty is that the association between the stock of flow of private investment and GNP per head reflects a two-way relationship that makes it difficult to sort out the cause and effect relationships. Among the important factors identified in my study as well as others as an important determinant of investment flows is the size and growth of the host-country market. On the other hand, a large or growing stock of capital might be expected to be associated with a larger or growing GNP per head. This two-way relationship makes it difficult to interpret not only the simple correlations given in Table 13.3 but also, I believe, the results of more elaborate estimates made by others in which this two-way relationship is not taken into account.

TABLE 13.3

Statistical Association between the Stock
of Direct Private Foreign Investment and GNP

	r(GNP/N, K/N)	n
All areas	.68	109
Latin America	.87	27
Africa, south of Sahara	.68	37
Middle East and North Africa	.90	18
Asia	.76	21
Extractive countries	.86	31
Nonextractive countries	.68	78

Notation: r = coefficient of correlation; GNP/N = gross national product per capita in 1968; K/N = stock of direct private foreign investment per capita at the end of 1967; n = number of countries in the sample. All estimates are significant at the 1 percent level.

Source: See Appendix B.

In order to gain some further insight into this relationship two additional steps were taken, both very unsophisticated. The first was to consider the association between the stock of private direct investment and exports, imports, and the trade balance. The results are shown in Table 13.4. Both exports and imports per head are positively and significantly associated with the per capita stock of investment for the total sample and the various subgroups. When one looks at the trade balance the picture is mixed. No association is evident in the aggregate. A strong negative association is evident, however, for Latin America and for countries where nonextractive industries are dominant. For Africa and countries where extractive industries are dominant a strong positive association is apparent. A weak association is indicated for Asia.

TABLE 13.4

Statistical Association between the Stock of Direct
Private Foreign Investment and Foreign Trade

	n	r(X/N, K/N)	4(M/N, K/N)	r(X/N − M/N, K/N)
All areas	95	0.62	0.65	−0.10[a]
Latin America	26	0.57	0.70	−0.91
Africa, south of Sahara	31	0.89	0.81	0.83
Middle East and North Africa	13	0.99	0.95	0.98
Asia	19	0.82	0.60	−0.28[a]
Extractive countries	26	0.85	0.56	0.41[b]
Nonextractive countries	69	0.57	0.70	−0.69

Notation: X/N = exports per capita in 1968; M/N = imports per capita in 1968; otherwise the same as in Table 13.3. All estimates are significant at the 1 percent level unless otherwise indicated.

[a]Not significant at the 5 percent level.
[b]Not significant at the 1 percent level but significant at the 5 percent level.

Source: Appendix B.

The second step was to examine time series evidence for a much more limited set of countries to see whether the lead-lag relationships between investment and GNP and trade flows might indicate something about causal relationships. The estimates presented in Table 13.5, generally speaking, are not very conclusive. There is some suggestion that capital flows lag behind GNP and lead exports and the picture for imports is highly ambiguous.

Although these and similar estimates are of some interest, I think they are little more than descriptive and demonstrate very little about the effects of direct investment on host countries. To sort out these relationships requires a very complicated model

TABLE 13.5

Lead-Lag Relationships
(simple correlation coefficients)

	Capital Flows Leading		Capital Flows Lagging	
n	Variables	r	Variables	r
11	$(GDP/N_{659}, US_mK/N_{615})$	.71	$(GDP/N_{615}, US_mK/N_{659})$	<u>.79</u>
27	$(GDP/N_{659}, PFI/N_{615})$	.38	$(GDP/N_{615}, PFI/N_{659})$	<u>.61</u>
22	$(GDP/N_{615}, PFI/N_{571})$	.50	(insufficient observations)	
11	$(X/N_{689}, US_mK/N_{658})$	<u>.63</u>	$(X/N_{658}, US_mK/N_{689})$	.53
11	$(X/N_{659}, US_mK/N_{615})$	<u>.70</u>	$(X/N_{615}, US_mK/N_{659})$	.59
27	$(X/N_{689}, PFI/N_{658})$	<u>.60</u>	$(X/N_{658}, PFI/N_{689})$	.33
29	$(X/N_{659}, PFI/N_{615})$	-.02	$(X/N_{615}, PFI/N_{659})$	<u>.40</u>
28	$(M/N_{689}, PFI/N_{658})$	<u>.80</u>	$(M/N_{659}, PFI/N_{689})$	.48
29	$(M/N_{659}, PFI/N_{615})$	.60	$(M/N_{615}, PFI/N_{659})$	<u>.70</u>
21	$(M/N_{615}, PFI/N_{571})$	<u>.45</u>	$(M/N_{571}, PFI/N_{615})$	.33
11	$(M/N_{689}, US_mK/N_{658})$	.65	$(M/N_{658}, US_mK/N_{689})$	<u>.77</u>
11	$(M/N_{659}, US_mK/N_{615})$	.48	$(M/N_{615}, US_mK/N_{659})$	<u>.77</u>

Notation: GDP/N = gross domestic product per capita; PFI/N = total private foreign investment inflows per capita; US_mK/N = value of the stock of U. S. direct investment in manufacturing per capita; X/N = value of host-country exports per capital; M/N = value of host-country imports per capita; subscripts identify years over which the value of the variable is averaged (for example, 629 = average from 1962 to 1969); n = number of countries in the cross-section sample. Data sources are described in Appendix B. The higher of the leading or lagging coefficients is underlined.

that is well beyond the data resources now available. In a companion study, H. C. Bos and some colleagues at the Netherlands Economic Institute have attempted to develop such a model. Not only did they run into enormous data problems but also they were confronted with the major difficulty of taking into account a variety of micro effects of foreign investment in a macro model.

EFFECTS OF FOREIGN OWNERSHIP

So much for my digression. I'd now like to return to the effects of the type of foreign investment on host countries. The figures shown in Table 13.6 attempt to identify the effect of the degree of foreign ownership and the export share of output in our sample projects on selected indicators of business practice. Consider first the effect of the type of investment. In general the higher the share of exports (1) the lower the percentage of the current workforce made up by local personnel, (2) the larger the increase in imports of all kinds from the parent, (3) the more of the initial financing, particularly in the form of debt, brought from abroad, (4) the greater share of sales to countries other than the home country, (5) the smaller the share of inputs purchased locally and the larger the share purchased from the home country, (6) the lower the relative cost of production.

Some additional evidence, which does not lend itself very readily to regression analysis, was also obtained on the effect of the type of investment on the transfer and adaptation of technology and skills. This is a very complex issue theoretically as well as empirically. In any event, our figures suggest that technology was adapted more frequently in projects geared to local markets as was product design and production techniques. The main reason appears to have been the need to scale down plant and equipment in the case of locally oriented projects to the low volume of demand. There were relatively few cases of adaptation in response to low labor costs and to the extent they occurred they were more prevalent for export-oriented projects. Other important factors conditioning adaptations for locally oriented projects were government regulations and the standards or the quality of raw materials and components purchased locally under mandatory requirements.

Apart from indicating some of the differences in the characteristics of different types of investment, this evidence suggests a number of policy implications that may be worth noting. First, it suggests that general policies that treat all investment more or less the same may have important differential effects. For example, policies that insist on majority ownership seem likely to discriminate against vertical-type export-oriented investment in favor of horizontal-type locally oriented investment. Second, given the role of the size

TABLE 13.6

Estimates of the Effect of the Degree of Foreign Ownership and the Export Share
of Output in Sample Projects on Selected Indicators of Business Practice

$$y_i = a + bO_i + cS_i$$

Equation Number	n	y_i = Indicator of Business Practice	O_i = Current Percent Ownership Held by Investing Firm	S_i = Export Percent of Output	a	R^2
1. Percent of current workforce made up of local employees:						
a	64	Production workers	0.02 (0.96)'	−5.29 (3.32)⊕	98.69	.15
b	65	Foremen & supervisors	0.03 (0.44)	−9.51 (1.91)°	94.39	.06
c	64	Clerical & accounting	0.05 (1.01)'	−10.22 (2.72)⊕	95.38	.11
d	53	Sales & marketing	−0.11 (0.83)'	−68.14 (5.65)⊗	102.18	.40
e	60	Management	−0.08 (0.58)	−16.62 (1.57)'	79.22	.06
f	60	Management	−0.13 (0.91)	n.i.	78.79	.01
g	58	Total workforce	0.0002 (0.006)	−6.35 (2.70)⊕	98.74	.12
h	58	Total workforce	−0.02 (0.65)	n.i.	98.70	.007
2. Change in exports of the investing firm to the host country ($ million):						
a	64	Same product line	−0.01 (1.79)°	0.91 (1.65)'	0.24	.07

b	63	Raw materials & supplies	0.03 (1.54)'	n.i.	0.02	.04
c	62	Complementary finished goods	-0.60 (0.93)'	-15.33 (0.35)	61.88	.02

3. Change in imports of the investing firm from the host country ($ million):

a	59	Same product line	0.003 (0.67)	1.21 (3.52)⊛	-0.16	.22
b	59	Same product line	0.009 (1.73)°	n.i.	-0.25	.05
c	59	Raw materials & supplies	0.01 (1.05)'	1.61 (2.52)⊛	-0.71	.15
d	59	Raw materials & supplies	0.02 (1.88)°	n.i.	-0.83	.06

4. Form of earnings (Percent of total earnings):

a	57	Dividends	-0.08 (0.53)	-1.33 (0.12)	29.32	.006
b	54	Royalties	-0.07 (1.09)'	-4.81 (0.98)'	12.06	.05
c	51	Fees	-0.07 (1.18)'	-3.60 (0.86)'	8.67	.06
d	51	Fees	-0.08 (1.44)'	n.i.	8.78	.04
e	52	Profit on sale of related materials	0.04 (0.43)	2.84 (0.43)	4.12	.01
f	54	Reinvested earnings	0.10 (0.54)	-17.86 (1.34)'	39.84	.03

(continued)

(Table 13.6 continued)

Equation Number	n	y_i = Indicator of Business Practice	O_i = Current Percent Ownership Held by Investing Firm	S_i = Export Percent of Output	a	R^2
5. Source of initial capital invested (percent of total capital)						
a	64	Equity from abroad	0.50 (4.03)⊛	-1.44 (0.15)	3.27	.22
b	61	Debt from abroad	-0.11 (0.96)▪	30.34 (3.46)⊛	23.65	.17
c	61	Debt & equity from abroad	0.41 (3.40)⊛	28.21 (3.21)⊛	26.55	.33
d	61	Debt & equity from abroad	0.49 (3.96)*	n.i.	26.56	.21
e	64	Equity from developing country	-0.26 (2.45)⊛	-15.25 (1.92)°	42.54	.17
f	61	Debt from developing country	-0.16 (1.46)▪	-13.06 (1.65)▪	32.01	.10
6. Distribution of project sales (percent of total):						
a	75	Other developing countries	-0.09 (1.61)▪	6.47 (1.63)▪	9.80	.05
b	73	Developed countries other than home country of investor	-0.04 (1.03)▪	6.10 (2.03)*	3.08	.06
7. Distribution of purchases of goods and services (percent of total)						
a	70	Indigenous local firms	-0.30 (2.03)*	-28.58 (2.76)⊛	66.87	.18
b	64	Locally based foreign subsidiaries	0.04 (0.42)	-6.21 (0.98)▪	6.81	.02
c	68	Parent company	0.20 (1.14)▪	30.64 (2.45)⊛	18.01	.12

d	66	Parent company suppliers	-0.09 (1.04)'	-1.17 (0.19)	12.72	.02
e	68	Other	0.09 (1.41)'	-9.91 (1.98)°	2.08	.07
8.		Number of local businesses brought into being because of project:				
a	17	Distributors & sales agents	0.13 (0.82)'	-11.92 (1.39)'	3.33	.17
b	13	Suppliers	-0.16 (0.26)	-15.33 (0.39)	44.11	.03
9. a	37	Training cost incurred to install corporate systems ($1,000s)	1.98 (0.49)	481.10 (1.83)°	-27.54	.12
b	37	Training cost incurred to install corporate systems ($1,000s)	4.60 (1.17)	n.i.	-76.16	.04
10. a	42	Cost of production in home country/ cost of production in developing country (index)	0.28 (1.09)'	81.80 (5.21)⊗	45.44	.51
b	42	Cost of production in home country/ cost of production in developing country (index)	0.87 (2.94)	n.i.	25.54	.18

⊗ * ° ' indicate coefficients statistically significant at above 2, 5, 10, and 50 percent levels respectively.

Source: Compiled by the author.

of the market, it is evident that for a large majority of developing countries horizontal-type investment in many industries is not very practical. In this connection it is noteworthy that in 1969 the GNP of only four developing countries—India, Brazil, Mexico, and Argentina—was larger than that of Denmark; in only a dozen was it half as large. Most developing countries wishing to attract foreign investment in industries that are capital-intensive will have to think in terms of export-oriented vertical-type investments unless of course they are prepared to pay whatever subsidy may be necessary to meet the supply price of capital. This latter policy, as already emphasized, may well cost more than the benefits are worth. On the other hand, if such countries wish to attract vertical-type investments, it may be necessary to accept some of the characteristics typical of such investments—such as relatively high levels of foreign control and a relatively weak bargaining position vis-a-vis the foreign investor. Moreover, this is the type of investment where such problems as profit transfers via pricing policies become especially important and may require substantially different policies than pursued in the past. For example, instead of trying, usually ineffectively, to cope with this by better tax administration, it may be much more effective simply to negotiate a tax rate based on the capital invested.

Third, in many of the cases of investment related to export markets the notion of alternatives to foreign direct investment is difficult to contemplate. It is sometimes suggested that the various components of the package of foreign investment might be unscrambled and that the developing countries might purchase only those portions that they are lacking. But in the case of vertically-integrated export-oriented investment this does not seem very feasible, which means that it is not a practical option for many developing countries in many types of industries. Indeed, even in horizontal-type investment it is questionable whether the various components may be obtained more cheaply and as effectively on a fragmented basis as on a packaged basis.

Finally, if it is correct that policies in many developing countries in recent years have been shifting somewhat away from self-sufficiency and toward a greater emphasis on international trade, then there may also be a corresponding shift in the relative importance, potentially at least, of vertical versus horizontal types of investment and all that that implies.

The other question to be considered here is the effect of foreign ownership on business practice or policy in host countries. Foreign control lies at the heart of much of the concern about direct investment. If it could be demonstrated that business policies and practices are the same irrespective of whether control rests in the hands of local or foreign investors, much of the concern about foreign investment would be substantially different—though

other concerns of course still remain. The concern about foreign
control is manifest in a variety of ways including demands for local
equity participation, local representation on boards of directors,
and so forth.

It is also evident from a wide range of evidence that investing
firms, whatever their nationality, generally have a fairly strong
preference for wholly owned or at least partially owned subsidiaries.
This preference is based upon the desire to avoid conflicts with
local partners because of differences in attitudes, objectives, and
the circumstances confronting foreign and local investors. Given
this manifest preference for control and the ample opportunities to
exercise—including not only other foreign countries but the home
economy as well—it seems very likely that attempts to restrict
foreign control have a considerable impact on the flow of foreign
investment in the manufacturing sector or induce a wide range of
compensatory concessions for the investors that overcome his
preference. Moreover, when forced to divest, the foreign investors
may be able to set a price that capitalizes much of the return he
will forego as a result of local participation—a point emphasized
in a recent unpublished paper by T. Horst. Moreover, the key
question for local owners once they are installed is not whether
the global profits of the firm should be maximized but rather what
share of global profits should be ceded to the minority interests
of the subsidiary, that is, how much tribute can they collect.

The figures shown in Table 13.6 attempt to identify the effect
of the degree of foreign ownership on selected indicators of business
practice given the effect of the export share of output. What do
the estimates show?

1. The evidence provides little or no reason for believing
that the percentage of the workforce made up of local personnel is
significantly influenced by the degree of foreign ownership. Those
instances where there is some suggestion that it may be a factor
can be largely discounted since there is very little variation in the
variables that stand close to 100 for all investments.

2. There is some evidence that the change in exports from the
investing firm to the developing country as a result of these projects
was significantly associated with the degree of foreign ownership—
negatively in the case of the same product line and complementary
finished goods and positively in the case of raw materials. On
the import side there is some suggestion of a positive association.
But all of these associations are weak and highly uncertain.

3. The form in which earnings are received by investing firms
also seems to be unaffected by the degree of foreign ownership
with the possible exception of fees and royalties. The figures
suggest that the greater the degree of foreign ownership the lower
the share of earnings taken in the form of fees and royalties. These
relationships are marginally significant.

4. The evidence indicates that the higher the degree of foreign ownership the greater the percentage of initial financing drawn from abroad.

5. Although the relationships are very weak, there is some indication that the higher the degree of foreign ownership the lower the percentage of sales made in foreign countries other than the home country.

6. The percentage of foreign ownership is negatively and significantly related to the percentage of purchases made from indigenous local firms and perhaps also the greater the share of purchases made from the parent firm.

7. Little or no relationship is evident between the degree of foreign ownership and the number of new local businesses being brought into being or training costs.

8. There is some evidence that the greater the degree of foreign ownership the more competitive by international standards are production costs.

The procedure followed distinguishes export-oriented and locally oriented projects on the basis of S_i. However, one may question whether this is the most appropriate procedure given the bimodal distribution of our projects between these two categories. As a check on the estimates, the relationships were rerun replacing S_i by T_i, a dummy variable with the value 0 when the export share was 10 percent or less and 1 when it exceeded 10 percent. In most cases the degree of statistical significance coincides closely with those shown in Table 13.6 though it is generally marginally higher. The main exception relates to equation 10(a) pertaining to the relative production costs. The alternative estimate shows a stronger relationship between production costs and foreign ownership.

$$RC_i = 31.6 + 0.53 \ 0_i + 56.39 \ T_i$$
$$(2.48) \qquad\qquad (4.44)$$
$$\bar{R}^2 = .43$$
$$n = 45$$

Summing all this up, one may say that differences in the degree of foreign ownership do not seem to be very significantly associated with the performance characteristics of affiliates in host countries. There is some evidence that a larger degree of ownership is associated with (1) an inflow of more capital from abroad, (2) a smaller share of purchases from indigenous firms, and (3) lower production costs. Even these relationships are not very robust. Moreover, these and the other marginal effects to the extent that they do exist seem about as likely on balance to be to the advantage as to the disadvantage of host countries.

In conclusion, what this evidence suggests to me is that policies that give primary attention to questions of ownership and control and alternative ways of doing the same thing may be largely misplaced, at least for many developing countries. A more rewarding strategy may be to allow foreign investment to proceed largely unfettered into those areas where it is viable by international standards and to make sure that the developing countries obtain their share of the earnings. This poses a serious policy question, however, in that competition for such investment by the developing countries may erode the benefits they obtain.

NOTES

1. Private Firms Investment in Development (Oxford: Clarenden Press, 1973). This paper draws heavily on the text of the larger study at a number of points.
2. Richard Caves, "International Corporations: The Industrial Economics of Foreign Investment," Economica 38 (February 1971):1-27.
3. Gustav Papanek, "Aid, Foreign Private Investment, Savings and Growth in Less Developed Countries," Journal of Political Economy 81 (January-February 1973):120-130.

PART

VI

FORGING POLICIES
FOR EFFECTIVE
MULTINATIONAL
BUSINESS-GOVERNMENT
RELATIONS

14

**MULTINATIONAL
BUSINESS-GOVERNMENT
RELATIONS: SIX
PRINCIPLES FOR
EFFECTIVENESS**
J. J. Boddewyn

While journalistic exposes of firms like ITT as well as of business associations, lobbyists, and "superlawyers" make it appear that large American firms are very proficient at government relations and are routinely "walking the corridors of power," the opinions of qualified observers as well as scholarly studies present a much less flattering or threatening portrait.[1]

In this context, some 200 parent headquarters and overseas affiliates of U. S. multinational enterprises at the national and regional levels have been interviewed by this author since 1969, and their experience suggests a set of emerging principles to guide the development of effective government relations in the multinational process of monitoring and influencing the actions of the authorities. These are not simple and uniform rules, but rather a set of reflections on some of the major obstacles encountered in this process and of the better attitudes and actions that are devised to cope with them.

GOVERNMENT RELATIONS ARE UNAVOIDABLE
AND IMPORTANT

It is significant that David Lilienthal's seminal 1960 paper on "The Multinational Corporation," which launched that now famous expression, practically starts with an extended analysis of "relations with governments" that takes up half of that rather long chapter to stress its importance and ubiquitousness.[2]

The same point can be made today since modern governments everywhere are major economic agents acting as legitimizer, planner,

J. J. Boddewyn is Professor of International Business, Baruch College, City University of New York.

regulator, economic developer, supplier of various scarce goods, customer, and competitor. These active governmental roles obviously invite if not necessitate active government relations. Besides, the relations between business firms and governments in the mixed economies of today is increasingly one of symbiosis[3] where they have to rely on each other in order to achieve their respective objectives. The situation is thus frequently one of a "positive-sum game" where both parties benefit from their relationships.

Government relations are thus largely unavoidable, and they are particularly important for multinational firms whose legitimacy and loyalty are frequently questioned by host governments at home and abroad. While most U. S. multinationals are still at a low level of awareness and preparedness in this area, the more effective ones are taking their government relations very seriously instead of assuming that the "low-profile" approach is always appropriate.

GOVERNMENT RELATIONS ARE
AN EARNING FUNCTION

Politics has an unfavorable connotation for many people as is evident in the contrasting of "political risks" with "market opportunities" in studies of foreign countries. Yet, there are also "political opportunities" and "market risks" as is evident from the respective examples of Outboard Marine, which has been very much helped through incentives and other measures by the Belgian authorities at the national, provincial, and municipal levels, while Raytheon's failure in Italy was based on its producing out-of-date television tubes for an already saturated market.

Because of this negative view of politics, there is a tendency to view government relations in a defensive manner and as a protective device against the machinations of political demagogues and power-hungry bureaucrats. The latter exist for sure, and guarding one's firm against unfavorable developments is certainly a critical component of the government-relations function.

Beyond this elementary observation, however, lies the more profitable realization that modern governments control scarce and valuable goods in their capacities as credit suppliers through state financial institutions, as partners through state enterprises, as customers through their purchases, as grantors of partial or complete monopolies through their selective distribution of permissions to invest, as subsidizers of research and training programs, as providers of public utilities and "law and order," and so on.

Government relations are thus much more than a "spending" function on the order of a night watchman who protects a firm's real sources of profits. They have real "earning" potential; and

they deserve as much executive attention as the other two pillars
of profitability, namely, efficient management within the company
and business effectiveness in the marketplace. Most importantly,
when conjugated with the other facets of the external-affairs function,
government relations contribute to obtaining and maintaining the
legitimacy—the "stamp of approval" of society—which ultimately
underlies the survival and prosperity of a particular firm and of the
business system in general.

This emphasis on earning, however, should not obscure the
fact that the effectiveness of government relations seldom can
immediately be measured in terms of their impact on costs, sales,
or return on investment. So many things contribute to profitability
that it is very difficult to single any one of them out. For example,
the usefulness of good personal relations with government officials
is not readily measurable although such relations may ultimately
be a crucial reason why a company received certain benefits or
avoided a particular problem.

For that matter, a goodly portion of government relations is
in the nature of a "reserve power" that prevents unwelcome outcomes.
This function thus resembles that of the military charged with keeping
the country out of war. Being ready, strong, feared, and/or respected
helps achieve this objective; but then when there is no conflict,
people wonder why armed forces are needed! This aspect of government relations must be understood lest it lead to the unwarranted
elimination or curtailment of a government relations staff.

Finally, government relations are no panacea and are usually
not sufficient to insure a firm's prosperity or survival even though
the Lockheed, Penn-Central, and Rolls-Royce cases illustrate the
life-saving contribution of this function. In any case, there usually
are limits to what dealings with the authorities can achieve. For
example, one U. S. firm that supplies public-telephone equipment
in several European countries can count only on a certain share of
government purchases because the authorities are anxious to keep
other firms going in order to insure competition and innovation.
No amount of government relations is likely to change that share
but it helps keep it, when coupled with internal efficiency and
market effectiveness, since government relations can be very
effective in magnifying the impact of these more traditional sources
of profitability and survival.

GOVERNMENT RELATIONS MUST BE MANAGED

Obviously, situations differ as to what response is needed in
the light of such factors as the size, age, experience, and tradition
of the company, its industry and the markets it serves, as well as
the political-ideological configuration and stage of economic development of the host country.[4]

To illustrate this point, one can reflect briefly on the different opportunities and problems encountered at the entry, operations, and exit stages of a foreign investment. At entry, government relations center on negotiating favorable conditions in light of the company's anticipated contributions and the country's needs. Headquarter executives and experts (legal, technical, financial, etc.) are actively involved as well as a number of intermediaries such as consultants, bankers, and lawyers. Ongoing operations, on the other hand, require a type of government relations focusing on the integration of the guest company into the host economy and society through the obeying of laws, the maintenance of employment, and the fitting into local patterns of influencing government policy; and local nationals, insiders, and collective action (for example, through business associations) play a greater role than at the entry stage. Exit, whether forced or not, is again different as government relations typically take place in a more hostile or at least tense context that requires that outsiders, experts, and/or hatchet men be brought in.

The major point here is that government relations have to be intelligently managed like any other function of the enterprise, rather than neglected, improvised, or let go wild. Doing nothing can be dangerous, and the "low profile" approach cannot be assumed to represent the epitome of good external relations in all cases. Complacency must also be shunned, as in the case of the executive who said, "The Chairman of our subsidiary in Italy is a good friend of the Prime Minister," implying that this took care of government relations in that country, as if governments did not change, and as if such an arrangement was sufficient in itself.

A key principle in this respect is that informed commitment is more important than any particular organizational structure or technique. Simply imitating some competitor's move, coping with a problem on an ad hoc and crisis basis, or succumbing to the entreaties of a consultant are poor ways of getting started in government relations. Those relations should rest instead on an understanding of the function's importance and on an appraisal of risks and opportunities in this area. Ultimately, this awareness and commitment must pervade the entire organization instead of being relegated to some specialized niche and personnel.

The techniques, for that matter, are not arcane or terribly sophisticated since the state of monitoring the nonmarket environment is still very primitive,[5] while the art of "making friends and influencing people" is age-old. It is seldom a matter of cloak-and-dagger machinations and dark conspiracies a la ITT in Chile but rather a matter of building good sources of information, useful contacts, valid arguments based on real contributions, and the necessary negotiating skills. Multinationals are also well advised to anticipate the normally downward course of their bargaining power over the life of an investment, and to renew it through new and well-publicized contributions to the host economy and society.

A mixture of professional, cultural, and ethical judgment has to be exercised here since ways and means vary over time and place. Government relations being a rather "polycentric" locally oriented function, American MNCs are well advised to stay within what local firms are doing in the way of creating favorable images, of influencing public policies, and of negotiating with government. In Rome, an American subsidiary cannot always do what the Romans do—for example, bargain for lower taxes in exchange for support for the ruling political party—but it can well import effective U. S. techniques such as those public-relations activities associated with a plant opening. Such imports must, of course, be fitted to the local situation, but this usually is a minor problem in government relations because, as one manager put it: "Americans are not in danger of exporting the wrong thing but of not doing anything at all since they do so little of it at home while most foreigners are much more accustomed to dealing with government!"

GOVERNMENT RELATIONS ARE
A TOP-MANAGEMENT FUNCTION

The fact that the number of Washington representatives as well as of vice-presidents and staffs for government relations (various names are used) is growing should not obscure the requirement that the top must be actively involved in planning and conducting government relations.

The fundamental reason for this situation is that nobody else can represent the corporation in the acquisition of legitimacy and community support typically bestowed by government, public opinion, and other legitimizing elites. This "institutional role" belongs to top management and is part of executive leadership almost by definition.[6] Normally, this task is carried out by the board of directors, and some American subsidiaries abroad use it for that purpose, particularly when local nationals must sit on such boards (as in Sweden and Indonesia). However, most U. S. subsidiaries have only nominal inside boards composed of executives from the parent company and the subsidiaries, so that this task has to be handled by the top executive(s) on the spot, whether consistently or on an ad hoc basis.

A more operational reason why external affairs cannot be delegated downward is that, as one executive put it, "Only real power can face power in important negotiations and deliberations with government and other groups." Staffs and lower-level managers can obviously prepare the ground and carry out routine or less crucial transactions, but only the man or men who know and represent the total firm and control its resources can speak with full authority when important matters are at stake.

This requirement is reinforced by the fact that in most countries there is a long tradition of centralized authority, whereby companies speak only through their top executives, for example, within trade associations and with government officials. Having a lesser executive represent the company in major external contacts is actually interpreted as a slur on the other party and is not conducive to open and productive deliberations. Protocol thus also requires top-management involvement in relations with government and other key groups.

Such a requirement has important implications for the selection and grooming of top executives whose experience is frequently inadequate for government relations—a function often spurned by production and marketing managers who tend to see it as not central to what a business firm is all about. The unfortunate practice of appointing rich political donors as U.S. ambassadors also reveals a belief that dealing with foreign governments requires no special competence and that success in the tough world of business is enough, when in fact this is not the case at all.

This problem is compounded by the importance of personal relations in government relations—a requirement often vitiated by the frequent rotation of expatriate managers and by their frequent lack of knowledge of the local language. Obviously, much greater attention has to be paid to that crucial aspect of executive leadership that can of course be assisted by various assistants and outsiders.[7]

GOVERNMENT RELATIONS ARE
A LEGITIMATE FUNCTION

Even if necessary, government relations will not be accepted unless they are also seen as proper. Here, many business executives feel ill at ease with the notion of dealing with government. Part of this attitude comes from lack of familiarity and experience, but it also stems from the idea that government relations are "not nice." For one thing, the tendency for business and government actors in the United States has been to conceive of their mutual relationships in the arm's length context of a laissez-faire economic system. Closer relations between the two, on the other hand, have been associated with other types of economic systems that they find objectionable for mixing what should remain separate spheres of specialized if complementary endeavor.

This relative underdevelopment of the government-relations function in the United States also reflects the background and mentalities of corporate executives. Particularly those with careers

centering on engineering, production, or marketing have tended to
view government relations as irrational and unbusinesslike when
compared to the traditional ideologies that stress efficiency, rational-
ity, innovation, and competitiveness through management, marketing,
and engineering.

In such a context, government relations are considered proper
only when the company needs to be protected or rescued by government, or when it must defend itself against some unconscionable
action on the part of the authorities. This view is akin to considering the government as a "partner of last resort" and to viewing
government relations as a "necessary evil" type of practice best
left to some remote Washington representative, some mysterious
special assistant to the president, or some hidden "Department of
Dirty Tricks."

Only readily accepted are the purely informative and liaison
roles of government relations in such matters as the monitoring
of legislative and administrative developments, the relaying of
company positions on pending legislation and regulation (for example,
at congressional hearings), and the applications for government
purchase orders and permits (to operate, export, hire, etc.),
provided they are done in an open and rational way on all sides.

Such "acceptable" activities are obviously essential and a
normal part of the government relations function, but I think that
more than that is justified by the notion of "corporate citizenship,"
which is so highly recommended nowadays. This principle includes
by definition both the duty to serve society (the part usually stressed)
and the right to be heard and heeded. This right of petition is
guaranteed by the First Amendment to the U. S. Constitution; while
abroad, many planning schemes make such relations a matter of
routine if not of obligation (for example, in corporative states such
as Spain and in the context of the formal "consultative bodies" of
countries like Belgium). Multinationals are thus entitled to press
actively for their views and needs.

Obviously there are acceptable and unacceptable ways of
monitoring and influencing governments, but occasional improper
practices do not invalidate the legitimacy of this function any more
than shady advertising claims or "yellow" labor contracts do not
obliterate the fundamental need for marketing and industrial relations
nor the societal contributions that these functions make.

Here, government relations are more likely to be accepted as
legitimate if they are seen as being related to the broad concerns
of society that governments everywhere make explicit and attempt
to satisfy,[8] rather than being only concerned with manipulating
the state and society for purely selfish personal and corporate
interests.

GOVERNMENT RELATIONS MUST BE VIEWED
IN A MUTUALLY BENEFICIAL PERSPECTIVE

The state is sovereign by definition, and companies are only subjects. Yet, there will always be some weak governments when it comes to influencing legislation or negotiating a new or an old investment. Such a situation may be chronic or evolve over time; but in either case, a very uneven relationship of the dictator-supplicant type is seldom fruitful in the longer run because it leads to ill feelings, recriminations, renegotiations, nationalizations, stagnation of investment, and/or divestment.[9]

Instead, the best gains are those that leave the other party satisfied too—now and for the foreseeable future. Hence, it is essential for MNCs to consider the problems and goals of governments and to couch their own approaches in terms of what they will contribute to the satisfaction and achievement of public objectives. Conversely, opposition to government policies must stress how they may be self-defeating or inferior in terms of what a country needs and wants.

This has been IBM's preferred stance in Europe where, in the best diplomatic tradition, it has usually chosen (with mixed success) to draw the attention of the British, French, and German governments to the fact that their policies of favoring national computer firms (ICL, CII, and Siemens) is not likely to result in good economics (mainly lower costs and larger exports) or technological superiority. That company is also increasingly attempting to even out its impact on balance of payments of host countries—for example, by locating IBM's European training facilities in Belgium where no major production facilities are contemplated but where IBM imports are high.

Many MNCs find it hard to adopt such a posture because of the near irresistible attractiveness of high profits and of getting something for nothing or little, and because MNCs prefer to compensate for higher overseas risks through quick and handsome returns. Still, "getting all one can get" with no thought for the morrow and the other party is inviting trouble overseas.

As Jack Behrman has argued, we can expect an increased emphasis on criteria of fairness and equity in the division of burdens and benefits; the MNCs should therefore try to get on the same side of the problems as the host government and to view them as ones for which mutually beneficial solutions have to be found.[10] What is good for General Motors is often good for the countries where it operates ("and vice-versa," as Charles E. Wilson correctly put it in his famous statement that unfortunately is often only partially quoted), but this beneficial relationship should not be assumed to exist too automatically. Instead, the good of the other side also has to be explicitly considered beyond the more natural tendency to think only of one's own. While host governments are increasingly requiring such explicit consideration of their country's needs and objectives, effective government relations demand that such a calculus be made even if it is not mandatory.

NOTES

1. For an analysis of the need for effective government relations in international business, and of the structures and processes developed for that purpose, see A. Kapoor and J. Boddewyn, International Business-Government Relations (New York: American Management Association, 1973); and J. Boddewyn and A. Kapoor, "The External Relations of U. S. Multinational Enterprises," International Studies Quarterly 16, no. 4 (December 1972):433-53 (part of the following analysis rests on these two publications). See also K. K. Bivens and H. S. Lambeth, A World-wide Look At Business-Government Relations (New York: Conference Board, 1967).

For the less flattering studies, see, for example, L. A. Dexter, How Organizations Are Represented in Washington (Washington, D. C.: Brookings Institution, 1962); and R. W. Miller and J. D. Johnson, Corporate Ambassadors to Washington (Washington, D. C.: American University, Center for the Study of Private Enterprise, 1970).

2. In Melvin Anshen and G. L. Bach, eds., Management and Corporations 1985 (New York: McGraw-Hill, 1960), pp. 119-58. The government-relations sections runs from pages 121 to 140.

3. Some economists have pointed out that besides the more obvious systems of "capitalism" and "socialism," there is an emerging third model of the "bargained economy" where major interest groups such as business and labor negotiate major economic decisions under the prodding and arbitration of government that acts as "king amidst his barons." See R. A. Solo, Economic Organizations and Social Systems (Indianapolis: Bobbs-Merrill, 1967), pp. 12ff. Analysis of the technostructure and/or military-industrial complex—whether marxist or galbraithian—is definitely related to this view of current economic systems.

4. For a more detailed analysis of the importance of these factors, see the various publications mentioned in the first part of note 1.

5. For evidence to that effect, see J. S. Schwendiman, "International Strategic Planning: Still in Its Infancy?" Worldwide P & I Planning, (September-October 1971), pp. 52-61, and his book Strategic Long-range Planning for the Multinational Corporation (New York: Praeger, 1973).

6. For scholarly arguments to that effect, see Talcott Parsons, Structure and Process in Modern Societies (New York: The Free Press, 1960); Philip Selznick, Leadership in Administration (Evanston, Ill.:

Row, Peterson, 1957); and J. Boddewyn, "External Affairs: A Corporate Function in Search of Conceptualization and Theory" (paper presented at the May 1973 CARI Conference Center of Business and Economic Research, Kent State University, to be published by the conference).

7. For a discussion of the types of people needed in government relations and external affairs, see J. Boddewyn, "Organizing the International External-Affairs Function: Critical Problems and Decisions," Working paper No. 73-42, Graduate School of Business Administration, New York University, July 1973.

8. Concern with societal needs is more correctly handled in the context of the external-affairs function that relates the firm's interests to those of society. Government relations constitute a crucial subpart of this function, which focuses on government as the major "public" in the "nonmarket environment" of the firm. For further elaboration on this distinction, see Kapoor and Boddewyn, op. cit.

9. R. D. Robinson has very aptly discussed the types (good and bad) of relations between business firms and governments in his International Business Policy (New York: Holt, Rinehart & Winston, 1964).

10. J. N. Behrman, "The Multinational Enterprise in 1976 and After: A Revolutionary View," in Management of the Multinationals, ed. S. P. Sethi and R. P. Holton (New York: The Free Press, 1974).

15

IMPLICATIONS OF
MULTINATIONAL
CORPORATIONS FOR
INTERNATIONAL
POLITICS
David H. Blake

A majority of the chapters in this volume focus on the linkage between multinational corporations and nation-states. This is reasonable since nation-states provide the critical and immediate environment within which multinational corporations must learn to operate. However, it is also important and useful to examine the ways in which multinational corporations by their existence and/or conscious policies influence international politics or the relations among states. This orientation is significant because multinational corporations are indeed international actors and as such their actions do have implications for interstate relations. Furthermore, specific nation-states have at times expressed concern over the ways in which these international enterprises have influenced negatively the relations among states. Moreover, in a much broader sense, the international political system also is an environment with which multinational corporations will have to contend both now and in the future. As examples, the patterns of relations within the Middle East certainly have importance for corporations and states. Similarly, the current Soviet-American detente has created new and exciting opportunities for international enterprises.

The thrust of this chapter, then, is to explore how multinational enterprises affect the international political system and the relations among political entities such as states and regional and international organizations. Figure 15.1 illustrates the approach of this study as opposed to the more frequent consideration of corporate and state relations. Unfortunately, this topic has not been subjected to

David H. Blake is Associate Professor of Business Administration and of Political Science, Graduate School of Business, University of Pittsburgh. This chapter is adapted from a chapter of a book authored by David H. Blake and Robert S. Walters, The Politics of Global Economic Relations.

FIGURE 15.1

The Political Implications of Multinational Corporations:
Two Perspectives

MNC nation-state orientation: the prevailing focus

MNC implications for relations among states

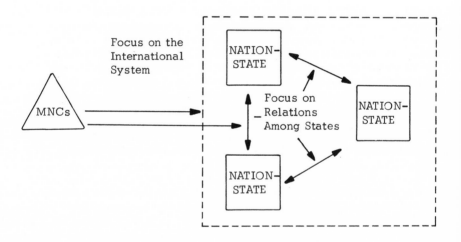

Source: Compiled by the author.

rigorous empirical investigation, and therefore the objective of this study can only be to identify ways in which multinational enterprises can affect the relations among states. First to be considered will be those consequences of international firms that tend to provoke conflict among states or groups of states. These, to my way of thinking, are negative or dysfunctional impacts on international politics. This will be followed by a brief discussion of the positive effects of multinational corporations; these are deemed to be positive in that they tend to reduce conflict among states.

NEGATIVE EFFECT ON
INTERNATIONAL POLITICS

The parent state-host state relationship is particularly suscep-tible to the emergence of conflicting issues as a result of multinational enterprises. Since both the parent and host states seek to utilize the international firm for their own objectives, very basic questions of sovereignty and jurisdiction arise in which the corporation may be caught in the middle. Antitrust provisions and the trading with the enemy act have often been mentioned as sore points injuring the relationship between the United States as a parent government and other countries as host states. These questions of jurisdiction have at several different times been raised in Canada and other states regarding legal demands of the U. S. government or its courts. For example, in 1950 the Canadian provinces of Ontario and Quebec tried to prevent U. S. subsidiaries from providing documents in compliance with U. S. court decisions by passing laws prohibiting such actions. At times, tangled diplomatic negotiations are necessary to unravel the complications resulting from jurisdictional disputes. In all these cases the existence of the transnational corporations brought into question the fundamental issue of which political entity had jurisdiction. It is not unreasonable to foresee that such problems will arise again.

The issue is complicated and exacerbrated by the fact that host states and parent states may have very different objectives for the same multinational enterprise. According to balance of payments calculations (one issue of obvious importance) a parent state trying to correct a deficit might enact regulations that seek to hasten and enlarge the repatriation of profits and management fees from the subsidiary, to hinder and restrict the outflow of new capital for investment thereby provoking the use of local sources of funds within the host state, and to expand the exports from the parent company and eliminate imports from the subsidiary. Of course, the host state troubled by a balance of payments deficit may institute regulations that have exactly the opposite effect from that desired by the parent state. Figure 15.2 illustrates the problem posed.

FIGURE 15.2

Parent State-Host State Conflict Matrix:
MNC Effect on Balance of Payments

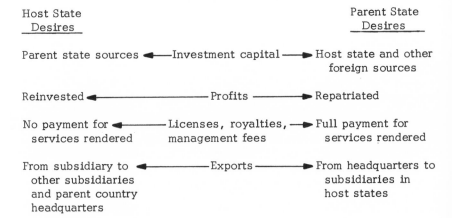

Host State Desires		Parent State Desires
Parent state sources ◄—Investment capital—►		Host state and other foreign sources
Reinvested ◄———————— Profits ————►		Repatriated
No payment for ◄———Licenses, royalties, —► services rendered management fees		Full payment for services rendered
From subsidiary to ◄———Exports————► other subsidiaries and parent country headquarters		From headquarters to subsidiaries in host states

Source: Compiled by the author.

Other issues involve the different objectives of parent and host states regarding trade, domestic employment problems, currency stability and valuation, national security issues and the impact of the location of research and development efforts, foreign policy matters, and other similar issues. For these and other issues it is possible to develop a conflict matrix such as that in Figure 15.2 to specify the differing objectives of host and parent states regarding the actions and effects of multinational corporations. A conflict matrix could also be constructed illustrating the various policy actions that could be undertaken by parent or host states in pursuit of their essentially conflicting objectives. The purpose of such an exercise and of this discussion is to emphasize that the behavior and existence of multinational corporations may be the source and vehicle of worsening relations between parent and host states as the result of each attempting to harness the corporation to advance their own interests.

Parent states and host states may also clash as a result of their attempts to influence the behavior of multinational corporations. The efforts of Cuba, Peru, Bolivia, and Chile regarding the nationalization of U. S. business enterprises in these countries had an obvious negative effect on the official government relations between these states and the United States. Somewhat similar problems have occurred involving French firms operating in Africa, and it is

highly probable that difficulties will emerge with Japanese enterprises in their Asian operations.

MNCs AS FOREIGN POLICY CONDUITS

Just as multinational corporations may be the source of conflicting relations between parent and host states, these firms may also
be the vehicle by which host or parent countries try to influence
the other. There is the much-talked-about fear with some justifying
examples that multinational corporations may serve as a conduit
for parent-state foreign policy actions. There is the example of
the U. S. government efforts to hinder the development of a French
nuclear force by prohibiting IBM from selling needed equipment.
Certainly, the well-known ITT-CIA case regarding the Allende
government in Chile heightens the fears and suspicions that multinationals may be the vehicle for U. S. foreign policy efforts.
The reverse is true also where the host state attempts to
influence the parent state through a multinational firm. In response
to President Nixon's August 1971 10 percent import surcharge, many
U. S. firms with subsidiaries in Latin America loudly decried and
sought the rapid repeal of the measure since Latin America was
already running a trade deficit with the United States. Whether
out of enlightened self-interest or direct requests from host-state
officials, it is clear that these firms were seeking to influence
U. S. policy on behalf of the Latin American host states. There
are similar indications that the Arab states are attempting to influence
U. S. and Western policy toward the Middle East via the multinational oil companies. The July 1973 letter to stockholders from
Standard Oil of California urging "understanding on our part of the
aspirations of the Arab people, and more positive support of their
efforts toward peace in the Middle East," is a good example of
a multinational's efforts to influence parent-state policy on behalf
of host states. As this pressure mounts and as the oil producing
countries begin to exercise their influence potential, one possible
result is that relations between the parent countries and host states
will worsen. Whether this happens or not, it is clear that the
multinationals will be right in the midst of the host state-parent
state relationship and as such are likely to have some effect on
relations.
The potential impact of multinational corporations on parent
state-host state relations is readily recognized, but there are
other relationships that multinational firms may adversely affect.
For instance, competition among parent states on behalf of their
own multinational firms may emerge in the near future. The expansion and success of American-based multinational corporations has
led a number of European states to counteract these challenges by

rationalizing and consolidating their own companies with the objective of forming sizable multinationals of their own to compete with
the foreign firms. As the creation of state policy, it is reasonable
to expect that the parent governments in some cases will seek to
insure that their firms are successful in their efforts by actively
supporting their firms to the detriment of international enterprises
of a different nationality. Moreover, some of the giant European
multinationals such as British Petroleum, Renault, and ENI are
partially owned by their respective governments, and the concept
of Japan Inc. suggests the very close relationship between the
Japanese government and its multinational enterprises.

A further stimulus to conflict among parent states stemming from
competition among multinational corporations is the current concern
about raw material and energy shortages. The lack of any domestic
supply of petroleum combined with the oil needs of a rapidly
growing economy in conjunction with the current efforts of the
Organization of Petroleum Exporting Countries (OPEC) to control
and coordinate policies regarding petroleum supplies has led the
Japanese government to help its firms explore for oil in other areas.
An oil-hungry and -dependent Europe might seek to establish new
sources of supply for itself and its own firms to the disadvantage
of Japanese and U. S. firms. Consequently, competition among
the multinational corporations of different nationalities for what
are thought to be vital scarce resources may well lead to conflict
among the parent governments of these firms.

Indeed, the international airline industry and the conflict to
be found there as the result of government support of private,
quasi-government, or totally government-owned firms may be the
forerunner of the conflict that may emerge as parent states seek to
advance the interests of their own international enterprises. The
day may not be too distant when competition among multinational
corporations from different countries will provoke political and
economic involvement by the respective parent governments. Perhaps
formal international negotiations involving both government and
corporate representatives of competing parent states periodically
will be necessary to achieve "peace."

COMPETITION FOR FOREIGN INVESTMENT
AS A SOURCE OF CONFLICT

Competition to attract the benefits of foreign investment may
lead to a degree of conflict between host states. Already, many
host states compete with each other by offering varying kinds of
inducements to foreign investors. During a 1971 visit to the United
Kingdom, Henry Ford made it clear to Prime Minister Heath and the
British people that the unsatisfactory labor-relations climate in

Great Britain might cause Ford of England to restrict new investment or even transfer some existing investment from Britain to other countries. The next day a group of Dutch businessmen and government officials voiced their invitation to Ford to consider further investment in the Netherlands. While this same episode might not happen today, among advanced industrial states and among the developing nations competition for foreign investment does exist.

There are several possible effects of this vying for multinational corporations. One result if the competition is severe enough may be to increase the various state incentive packages and/or reduce the investment risks and costs for the corporations. If states are actively pursuing foreign investment, they may undercut each other in offering inducements thereby generally reducing the level of their returns or benefits they can expect from such investment.

Moreover, the uneven pattern of foreign investment in the world or within a region may help to sour relations among nearby states. For example, within a particular region the combination of natural and human endowments, locational advantages, government policies, and other factors may mean that one or two states receive much of the foreign investment and other states very little at all. To the extent that multinational corporations are thought to bring more advantages than disadvantages, it may be that the less fortunate states will seek to gain a greater share of the foreign investment through political efforts directed toward the more successful host countries.

REGIONAL BLOCS AND FOREIGN INVESTMENT

As a result of competition for investment and concern about the unequal distribution of such investment, some states in a particular region may seek to form a regional grouping to distribute more equitably and purposefully foreign investment, to harmonize the laws and incentives regarding these enterprises, and to reduce generally the possibility of intraregion conflict because of these firms. Among other reasons, the desire to present a united front to foreign investors was a major stimulus for the formation of the Andean community involving the six states of Venezuela, Columbia, Ecuador, Peru, Bolivia, and Chile. Thus, in almost a dialectical fashion, competition among host states as a result of multinational enterprises may lead to the development of regional strategies designed to prevent this conflict.

However, similar regional or international efforts to contain interstate conflict may be perceived by some host states as interfering with their ability to try to attract foreign investment or at least to determine their own policies on these issues. Columbia and Venezuela had some hesitancies about joining the Andean pact because both countries have had relatively satisfactory experiences with a sizable foreign investment sector. Host-state conflict with international or regional organizations emerges from the assessment of the former that it will be able to obtain a greater amount of foreign investment and resultant benefits by not subscribing to the international or regional agreement. Such an agreement establishes a common policy toward multinational corporations. Therefore, a state with a relatively attractive environment for foreign investment may, following the logic presented by Mancur Olson, adopt a strategy and policies that are less restrictive and onerous than those of the regional or international organization.[1]

Moreover, following the same kind of logic, a member state of such a group that feels disadvantaged by its participation may well determine to drop out of the regional or international organization in order to pursue its own objectives in its own way. For example, if one of the members of the Andean community feels that the reduced flow of new foreign investment is largely responsible for a smaller economic and industrial growth rate than was expected, then it may decide to withdraw from the arrangement. If the costs of membership outweigh the benefits derived, there is little point in continuing to participate. Of course, any attempt by the regional or international group to force compliance involves conflict—precisely that which such an arrangement seeks to avoid. The point of this discussion is that to some states the benefits accompanying foreign investment are something worth obtaining, and regional or international arrangements that hinder states in these efforts are likely to foment conflict.

Similarly, regional or international efforts to control multinational firms may provoke conflict between the parent states of these enterprises and the international organization. Depending upon the composition of the regional or international group, the parent states may be excluded from the process by which the controls are developed and implemented. In other cases the very small number of important parent states may be outvoted by the more numerous host states. In both cases the parent countries may well object to the outcome of a procedure in which they have little influence.

Furthermore, the conflict between regional or international organizations and parent states is likely to be even more severe to the extent that specific parent states are deeply committed to the success of their multinational corporations. Where state ownership of international firms is large or where the state perceives these enterprises as playing a crucial role in securing needed natural resources for the parent state economy, these states are likely to interfere in the efforts of a group of host countries to impose severe restrictions. Evidence of this concern is apparent in the conflict between the major petroleum countries and the

Organization of Petroleum Exporting Countries. Parent states such as the United States, Great Britain, France, and Japan have to varying degrees become involved in the several negotiations and the relationship more generally.

Somewhat similar developments may emerge should the developing countries as a whole or in regional groupings seek to impose extensive and general restrictions on multinational enterprises. Regardless of state ownership or national security concerns, it is probable that some of the parent states might use their economic and political strength to modify the conditions proposed. As multinational enterprises become more integrated internationally, thereby increasing the interdependency of parent-state economies with that of host states, then parent states may feel that they have a vested interest in insuring the relatively free flow of investment and goods among states. In sum, for a variety of reasons, parent states may seek to insure that the proposals of groups of host states to restrict multinational enterprises are not injurious to the national interests of the capital exporting countries. Obviously, conflict may ensue if parent states and the regional or international organizations disagree over objectives or methods of achieving these objectives.

Multinational corporations might eventually provoke competition among different international, regional, or functional groupings. One form of conflict might occur because of the desire of different groups of states to compete for foreign investment. While this has not occurred yet (and may not), it is theoretically possible, for example, that the Caribbean Free Trade Area states and the Central American Common Market states would be attempting to attract the same foreign investment. Conflict and competitive policies might ensue.

Perhaps a more likely source of conflict between two international or regional groups would involve an organization more or less representative of capital exporting countries and one representative of the developing countries. Over the issue of multinational corporations, UNCTAD and the OECD might find themselves in substantial disagreement. Other groups or organizations such as the General Agreement on Tariffs and Trade, the International Monetary Fund, various U. N. agencies, and even an international organization designed specifically to deal with foreign investment might find themselves involved in interagency disputes. Furthermore, conflict between an international organization and a regional one that had a quite different set of policies might emerge.

This section of the chapter has attempted to indicate the many ways in which multinational corporations as a matter of policy or merely because of competition for their benefits have and may affect adversely the patterns of relations among states and international or regional organizations. While it is impossible for conceptual as well as methodological reasons to determine precisely the impact of these enterprises on international politics either in specific cases or generally, it is important to be aware of the possible implications for the relations between states. Multinational corporations are crucial international actors, and any attempt to analyze international politics should also incorporate an assessment of the impact of these firms, both individually and collectively.

POSITIVE EFFECT OF MULTINATIONAL CORPORATIONS ON INTERNATIONAL POLITICS

Some students of the multinational corporation claim that these enterprises have had and will continue to have a beneficial impact on the relations among states. In several different ways, multinational enterprises are thought to contribute to regional or functional integration and other cooperative efforts. In the first place, the existence of multinational corporations may directly cause political entities to adopt common policies to counteract, adapt to, or get the most benefit from the activity of multinational corporations. Concerns about the ability of multinational enterprises to exploit a common market situation led the Andean community to adopt a set of stringent barriers and regulations designed to closely control the ability of such firms to do business in this regional market. In another example the OPEC countries have joined together to present a united front to the giant multinational oil companies. In these cases and others the multinational enterprise has had a catalytic role in the formation of coordinated efforts among states.

Secondly, multinational corporations as a result of their own integrated nature and their impact on other social units may help to provide an environment that is conducive to the promotion of integration among states. The ability of these enterprises to surmount national boundaries in the production and marketing of a product contributes to the establishment of a common regional culture and life-style. Integrated production means that workers in a number of different states are closely linked to one another in terms of their work and of course to their employer, and in Europe particularly, regional union organizations are springing up to represent these regionwide interests. Management personnel in Europe are beginning to develop a European perspective and perceive of themselves as having interests and opportunities that range beyond their own country.[2] Also within Europe there are many products, brand names, and advertising efforts that are common to several different states. In sum, the multinational corporation may help to break down the barriers of separateness and to provide some of the common interests and culture that foster regional interest groups and regional orientations.

Some supporters of the multinational corporation claim that it
is a force for peace among states since it represents an extremely
successful form of internationalism that does link states more
closely together. In spite of the political impediments of different
national systems and national characteristics, the corporation has
succeeded in overcoming these barriers to make states somewhat
more interdependent and thus less likely to engage in violent
conflict. The president of the Bank of America had many supporters
when he wrote with great clarity:

> the idea that this kind of business enterprise can be a
> strong force toward world peace is not so far fetched.
> Beyond the human values involved, the multinational
> firm has a direct, measurable, and potent interest in
> helping prevent wars and other serious upheavals that
> cut off its resources, interrupt its communications,
> and kill its employees and customers.[3]

This quotation reflects the belief of many that multinational corporations are the most effective and operational international institutions
in existence today.

Up to this point in the chapter multinational corporations have
been examined largely in terms of their impact on nation-state
relations. However, a different perspective is useful, for not
only do these firms have important consequences for state actors,
they also have stimulated the development of other nongovernmental
actors in the international system. While the former relationship
is the source of so much concern and comment about multinationals
by scholars and policymakers, it is in the latter area where some
far-ranging and basic changes may be emerging. To oversimplify
things a bit, it appears that an international economic and political
system may be emerging with the multinational corporation being
both the major institution of this system as well as the prime
stimulus for the development of other structures. However, all
this is occurring without a corresponding political focal point.

MNCs AS VEHICLES OF A NEW
INTERNATIONAL ECONOMIC ORDER

Because of the importance of the international economic system,
various international groups formed about common interests are
beginning to participate in the system as their domestic counterparts
do in individual states. The reason for this activity is the simple
fact that the international economic transactions have important
consequences for the interests of these groups, and as a result
they seek to influence these transactions. Nation-states have not

been particularly responsive or effective in controlling the impact of the international economic system; strictly domestic-oriented groups are relatively powerless in the light of the internationalness of the system; and few meaningful international government mechanisms exist. Thus, there is a need to develop an international capability.

The lack of a systematic investigation of this phenomenon requires us to illustrate this point by specific examples. The Council of the Americas is an example of a business-oriented group somewhat analogous to a lobbying organization in that it seeks to promote actions by Latin American governments that favor multinational corporations. Also the council seeks to aid and educate American corporations regarding the problems and prospects of doing business in Latin America. In addition to the council and a number of other similar organizations, there are various international trade associations of some importance. More broadly, the International Chamber of Commerce has made a significant effort to develop a proposed set of guidelines for multinational corporations, parent governments, and host governments. Quite clearly, the International Chamber of Commerce hopes that its ideas will be largely incorporated into other efforts of this sort mounted by states or international organizations.

Recognizing the many business-oriented organizations in this emerging international system, probably the more interesting developments involve those groups seeking to offer a countervailing force to the multinational corporation. The efforts of international labor union organizations in this regard are most revealing, for the patterns of response that are being established may prove to be some sort of a model for the actions of other groups. The various national labor movements feel themselves to be somewhat helpless in the face of the international mobility, flexibility, and strength of the multinational corporations. For a variety of reasons, the strategies and tactics used by unions on domestic employers are frequently less effective on multinational employers.[4]

To overcome this disadvantageous relationship, a number of activities have been designed to exert some control over the corporations.[5] At the national level, unions from two or more different states have cooperated to aid each other in their conflicts with the same multinational employer. At times this has meant the holding of meetings to exchange information and plan strategy for eventual confrontations with management. In other instances, this has resulted in actual coordinated action against the employer in several different countries. At the regional level, groups of unions have formalized their efforts to coordinate some actions regarding the corporations. Through the leadership of the European Metalworkers' Federation, representatives of unions from several states have met with the management of such multinational employers as Philips, AKZO, VFW-Fokker, and others to discuss various issues.

Moreover, where a union in one country has struck a multinational employer sometimes counterpart unions in other countries have refused to work overtime to take up the slack caused by the disruption in production and have applied similar types of pressure to the common employer.

At the international level, similar activities have occurred. A number of the international trade secretariats—international union organizations organized according to type of industry, such as the International Metalworkers' Federation and the International Chemical and General Workers' Federation—have formed company councils composed of many of the unions associated with the same multinational employer. Information exchange, consultation and planning, and joint solidarity actions have been planned and coordinated by these international trade secretariats.

While these activities do not represent the prevailing pattern of union responses to multinational corporations and the international economic system, they do represent efforts of both a formal and informal sort to confront multinational corporations on a regional and international level. To a limited but increasing extent, industrial relations are being internationalized.

It is this type of development, stimulated by multinational corporations, that is leading to the emergence of an international economic and political system. Processes and procedures formerly limited to nation-states are being introduced at the regional and international level as a matter of necessity because of the international nature of the firms. While this is clearly a slow process, there is enough evidence to suggest that this may well be one of the most important long-run effects of the multinational corporations. It has provoked an internationalism of an operational sort before the formal political mechanisms are able to be similarly international in nature. Probably, in the long run, the stimulation of an emerging international system will have positive effects for international peace and cooperation but undoubtedly there will be many instances of conflict fostered by these developments.

CONCLUSION

The multinational corporation has wide-ranging implications for a variety of political and nonpolitical actors and systems. The importance of the corporation/nation-state link is well known and has immediate repercussions for state and corporate policy. Much less attention, though, is paid to the impact of these firms on the relations among states. Except for rather self-serving and unsubstantiated claims that multinational corporations are a force for peace by creating interdependencies among states and reducing somewhat the vehemence of nationalism, little analysis of this issue by either scholars or policy makers has been undertaken. However, in the long run the nature of political relations among states determines the ability of corporations to operate internationally. A world or region rife with conflict or the existence of extremely hostile relations between two or more states cannot help but hinder multinational business activities by corporations. Consequently, corporate and state policy might well benefit from a sensitivity to the kinds of problems raised in this study.

NOTES

1. Mancur Olson, The Logic of Collective Action (New York: Schocken Books, 1968).

2. See Bernard Mennis and Karl P. Sauvant, "Multinational Corporations, Managers, and the Development of Regional Identifications in Western Europe," The Annals 403 (September 1972):22-33.

3. A. W. Clausen, "The Internationalized Corporation: An Executive's View," The Annals 403 (September 1972):21.

4. See David H. Blake, "Trade Unions and the Challenge of the Multinational Corporation," The Annals 403 (September 1972):36-38 for a discussion of trade union weaknesses.

5. See David H. Blake, "The Internationalization of Industrial Relations," Journal of International Business Studies 3 (Fall 1972): 17-32 for an examination of union efforts to counteract the advantages of the corporation.

16

**BUSINESS-GOVERNMENT
RELATIONS IN AN
INTERNATIONAL CONTEXT:
AN ASSESSMENT**
Hans Schollhammer

The challenge of balancing the advantages of free entrepreneurship and corporate initiative with the necessity for some form of
regulation of business activities to safeguard the public interest
has been the subject of intense debate over a long period of time
and it still remains a controversial issue. There is, however,
agreement that one of the most critical problems in both the
industrial and the emerging nations is that of bringing about improved
understanding and cooperation between business and government.
The intensity of this problem is particularly apparent with regard
to the international business operations of multinational enterprises.
These operations have become massive in scale, continue to expand
rapidly, and are essentially governed by considerations beyond the
range of national interests that individual governments tend to
accept as guidelines for their social and economic policies. It
has been pointed out that the necessarily global orientation of
truly multinational firms on the one hand, and the pursuit of strictly
national interests by sovereign governments on the other hand,
create a fundamental conflict situation that cannot entirely be
eliminated, although experts advocate various means for minimizing
or containing the conflicts. With the increasing magnitude of
multinational business operations this basic dichotomy becomes
more and more pronounced. Multinational firms are now frequently
viewed with suspicion and their operations are increasingly restrained
by a variety of governmental, legal regulations.
There are observers who strongly believe that this situation is
to a large extent the consequence of a lack of cooperation and of
underdeveloped relationships between multinational firms and the

Hans Schollhammer is Associate Professor of Management and
International Business, University of California at Los Angeles.

governments of the countries in which they operate or plan to operate. In addition, it is felt that the future growth of multinational business activities depends on efforts being made to improve the multinational firms' interactions with governments while there is still time. Much is at stake and the seriousness of the problem must be recognized.

THE PRESENT STATE OF MULTINATIONAL BUSINESS-GOVERNMENT RELATIONS

Business-government relations by multinational firms reflect a diversity of experiences ranging on a scale from critically strained to close cooperative. In a limited empirical survey among 14 U. S.-based and 12 European-based multinational firms, top-level executives were asked to register their perception of their firm's present government relations for the various countries in which they maintain manufacturing facilities on the following scale:

Our firm's government
relations in (country) are: critically   inexistent   close
                                strained   coopera-
                                                              tive

The results show that on the average executives of three-fourths of the firms (20 out of 26 companies) ranked their company's government relations in close proximity to "inexistent." The results did not differ markedly between the U. S.-based and the European-based firms—although the European-based firms were slightly more positive in their assessment (the mean of the responses being to the right of "inexistent" on the above scale) than the U. S.-based multinational companies (the mean of their responses to the left of "inexistent" on the above scale). In explaining their company's approach a majority of the responding executives pointed out that in general they would take steps toward some form of government relations only when circumstances would warrant this in order to avoid or minimize aggravating negative effects of government actions, but not as part of a more systematic, continuing effort. However, about two-thirds of the responding executives indicated that they would find it desirable to develop a better understanding and cooperation between government officials (at various levels of government) and executives of multinational firms.

In order to achieve this goal it is necessary for multinational firms to adopt an explicit policy that commits them:

1. To develop and maintain open channels of communication between company executives and government officials on a continuing basis (and not only on an ad hoc basis),

2. To develop a cooperative attitude for solving specific
   public interest problems whenever and wherever it is
   in the power of the company to make a contribution,
3. To foster the idea of partnership between business and
   government in the formulation of short- and long-range
   interdependent objectives.

An example of this latter point is the French national economic
planning system, which invites business executives to work on
planning committees whose function it is to develop sectoral plans.
There exists evidence that executives of foreign-owned French
firms show little interest or effort to work on these planning committees or to make corporate decisions that are in support of the national
planning objectives. It is this type of situation that is at the root
of the accusation that multinational firms tend to be "irresponsible"
and slow or reticent to work with governments toward common
objectives. On the other hand, multinational firms point to a
range of frequently discriminatory regulations or measures with
significant negative effects. International executives generally
fear the power of governments and frequently mistrust the motives
of government actions.

In summary, the present state of the interrelationships between
multinational firms and governments is characterized by a widespread
mutual mistrust, inexistent or ineffective channels of communication,
and, with respect to the large majority of multinational firms, an
absence of an explicit, systematic policy that could contribute
to an improvement of this situation. If a better understanding is
to be achieved, then the executives of the multinational firms
will have to take the initiative.

SOME GENERAL GUIDELINES FOR IMPROVING
GOVERNMENT RELATIONS OF MULTINATIONAL FIRMS

About 80 percent of the executives of the 26 multinational firms
that responded to the survey described above indicated that they are
looking for ways to make their relationships with government officials
more effective. Their stated aim is generally to create a climate
that is conducive to a better understanding so that mutual problems
can be satisfactorily approached and settled. There is a high
degree of consensus among the responding executives that in order
to achieve this aim, the following initiatives should be given priority:

1. Efforts to generate a better awareness of the positive
   contributions of multinational business operations
2. Efforts to establish and maintain as many formal and informal
   contacts and channels of communication between executives and government officials at all relevant administrative
   and legislative levels

3. Support of legislative proposals that deal intelligently
   with issues affecting multinational business operations

Beyond these three general initiatives the responding executives advocated (in the order of diminishing importance) the following more specific measures:

4. Fair competition with local (national) competitors
5. Sound investment and financing policies with a view toward
   supporting governmentally established development needs
6. Strict conformance with local labor and industrial relations
   practices
7. Prompt disclosure of corporate plans for future programs that
   are of public interest
8. Contributions of money, personnel, and facilities for
   local civic projects

Although these are broad and somewhat vague measures, they are indicative of the type of endeavor that executives of multinational firms feel are appropriate in the pursuit of improved multinational business-government relationships. The configuration of the various measures listed above leads one to three observations: (1) Government relations of multinational firms are considered to be a very complex task requiring a broad range of corporate activities and behavioral patterns that in effect try to meet the demands for "good corporate citizenship"; (2) There seems to exist a high degree of uncertainty about the actual effectiveness of the various measures that were mentioned; (3) Government relations and public relations are viewed as largely overlapping endeavors.

MEANS FOR AFFECTING MULTINATIONAL BUSINESS-GOVERNMENT RELATIONS

There is agreement that effective communications with government officials, politicians, and the public at large are a very essential element in any government relations program that multinational companies adopt. In addition it is emphasized that any informational effort should focus on a "continuing dialogue" and involve the use of a variety of communications media such as regular press releases, widely distributed reports about company activities, or even sponsorship of research and educational programs at universities.

Besides these more technical considerations, the dissemination of objective information about corporate activities and endeavors has to be supported by mutual trust and respect stemming from personal contacts between company executives and relevant government officials. For this purpose it is important to seek opportunities for face-to-face meetings in which both sides can express openly matters of mutual interest and can clarify issues under dispute. Since governments frequently need the services of outside experts,

it is felt that membership in certain advisory councils to government
agencies are an appropriate and effective setting for personal
contacts.

IMPLEMENTATION OF MULTINATIONAL
BUSINESS-GOVERNMENT RELATIONS

The actual implementation of a business-government relations
program depends on an organized effort that can take place at three
levels: (1) collective action by a group of multinational firms
with similar interests, (2) efforts by an individual company, and
(3) activities of individual executives. Ideally, all three avenues
could be used for achieving a better understanding between business
and governments. In reality, however, collective cooperative
actions by a group of multinational firms are apparently neither
used nor favored as a potential approach to affect business-government
relations. Of 26 firms providing information, only four European-
based firms admitted their cooperation in a collective effort in the
area of government relations. On a national level one finds a wide
variety of trade and industrial associations that become frequently
the institutional vehicle for defending the interests of their members
when faced, for example, with specific legislative proposals that
affect them. In contrast, multinational firms have not yet evolved
at forming a similar organizational set-up on a supranational level
for representing joint interests toward national governments or
international organizations. As of now there are obvious reasons
for this situation: (1) multinational firms attempt to emphasize
their local identification and do not want to give the appearance
of a "pressure group"; (2) large multinational companies have
traditionally been strictly "individualistic" in the pursuit of their
corporate interests and cognizant of their own relative power.

From among the various possible approaches, the individual
company acting by itself is the most common way by which multinational firms try to achieve the government-relations objectives
they may have set for themselves. The problem with this approach
is that top executives are generally preoccupied with internal
operating problems and the establishment of meaningful contacts
with government officials tends to become a challenge of secondary
importance. To ameliorate this situation multinational firms ought
to create positions in the organization whose primary responsibility
it is to deal consciously and continually with government affairs
and to seek channels for an improved dialogue with government
officials. In this way the task of improving a firm's government
relations becomes institutionalized in the organization structure.
A full-scale government-relations program requires that someone
in the organization should be responsible for keeping the management

of the company informed about relevant legislative and government proposals and for affecting the external aspects of the program.

In only 5 of the 26 multinational firms providing information is the functional responsibility for government relations clearly established as the exclusive task of an organizational unit. In all other companies government relations are part of an ill-defined role structure that encompasses a variety of responsibilities among which government relations get little or only sporadic attention.

CONCLUSIONS

There is general agreement among multinational companies that, in the light of continuing expansion of international business activities and because of increasing government interference, the issue of creating more effective business-government relations is a very important one. The initiative for the establishment of conducive government relations rests essentially with the business sector. There is evidence that thus far multinational firms have shown little creativity or ingenuity in fostering a better understanding and cooperation with governments. At present, the interrelationships between governments and multinational firms are frequently characterized by an expression of mutual mistrust, ineffective communications, and a lack of a clear policy for improving this state of affairs. Although the observations presented in this study are based on only a very limited empirical survey, they seem nevertheless to be representative. This situation then is indicative of the substantial and organized effort that will have to be made to achieve better business-government relations.

International executives tend to agree that the range of corporate endeavors frequently circumscribed by the term "good corporate citizenship" is universally valid and applicable for improving business-government relations. In addition, it is recognized that a greater exchange of objective information and more frequent personal contacts are important elements in a business-government relations program in all countries. While specific communication techniques in the government relations area may differ substantially from country to country, it is important to have a unified approach and a consistent policy for a continuous, planned effort to achieve satisfactory government relations in an international context.

TABLE A.1
Basic Trade and Domestic Shipments Data Used In Chapter 8
(millions of U.S. dollars)

Industry*	A. Levels Of Trade In 1970					B. Changes In Trade, 1966-70				
	MNC Exports	MNC Imports	U.S. Exports	U.S. Imports	U.S. Domestic Shipments	MNC Exports	MNC Imports	U.S. Exports	U.S. Imports	U.S. Domestic Shipments
Petroleum refining	330	430	538	1,552	24,145	185	254	19	530	4,205
Grain mill products	227	48	197	54	10,760	6	18	-24	31	1,518
Beverages	58	140	23	724	12,153	2	-38	11	226	3,806
Other food products	777	502	382	2,784	74,735	298	33	57	1,634	12,529
Paper and allied products	609	671	1,123	1,548	24,659	196	192	446	130	4,245
Drugs	361	101	420	163	6,793	127	168	151	88	1,967
Soaps and cosmetics	130	24	120	26	8,184	27	6	27	7	2,076
Industrial chemicals	1,198	282	1,590	710	15,895	291	32	556	231	2,038
Plastic materials	318	185	653	184	8,786	51	43	180	124	1,382
Other chemicals	335	215	1,042	172	9,596	-110	20	234	-152	1,010
Rubber products	383	146	485	661	15,388	75	38	58	491	3,412
Primary metals (excluding aluminum)	976	305	1,518	3,184	39,274	485	40	842	1,239	1,314
Fabricated metals (excluding aluminum, copper, and brass)	554	121	810	798	38,754	198	79	137	482	8,246
Primary and fabricated aluminum	627	25	390	233	4,490	351	0	83	-421	473
Other metal industries	80	62	267	500	5,487	61	12	142	148	363
Farm machinery and equipment	392	128	628	308	4,367	8	21	-1	-17	45
Industrial machinery and equipment	1,694	225	4,325	705	22,329	427	-72	1,416	39	2,916
Office machines	576	99	978	566	2,286	393	37	693	447	473
Electronic computing equipment	399	329	570	1,031	5,232	104	292	298	958	1,081
Other nonelectrical machinery	734	105	1,871	492	21,646	250	74	328	-2	4,751
Household appliances	157	65	119	271	6,053	67	15	-11	231	933
Electrical equipment and apparatus	978	104	700	243	9,524	230	64	156	53	1,377
Electronic components, radio, T.V.	734	490	1,203	1,706	24,544	224	236	619	1,118	3,535
Other electrical machinery	191	67	978	405	8,017	95	13	337	207	1,451
Transport equipment	6,750	3,802	6,504	6,362	71,457	2,968	2,478	2,789	4,227	-193
Textiles and apparel	244	154	927	2,346	45,824	120	82	123	766	6,253
Lumber, wood products, furniture	352	426	397	1,230	21,976	311	243	141	442	3,719
Printing and publishing	144	19	327	176	25,741	50	6	65	79	5,540
Stone, clay, and glass products	267	1,208	350	542	16,893	59	281	72	250	444
Instruments	848	244	1,127	661	11,723	430	79	389	264	2,890
Ordnance, leather, tobacco, and other	625	410	1,736	2,011	28,865	216	292	129	584	4,508

*See Table A.3 for designation of Industries by SIC (Standard Industrial Classification) codes.

Source: U. S. Tariff Commission report to Committee on Finance, U. S. Senate, Implications of Multinational Firms for World Trade and Investment and for U. S. Trade and Labor, 1973 (T. C. pub. 537), pp. 360-61, 307-78, 691-92.

TABLE A.2

Industry Characteristics Data Used in Chapter 8[a]

Industry[b]	Capital-Labor Ratio	Labor-Intensity Ratio	Human Skills (A)	Human Skills (B)	Productivity	Scale Economies	Concentration Ratios	Product Differentiation	First Trade Date	Profitability	Growth In: Shipments	Growth In: Value Added	Growth In: Employment
Petroleum refining[c]	96,514	.231	134,742	30.2	27.66	NA	57.2	NA	NA	6.6	3.9	6.6	-1.7
Grain mill products	24,141	.263	108,757	30.4	18.22	.136	68.8	29.5	1,936.6	6.7	3.8	5.0	-0.4
Beverages	19,379	.307	98,050	48.2	22.82	.129	61.3	52.0	1,932.9	7.4	7.0	6.3	-0.9
Other food products	9,610	.440	99,644	31.6	11.21	.001	43.4	36.2	1,940.1	2.9	3.7	4.3	-0.8
Paper and allied products	25,872	.454	124,102	20.6	9.63	.053	52.1	78.7	1,947.1	7.6	5.5	6.1	1.5
Drugs	17,291	.230	132,542	44.7	33.32	.167	61.3	147.4	1,948.0	15.3	7.1	7.9	2.6
Soaps and cosmetics	14,545	.171	125,990	39.3	35.93	.182	55.8	76.2	1,943.0	12.4	7.7	8.5	2.8
Industrial chemicals	63,165	.273	130,389	35.3	24.51	-.045	69.2	82.8	1,939.4	10.3	5.9	5.9	0.5
Plastic materials	39,818	.308	128,882	28.5	17.83	.084	79.8	40.7	1,953.4	10.3	7.4	7.7	3.7
Other chemicals	21,110	.335	112,079	33.4	15.82	.056	57.1	77.4	1,939.8	8.4	5.1	5.6	1.6
Rubber products	11,641	.479	120,897	20.6	8.83	.042	61.0	73.1	1,941.4	7.9	7.3	8.2	3.9
Primary metals (excluding aluminum)	28,897	.500	149,148	19.9	10.03	-.023	55.0	69.8	1,944.8	5.3	5.7	5.3	1.2
Fabricated metals (excluding aluminum, copper, and brass)	9,368	.515	128,249	21.4	8.90	.003	38.2	104.1	1,946.5	7.1	6.1	6.8	1.9
Primary and fabricated aluminum	36,337	.450	133,935	18.5	12.88	.016	70.0	75.0	1,947.0	NA	7.1	6.6	3.3
Other metal industries	17,878	.250	129,911	17.8	11.60	-.082	59.0	95.9	1,946.0	NA	7.6	7.1	0.8
Farm machinery and equipment	9,157	.475	116,523	24.6	10.64	-.077	56.0	56.5	1,950.7	3.8	5.0	5.4	1.2
Industrial machinery and equipment	9,307	.421	120,251	31.3	10.85	.004	45.2	121.5	1,947.9	8.7	7.0	7.5	2.4
Office machines	7,466	.454	121,138	32.2	12.25	.102	81.7	59.6	1,946.1	19.9	7.2	7.2	1.4
Electronic computing equipment	7,423	.445	138,940	41.1	16.34	.089	95.0	59.6	1,946.1	19.9	13.3	13.4	6.8
Other nonelectrical machinery	9,171	.466	130,088	24.8	9.91	.018	45.0	112.4	1,949.8	7.2	7.9	8.2	3.0
Household appliances	7,762	.415	124,328	19.4	10.58	.064	82.0	53.2	1,948.8	8.6	5.2	5.9	1.7
Electrical equipment and apparatus	7,506	.504	115,735	30.4	10.13	.031	62.9	161.1	1,947.9	8.4	6.0	6.3	2.2
Electronic components, radio, T.V.	5,942	.536	125,252	26.8	9.92	.015	70.6	96.1	1,948.7	6.0	9.4	9.6	5.2
Other electrical machinery	7,782	.456	123,217	22.0	9.72	.051	63.1	157.9	1,945.6	NA	7.2	7.8	2.9
Transport equipment	8,993	.510	139,263	27.0	11.39	.028	59.5	71.2	1,950.4	7.9	5.3	5.4	0.6
Textiles and apparel	5,499	.541	105,401	11.4	5.11	-.074	41.9	57.0	1,945.8	4.9	5.1	5.6	0.6
Lumber, wood products, furniture	6,845	.524	116,309	13.4	6.15	.028	34.5	65.3	1,947.4	7.3	5.0	5.6	0.6
Printing and publishing	8,291	.498	103,542	38.9	12.73	-.044	33.2	134.7	1,947.1	9.0	6.1	6.7	1.9
Stone, clay, and glass products	19,320	.441	112,748	20.5	9.69	.018	57.0	74.6	1,943.8	7.3	4.7	5.3	1.1
Instruments	8,151	.427	127,928	33.6	13.39	.041	59.0	130.5	1,948.0	14.1	8.5	9.1	2.9
Ordnance, leather, tobacco, and other	5,934	.462	120,352	21.4	10.83	d .003	64.0	d 62.8	d 1,938.6	8.1	4.6	5.7	0.7

NA = Not Available.

[a]See appendix text for description of characteristics series and units in which they are stated.

[b]See Table A.3 for SIC codes designating the industries.

[c]Data cover only SIC Industry No. 29.

[d]Data do not include ordnance (SIC 19).

Source: U. S. Internal Revenue Service, Corporation Income Tax Returns, Statistics of Income 1968 (Washington, D. C., 1972) (pub. 16-3-72); Gary Hufbauer, "The Impact of National Characteristics and Technology on the Commodity Composition of Trade in Manufactured Goods," in The Technology Factor in International Trade, ed. R. Vernon (New York: National Bureau for Economic Research, 1970), pp. 145-231; U. S. Tariff Commission, Competitiveness of U. S. Industries (Washington, D. C., 1972) (TC Pub. 473); U. S. Bureau of the Census, Annual Survey of Manufactures, Industry Profiles (Washington, D. C., 1972) (pub. No. M70 (AS)-10).

Standard Industrial Classification (SIC) Codes
for Industries Listed in Tables A.1 and A.2

Industry	SIC Code
Petroleum refining	138,29,44,4612,4613
Grain mill products	204
Beverages	208
Other food products	(201,202,203,205,206,
	(207,209
Paper and allied products	26
Drugs	283
Soaps and cosmetics	284
Industrial chemicals	281
Plastic materials	282
Other chemicals	285,286,287,289
Rubber products	30
Primary metals (excld. aluminum)	(33, excld. 3331,3334,
	(3351,3352,3361,3362*
Fabricated metals (excld. alum.,	
copper and brass)	(34, excld. 3432,3334,
	(3352,3361*
Other metal industries	3331,3351,3362,3432*
Farm machinery and equipment	352
Industrial machinery and equipment	353,355,356
Office machines	357 excld. 3573
Electronic computing equipment	3573
Other nonelectrical machinery	351,354,358,359
Household appliances	363
Electrical equipment and apparatus	361,362
Electronic components, radio, and T.V.	365,366,367
Other electrical machinery	364,369
Transportation equipment	37
Textiles and apparel	22,23
Lumber, wood and furniture	24,25
Printing and publishing	27
Stone, clay, and glass products	32
Instruments	38
Ordnance, leather, tobacco, and	
other manufacturing	19,21,31,39

*Excludes SIC 333 from MNC data when related to mining operations in the same country.

Source: Bureau of Economic Analysis, U. S. Department of Commerce. See also, U. S. Tariff Commission, op. cit.

Descriptions and Sources for the Industry
Characteristics Measurements Used in This Paper

Arrays of industry characteristics data for U. S. manufacturing
industries are becoming available fairly rapidly, in a variety of
primary sources and analytic studies. Researchers working with
them will recognize that these kinds of measurements are the more
defensible, the deeper the extent of disaggregation of industry
detail—that is, there is greater certainty that one is indeed measuring
what he seeks when his characteristics truly describe conditions
in a specific, narrowly defined industry. All processes of aggregation involve some arbitrariness in assigning characteristic values,
or some averaging procedure that may produce a less than definitive
measurement. Because the key dependent variables in this study—
namely, the trade performance figures for the MNCs—are available
only in a highly aggregated array of 31 industries corresponding to
two- or three-digit SIC classes at best, the problems of aggregation
were severe. Hence, particular attention is invited to the descriptions, given below, of the various aggregation procedures that were
used for each characteristic measurement.

Nearly all of the industry characteristics used here, plus
several others, are the subject of an intense data collection and
preparation effort now underway in the U. S. Tariff Commission as
part of a large research project on the determinants of competitiveness
in U. S. manufacturing industries vis-a-vis exports and imports.
This research is now well along toward the objective of yielding
complete arrays of industry characteristics data at the 4-digit SIC
industry classification level. It is our hope that it will ultimately
become one of the more complete collections of its type in the
nation.

Capital-Labor Ratio. This series provides a measure of the
book value of assets per employee, in dollars, in 1968. It is
derived from the U. S. Census Bureau's Industry Profiles (1972).
Where necessary, aggregation was accomplished by calculation of
the simple mean values of capital per man for the various industry
combinations making up a group in the 31-industry set.

Labor Intensity Ratio. Also taken from the Census Bureau's
Industry Profiles (1972), this series is a ratio of payroll to value
added by manufacturing. The data are for 1968 and, again, any
necessary aggregation was accomplished by using simple means.

Human Skills (A). The Census Bureau's Industry Profiles (1972)
provide enough data to allow calculation of average wages paid
(in dollars) per nonproduction worker in each industry in 1968. The
series used represents these values, capitalized at an arbitrarily
chosen rate of 8 percent, and aggregated when necessary by simple
averaging. Thus, partially following Kenen (1965), this series
really is an estimate of the stock of human capital engaged in

nonproduction activities (that is, primarily R&D, technical services, and marketing) in each industry.

Human Skills (B). This is a more direct measure of the inputs of nonproduction skills required in the various industries, being simply the percentage of nonproduction workers in each industry's labor force in 1968. Once again, it comes from the Census Bureau's Industry Profiles (1972), and the aggregation problem was resolved by simple averaging where needed.

Productivity. The Industry Profiles (1972) give a ratio measuring, in dollars, value added in each industry per production-worker man-hour. Values for 1968 are used and averaged where necessary.

Scale Economies. These values are derived from a complete series for all 4-digit SIC industries recently completed by the Tariff Commission. The series is based on Industrial Census data for 1967 and calculated from a formula developed by Hufbauer. In Hufbauer's formulation, "Scale economies were equated with the exponent in the regression equation $v = kn^a$, where v is the . . . ratio of value added in plants employing n persons to average value added (for the industry), and k is a constant." (Hufbauer, 1970, p. 221). The values for industry groups used here were calculated as weighted means of the values for all 4-digit industries falling within the groups, with values of 1968 shipments used as weights.

Concentration Ratios. These values, which relate to 1968, give the percentages of total industry shipments accounted for by the eight largest firms in each industry. Aggregated values, again, are simple averages of these values. The source is the Census Bureau's Industry Profiles (1972).

Product Differentiation. This is a much-modified series. It traces to a series developed by Hufbauer, wherein product differentiation "is measured as the coefficient of variation in unit values of 1965 United States exports destined to different countries. Differentiated goods are marked by higher coefficients of variation." (Hufbauer, 1970, p. 222.) Hufbauer's data were developed for 3-digit SITC groups, and they were originally converted to a 4-digit SIC basis for an earlier Tariff Commission study on industrial competitiveness (USTC, 1972), using a concordance developed by Hufbauer and published in an appendix to his work. Simple averages of this derived series are the ones used here.

First Trade Dates. Again, we are indebted to Hufbauer. The first trade dates "were found by examining successive issues (beginning in 1917) of the United States Census Bureau Schedule B (the detailed schedule of exportable goods) for the first appearance of specific commodities. The 3-digit SITC estimates represent a simple average of all 7-digit commodities belonging to the 3-digit group." For use in the earlier USTC study (1972), these values were converted into a 4-digit SIC basis as described above for the product differentiation series, and the values used in Table A.2 are again simple averages of these 4-digit values.

Profitability. These figures, for 1968, come from the Internal
Revenue Service (IRS, 1972). They measure net profits in each
industry as a percentage of total sales. The form in which IRS
presented the profits and sales data very closely approximated the
industry classification scheme used here, so that little or no
aggregation was needed.

Growth Measures. These are average annual rates of growth
in shipments, value added, and total employment, respectively, for
the 1958-70 period, as given in the Census Bureau's Industry
Profiles (1972). Any necessary aggregation was accomplished by
simple averaging, for the series used here.

TABLE B.1

Distribution of Sample Projects by
Type of Investment, Home Country of Investor,
Host-Country Areas, and Entry Status

	Export[a] Oriented	Market[b] Development	Government[c] Initiated	Total
Home country of investor				
Europe	5	18	11	34
North America	13	9	5	27
Japan	8	5	6	19
Host country areas				
Latin America[d]	6	14	8	28
India	2	6	5	13
Far East[e]	12	6	2	20
Other[f]	6	6	7	19
Entry status				
Green field investments	24	20	20	64
Expansion investments	2	12	2	16
Total	26	32	22	80

[a]Over 10 percent of the project's output is exported.

[b]Project undertaken at the investor's initiative with the primary motivation of achieving greater penetration of host country markets.

[c]Project initiated by developing country government directly.

[d]Argentina, Colombia, Brazil, Chile, Costa Rica, El Salvador, Mexico, Venezuela.

[e]Hong Kong, Indonesia, Korea, Taiwan, Malaysia, Thailand, Singapore.

[f]Cameroon, Ethiopia, Iran, Jamaica, Ghana, Greece, Kenya, Madagascar, Mauritania, Nigeria, Sierra Leone, Tanzania, Turkey, Uganda.

229

ABOUT THE CONTRIBUTORS

PATRICK M. BOARMAN served as Director of Research and Senior Economist of the Center for International Business, Pepperdine University, Los Angeles, from 1972 to 1975. Currently, he is President of a newly formed group of international business consultants, Patrick M. Boarman Associates, Palos Verdes, California. He previously had served as professor of economics on the faculties of the University of Wisconsin, Long Island University, Bucknell University, and the University of Geneva (Switzerland). Other experience includes economic consultantships with the Office of the Secretary of the Treasury, the Federal Pay Board, the World Trade Institute (New York), General Electric Company, the American Telephone and Telegraph Company, and the U. S. House of Representatives.

Dr. Boarman is the author of numerous books and articles in the field of international economics and is the recipient of many awards in the United States and abroad for his scholarly contributions, including the Distinguished Service Cross of the Order of Merit of the Federal Republic of Germany. He holds a Ph.D. in economics from the Graduate Institute of International Studies of the University of Geneva. Dr. Boarman is a fellow of the Royal Economic Society and a member of the American Economic Association, the International Economic Association, and the National Association of Business Economists.

HANS SCHOLLHAMMER is Associate Professor of Management and International Business, University of California at Los Angeles. He did undergraduate work in Germany and received MBA and DBA degrees from Indiana University. He has taught at the European Institute of Business Administration (INSEAD), Fontainebleau, France, 1963-66, at Indiana University, 1966-67, and at Columbia University, 1970-71. He is a member of the American Economic Association, the Institute of Management Science, the Academy of Management, the Association for Education in International Business, and the editorial board of International Studies of Management and Organization.

Dr. Schollhammer's publications include Readings in International Business, Locational Strategies of Multinational Firms, and articles in professional journals in the United States, Europe, and Latin America.

HOWARD J. AIBEL, Senior Vice President and General Counsel of International Telephone and Telegraph Corporation, is a graduate of Harvard College and Harvard Law School (cum laude). He was associated with the New York law firm of White & Case from 1952 to 1957. In 1957 he joined General Electric Company's Legal Department as Trade Regulation Counsel, a position he held until 1960. Thereafter, he served as Litigation Counsel until 1964 when he joined International Telephone and Telegraph as Trade Regulation Counsel. In 1965 he was named Antitrust and Government Regulatory Counsel and in 1966 was elected a Vice President and Associate General Counsel, becoming ITT's General Counsel in 1968. In 1969 he was elected a Senior Vice President of ITT.

DONALD I. BAKER holds law degrees from Cambridge and Harvard. After a period of private law practice he joined the Antitrust Division of the Department of Justice, where he became Chief of the Evaluation Section and subsequently Deputy Director of Policy Planning and Deputy Assistant Attorney General. He is a recipient of the Attorney General's Distinguished Service Award for "his role in developing and extending the antitrust laws into new areas of the private sector." His publications include several articles on antitrust law.

JACK N. BEHRMAN is Professor of International Business at the University of North Carolina Graduate School of Business Administration. He holds a Ph.D. in economics from Princeton. He has acquired a variety of experience in several academic, business, and government posts, including service as Assistant Secretary of Commerce for Domestic and International Business and as Visiting Professor at the Harvard Business School. He has lectured in the United States and abroad on international investment and foreign licensing and has published extensively on the multinational firm and on the role of foreign investment in economic development. His major works include Some Patterns in the Rise of the Multinational Enterprise and National Interests and the Multinational Enterprise.

JOEL BELL served as Chairman of the Working Group on Foreign Investment in Canada, which prepared a report on that subject and the recently enacted Foreign Investment Review Act. Currently an advisor in the Office of the Prime Minister, he has served as Advisor to several government departments, most recently the Department of Energy, Mines and Resources. Mr. Bell is trained in both law and economics.

DAVID H. BLAKE received his Ph.D. in political science from Rutgers. He is currently Associate Professor of Business Administration and of Political Science at the Graduate School of Business of the University of Pittsburgh, where he teaches a number of courses relating to the multinational corporation. He has been the recipient of several research awards and has a wide range of consulting experience. His publications include articles on the multinational firm and on related issues of collective bargaining and industrial relations.

J. J. BODDEWYN is Professor of International Business in the Baruch College of the City University of New York. A Ph.D. of the University of Washington, he has taught at New York University and the University of Portland. His major publications include International Business-Government Relations, World Business Systems and Environments, Public Policies Toward Retailing, and Comparative Management and Marketing. His current research interests center on the organization and performance of the government-relations and external-affairs functions in multinational firms.

WALTER A. CHUDSON is Adviser on Foreign Investment in the United Nations Department of Economic Affairs. He has worked as a consultant to ministries and special agencies of developing countries concerned with incoming direct investment and commercial technology and has participated in a number of U. N. projects on private foreign investment and multinational corporations. Dr. Chudson was a Rhodes Scholar at Oxford and received his Ph.D. in economics from Columbia University. He is the author or coauthor of several books, including Nationalism and the Multinational Enterprise and The International Transfer of Commercial Technology.

ROBERT A. CORNELL was educated in economics and business administration at Columbia University, New York University, American University, and Pacific Lutheran University. His career includes long government service as an international economist and research manager, plus experience in international banking, multinational business, and consulting. Since 1971 he has been Deputy Director of the U. S. Tariff Commission's Office of Economic Research. Mr. Cornell is the author of several articles, and he served as Project Director for the Commission's study on The Implications of Multinational Firms for World Trade and Investment and for U. S. Trade and Labor, prepared for the Committee On Finance, U. S. Senate, and published in 1973.

NEIL H. JACOBY, Professor Emeritus of the Graduate School of Management of UCLA, of which he was the founding dean, has combined the careers of scholar, administrator, and corporate director. Born in Canada, he holds an LL.D. degree from the University of Saskatchewan and in 1938 he received the Ph.D. degree in economics from the University of Chicago, where he later became Professor of Finance and Vice-President. For the past 25 years he has been at UCLA. He served on President Eisenhower's Council of Economic Advisers, was U. S. Representative in the Economic and Social Council of the United Nations, headed official missions to India, Laos, and Taiwan, and has been a member of the Pay Board. Dr. Jacoby was president of the American Finance Association in 1949 and was on the Executive Committee of the American Economic Association in 1963-66. He has been an organizer or director of several corporations, including one of the largest multinational firms. He is author or coauthor of more than 15 books, including United States Monetary Policy, United States Aid to Taiwan, European Economics—East and West, and Corporate Power and Social Responsibility. Dr. Jacoby is an Associate of the Center for the Study of Democratic Institutions at Santa Barbara and a frequent contributor to The Center Magazine.

S. STANLEY KATZ is Deputy Director of International Economic Policy and Research in the U. S. Department of Commerce. Dr. Katz holds a Ph.D. in economics from the American University. He has written extensively in the areas of international finance and multinational corporations and has participated in numerous government, academic, and business conferences, both in the United States and abroad. Before he joined the Commerce Department he was a senior economist with the World Bank in Washington and with the Organization for Economic Cooperation and Development in Paris.

MARSHALL T. MAYS was named by President Nixon in August 1973 to serve as President of the Overseas Private Investment Corporation, in which he had previously served as Vice President for Insurance and as General Counsel. Mr. Mays is a graduate of the U. S. Naval Academy and the University of South Carolina Law School. He was engaged in the private practice of law in Greenwood, South Carolina, before entering government service in 1969.

ANANT R. NEGANDHI is Professor of Organization Theory and Behavior and Director of the Center for Business and Economic Research, College of Business Administration at Kent State University. He received his Ph.D. from Michigan State University and has engaged in extensive research in the areas of comparative management and international business. He is currently engaged in cross-cultural studies of ten developing countries, the results of which appeared in Comparative Management (with S. B. Prasad), Management and Economic Development: The Case of Taiwan, and Organization Theory in an Open System Perspective (in press).

GRANT L. REUBER is a Canadian economist with a distinguished record of research in the economics of development. His Ph.D. is from Harvard University and he is the author of a number of studies of the Canadian economy, including <u>Britain's Export Trade with Canada</u> and <u>Capital Transfers and Economic Policy; Canada, 1951-62</u>. Since 1957 he has been Professor of Economics at the University of Western Ontario.

STEFAN H. ROBOCK is on the faculty of the Graduate School of Business, Columbia University, and currently holds the Robert D. Calkins Professorship in International Business. He is the author of <u>International Business and Multinational Enterprises</u> (with Kenneth Simmonds) and other books and professional articles in the fields of international business and economic development. Professor Robock has undertaken many technical assistance assignments for the United Nations and the U.S. government in Brazil, India, Bolivia, the Philippines, Liberia, Malawi, and other countries.

A. E. SAFARIAN is Professor of Economics and Dean, School of Graduate Studies at the University of Toronto. From 1956 to 1966 he was at the University of Saskatchewan, and from 1950 to 1955 he was a statistician with the Dominion Bureau of Statistics in Ottawa. His main published works are <u>The Canadian Balance of International Payments in the Post-War Years, 1946-52</u>, (joint author), <u>The Canadian Economy in the Great Depression</u>, <u>Foreign Ownership of Canadian Industry</u>, and <u>The Performance of Foreign-Owned Firms in Canada</u>. In 1967-68 he was a member of the Government of Canada Task Force that published <u>Foreign Ownership and the Structure of Canadian Industry</u>.

MULTINATIONAL CORPORATIONS AND
EAST EUROPEAN SOCIALIST ECONOMIES
Geza P. Lauter and Paul M. Dickie

FOREIGN DISINVESTMENT BY U. S.
MULTINATIONAL CORPORATIONS
Roger L. Torneden

THE NATION-STATE AND TRANSNATIONAL
CORPORATIONS IN CONFLICT: With Special
Reference to Latin America
edited by Jon P. Gunnemann

TRADE WITH CHINA: Assessments by Leading
Businessmen and Scholars
Patrick M. Boarman, with the assistance
of Jayson Mugar

THE MULTINATIONAL CORPORATION AND SOCIAL
POLICY: Special Reference to General Motors
in South Africa
edited by Richard A. Jackson;
introduction by Charles W. Powers

MANAGING MULTINATIONAL CORPORATIONS
Arvind V. Phatak

AMERICAN LABOR AND THE MULTINATIONAL
CORPORATION
edited by Duane Kujawa

INTERNATIONAL CONTROL OF INVESTMENT:
The Dusseldorf Conference on Multinational
Corporations
edited by Don Wallace, Jr., assisted
by Helga Ruof-Koch